MOUNTAINS OF THE MIDDLE KINGDOM

MOUNTAINS OF THE MIDDLE KINGDOM

Exploring the High Peaks of China and Tibet

GALEN ROWELL

Sierra Club Books, San Francisco
IN ASSOCIATION WITH THE AMERICAN ALPINE CLUB

COVER *Rainbow over the Potala Palace, Lhasa.*

FRONTIS 1 *The author's first look at the mountains of China from the northwest ridge of K2 in 1975.*

FRONTIS 2 *Sunrise on the Pamirs across the Kashgar plain.*

A YOLLA BOLLY PRESS BOOK

Mountains of the Middle Kingdom was produced in association with the publisher at The Yolla Bolly Press, Covelo, California. Editorial and design staff: James and Carolyn Robertson, Dan Hibshman, Diana Fairbanks, Joyca Cunnan, Juliana Yoder, and Barbara Youngblood.

The Sierra Club, founded in 1892 by John Muir, has devoted itself to the study and protection of the earth's scenic and ecological resources—mountains, wetlands, woodlands, wild shores and rivers, deserts and plains. Its publications are part of the nonprofit effort the club carries on as a public trust. There are more than fifty chapters coast to coast, in Canada, Hawaii, and Alaska. For information about how you may participate in the club's programs to enjoy and preserve wilderness and the quality of life, please address inquiries to Sierra Club, 530 Bush Street, San Francisco, California 94108.

Mountains of the Middle Kingdom was first published by Sierra Club Books in 1983.
First softcover edition: 1984.

Library of Congress Cataloging in Publication Data

Rowell, Galen A.
Mountains of the Middle Kingdom.

"A Yolla Bolly Press book."
Bibliography: p. 187
Includes index.
1. Mountains—China—Description and travel—History.
I. Title.
DS706.3.R68   1983   915.1'0943   82-19508
ISBN 0-87156-829-2 (pbk.)

PHOTO CREDITS

Richard Burdsall (courtesy of Terris Moore), p. 119; Richard Burdsall (courtesy of the National Geographic Society), pp. 115, 117; Leonard Clark (courtesy of Vern Appleby), pp. 135, 140, 143, 144, 147, 148, 152, 155, 159; Brooke Dolan (courtesy of the Academy of Natural Sciences of Philadelphia), pp. 55, 61; Heinrich Harrer (courtesy of Confida and National Geographic Society), pp. 52, 54, 62; Harold Knutson, p. 100; Terris Moore, p. 118; John Noel (courtesy of the Royal Geographical Society), pp. 84, 86, 104; the National Geographic Society, pp. 52, 54, 62, 136; Joseph Rock (courtesy of the National Geographic Society), pp. 116, 123, 135; the Royal Geographical Society, pp. 6, 10, 38, 58, 83, 84, 86, 87, 102; Galen Rowell, pp. 9, 17, 24, 26, 42, 72, 96, 99, 104, 164, 167, 168; and Ilya Tolstoy (courtesy of the Academy of Natural Sciences of Philadelphia), p. 138.

Yambulak Glacier, Mustagh Ata.

Stormy evening in the foothills
of Anye Machin.

Contents

Namche Barwa, world's highest unclimbed peak, seen from the air at upper left over the Great Bend of the Tsangpo.

Preface

This is not a mountain book. Nor is it a travel narrative. It is a *rediscovery* of mountain regions lost in history, created by a blend of past and present, exploration and politics, mountains and people. After the Communist Liberation of China in 1949, the mountains of the ancient Middle Kingdom receded once again into legend and mystery. All visits by outsiders were prohibited; a virtual blackout on news ensued. The few Chinese publications were (and continue to be) undependable propaganda. Yet during the same period the peoples of these mountain regions and the mountains they live in underwent greater change than in all prior human history.

The closure of a mountain region in Asia is not unusual; governments rise and fall like monsoon clouds. Mountaineers and explorers must bide their time, waiting to penetrate closed areas. The difference in this instance is that the Chinese acted on a grander scale than ever before, closing off a billion people and the highest, broadest, and most varied mountains on earth.

The resulting gap in mountain literature is far greater than even this long closure might indicate. The most poignant reason the Chinese haven't chronicled what happened in their own mountains is that their Cultural Revolution (1966 to 1976) erased the potential of their intelligentsia. This darkest cloud of all sent poets into coal mines, writers into wheat fields, and much of Chinese culture up in smoke. The damage could not be undone by simply lifting the cloud, and it left a generation gap unlike anything imaginable in the West. Our generation gaps are factors of age, trends, and progress; China has the dreadful reality of an entire generation of young adults whose formative years of education were in a cultural void, where the skills that give perspective to literature, art, and history were cast to the winds. The stigma of these years of oppression breaks the continuity of true expertise in every field of endeavor. Without reliable historians, written source material, and the tools of a liberal arts education, the very people within China who might have investigated and written about their nation's mountains have been left with impotent pens.

Another gap in the literature is more subtle. Styles of expeditions have changed in the past thirty years. Broad exploratory objectives have given way to specialized efforts. Mountaineers no longer travel mainly in the company of surveyors, anthropologists, geologists, and zoologists who scribble field notes on the move. Today they are more likely to travel with doctors, lawyers, and businessmen who can afford the requisite time and money. The day of large caravans moving across Asia, crossing borders with abandon, is long gone.

Information from early expeditions to China is now hopelessly dated: maps drawn without reference to aerial or satellite photography; geological interpretations made before the acceptance of continental drift; cultural assessments made before great influxes of Hans (the ethnic name for Chinese; a word, unlike American, that applies to only one race) scrambled traditions of mountain peoples into communal life.

When China opened her mountains to a limited number of expeditions in 1980, I longed to find a book that accurately portrayed the modern condition of these areas. I had never considered writing such a book. I was lucky enough to join the first American expedition ever allowed to climb in the People's Republic of China, but was all too aware that in our success we broke no new ground. Other Americans had climbed in old China before the People's Republic. Soviets and Chinese had reached the summit of our chosen peak. Eight days in the exotic culture of Kashgar on the ancient Silk Road hardly matched Eric Shipton's years of service there as British consul in the forties.

I returned home in such a state of confused humility that I didn't even write a magazine article on my journey, although I normally write multiple accounts of my successful foreign expeditions.

In 1981, before leading the first American group through Tibet to the north side of Mt. Everest, I faced a similar problem of lack of information. This is hallowed ground to mountaineers, yet with the exception of reports on modern Lhasa, none of the texts in English or Chinese went much beyond the basic propaganda of political conversions and the simple geography already available in my father's 1920 encyclopedia.

Our Chinese hosts had few answers to our questions, more often than not erroneous. I began to put myself in the place of a person traveling through the wilderness shrines of America—Yosemite, Yellowstone, the Grand Canyon—who spoke a foreign language and was denied all explanation and history of what he saw. Secretly I began to wish my hosts just such a reciprocal visit, until I realized that rarely were they denying me; they simply didn't know.

Journalism in China is vastly different from the strange brand we have engendered in the United States. Their newspapers are filled with pleasant, boring political trivia. Crimes, accidents, or tragedies rarely make print, because the Chinese are used to the separation of "written news" and "road news." The dissemination of road news is extremely logical: by word of mouth people learn of the accidents and events that concern them directly. If something isn't personally important, it simply doesn't get passed on. There is much to be said for this system. After six weeks in China I was depressed to again be subjected to our media's barrage of other people's sufferings. I had lived perfectly well, in fact, better, without such "knowledge."

The dark side of Chinese journalism is that the Chinese have denied themselves any repository of fact and opinion on news outside politics. This has not only led to distortions of their own history, but also to errors of interpretation in the rest of the world. A Chinese journalist can find plenty of information on Nixon's visit, but virtually nothing on the massacre of thousands of Mao's troops by Golok Tibetans in the fifties, an almost unknown event that abetted the Tibetan Rebellion, the defection of the Dalai Lama, and the 1962 Sino-Indian War. We will never know how many other lost tidbits of history explain the destiny of China's mountain regions.

There are plenty of books on Chinese society, but few on basic geography. Most visitors from the United States never learn of the uncanny geographical similarities between the two nations. In land area China and the United States differ by less than 1 percent. Both have populous eastern regions and sparsely settled Wild Wests. Both Easts have no significant mountains; both Wests have multiple high ranges separated by desert basins, many of which have no drainage to the sea. In the American West, an unusual number of ranges crest out at 14,000 feet; in China, an unusual number of ranges crest out at 25,000 feet. The high points of the exceptions are at the extreme edges of each nation—20,320-foot Denali in Alaska; 29,028-foot Chomolungma (Everest to us) on the Tibetan-Nepalese border. Both peaks are the high points of their respective continents, North America and Asia.

In 1981, after traveling through eight provinces on four treks and expeditions, I realized that no foreign writer had recently seen as much of China's mountain regions as I. Although my information was limited, I was in a position to create the very book I had not been able to find before my journeys. But I wanted to avoid writing an entirely personal narrative, which would restrict the text immensely, or a reference book, which, given such a paucity of data, could hardly be definitive.

What I at length realized I wanted was to *rediscover* these regions, to blend their history, geography, culture, and environmental and political change during the Communist regime into a modern parallel of an old-style expedition narrative. This would give me a clear mandate to go far beyond my own minor travels and exploits. I decided to recreate the past journeys of explorers and mountaineers in six major mountain regions, then to follow each with my own modern counterpart. With these pairings I have tried to show how the land, the peoples, the wildlife, and mountain experiences have changed.

GALEN ROWELL
Berkeley, California

Acknowledgments

The broad scope of this work is the result of the input of many people. I am struck as I reread the manuscript by how much I owe to various individuals and sources. I have leaned heavily on the words and letters of Heinrich Harrer, Richard Leonard, George Mallory, Terris Moore, Joseph Rock, George Schaller, Eric Shipton, S. B. Sutton, H. W. Tilman, and Walt Unsworth. I have selected phrases and impressions from my traveling companions, including, but not limited to, Dick Dorworth, Ned Gillette, John Harte, Ben King, Doug Powell, Jan Reynolds, Jo Sanders, Orville Schell, and Kim Schmitz. Four of my fellow adventurers—Tom Cole, Rod Jackson, Harold Knutson, and John Thune—have gone a big step beyond by sending me, usually unsolicited, information that is exciting to them about China and Tibet. Parts of Chapter 12 appeared in the *American Alpine Journal*, 1982.

Beneath the underground network that helped me write this text is yet another that made it possible in the first place by supporting or underwriting my travels in various ways. My thanks go to Calvin Klein Menswear; Coca-Cola; Himalaya, Inc.; Kastinger U.S.A.; the National Geographic Society; Nike-BRS, Inc.; Nikon, Inc.; The North Face; Oregon Freeze Dry Foods; and Recreational Equipment, Inc. I also wish to thank Mountain Travel and Nick Clinch for the use of their fine libraries, and the U.S. Embassy in Peking for additional information.

The greatest single input unquestionably came from John Martinek, who researched the bibliography and "A Chronology of Mountain Exploration," which appear at the end of the text. The chronology provides a concise framework of Chinese mountain history that is notably absent from the literature. My days of writing were frequently punctuated by free-ranging discussions over lunch with John, whose fluency in the Tibetan language and broad knowledge of the culture helped guide me through the murky depths of Buddhism.

Jim Robertson and Dan Hibshman of the Yolla Bolly Press helped me develop the original concept of this book and followed it through each stage to completion, including a most sensitive job of editing. Barbara Youngblood maintained this high standard in her part of the editing as well. Three of America's most literate mountaineers— H. Adams Carter, Nick Clinch, and Bob Craig—gave of their most valuable time to critique the entire manuscript.

For permission and assistance in obtaining the black-and-white historical photos my thanks go to Vern Appleby, Tom Dolan, Heinrich Harrer, T. I. M. Lewis of *Mountain* magazine, Terris Moore, John Noel, Bill O'Connor, Robert Peck of the Academy of Natural Sciences of Philadelphia, the Royal Geographical Society, and Barbara Shattuck of the National Geographic Society.

Others who have helped in special ways include Lloyd Alexander, H. Adams Carter, Bob Gilka, Anne Kobor, Tarthang Tulku Rimpoche, Caspar Weinberger, Bradford Washburn, and Peter White.

I dedicate this book to the marriage I lost during the intense months of writing and found again in the mountains of Asia soon afterwards.

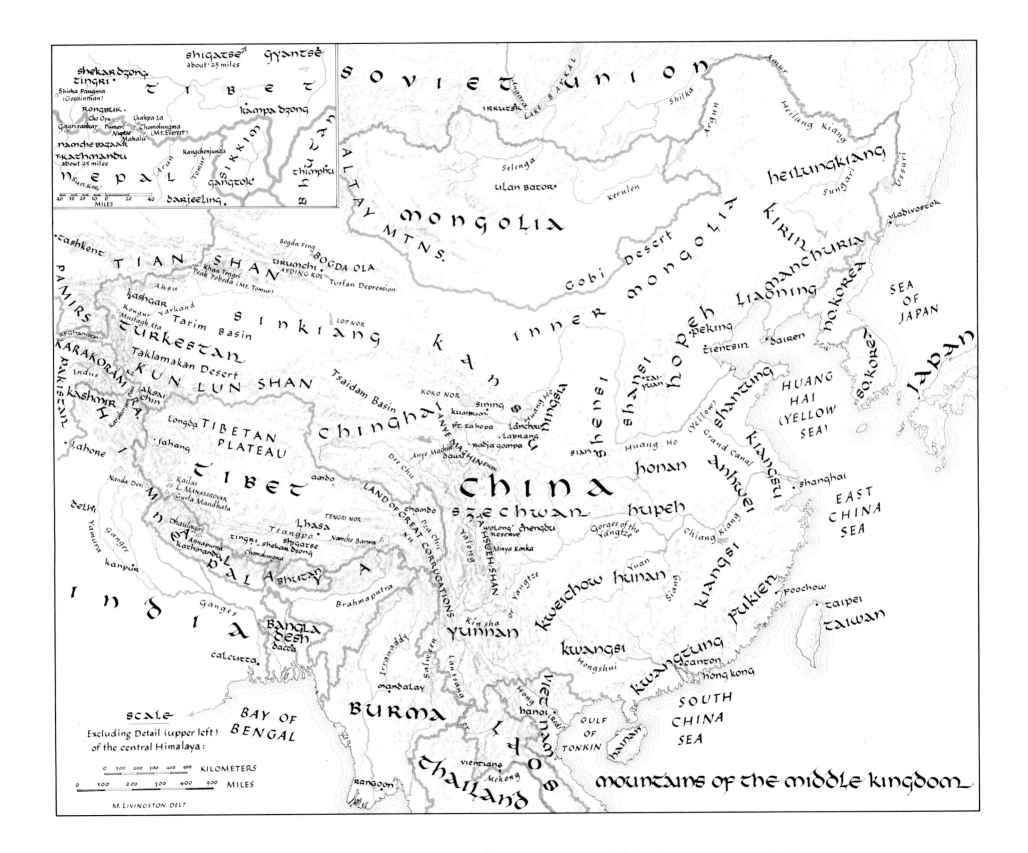

Detail inset (upper left):

SHIGATSE
about 25 miles
GYANTSE

SHEKAR DZONG
TINGRI

TIBET

Shisha Pangma
(Gosainthan)

KAMPA DZONG

RONGBUK
Cho Oyu
Gaurisankar Pumori Lhakpa La
Makalu Nuptse Chomolungma
(Mt. Everest)

NAMCHE BAZAAR

KATHMANDU
about 25 miles

SIKKIM

Kangchenjunga

Arun

Tamur

Sun Kosi

NEPAL

GANGTOK

THIMPHU

BHUTAN

MILES
40 30 20 10 0 40

DARJEELING

Main map:

SOVIET UNION

Angara

IRKUTSK

LAKE BAIKAL

Shilka

Amur

Argun

Heilung Kiang

MONGOLIA

Selenga

ULAN BATOR

Kerulen

Gobi Desert

INNER MONGOLIA

Sungari

Ussuri

VLADIVOSTOK

HEILUNGKIANG

KIRIN

MANCHURIA

LIAONING

N. KOREA

SEA OF JAPAN

Tashkent

TIAN SHAN

Bogda Feng
BOGDA OLA
Khan Tengri URUMCHI
Peak Pobeda (Mt. Tomur) AYDING KOL
Aksu Turfan Depression

PAMIRS

Kashgar Kongur Yarkand
Mustagh Ata

TURKESTAN

Tarim Basin

SINKIANG

LOP NOR

KAN

HOPEH

SHANSI
Tai-yuan

PEKING

Tientsin
Dairen

SHANTUNG

HUANG HAI
(YELLOW SEA)

KARAKORAM

KUN LUN SHAN

Taklamakan Desert

Tsaidam Basin

KOKO NOR

SINING
Kumbum
Ft. ta ho pa
Lanchow
LABRANG
RADJA GOMPA

Huang Ho

NINGSIA

SHENSI

Sian

Huang Ho
(Yellow)

Grand Canal

KIANGSU

Shanghai

EAST CHINA SEA

Afghanistan

Indus

PAKISTAN

KASHMIR
Aksai
Chin
Karakoram P.

Lahore

Longda TIBETAN PLATEAU

Jahang

CHINGHAI

Anye Machin
ANYE MACHIN SHAN
DAWU

HONAN

ANHWEI

Nanda Devi

Kailas
L. MANASAROVAR
Gurla Mandhata

TIBET

Aando

CHINA

SZECHWAN

HUPEH

Delhi

Yamuna

Ganges

Kanpur

Dhaulagiri
Annapurna
NEPAL
Kathmandu

TENGRI NOR

Lhasa
Tsangpo
Tingri Shekar Dzong
Chomolungma

LAND OF GREAT CORRUGATIONS

Chamdo
Dza Chu
Niu
Namche Barwa

Dre Chu

Chengdu
WOLONG Reserve
Minya Konka

Gorges of the Yangtze

Chiang Kiang

Yalong

TA HSUEH SHAN

Yangtze

or

KWEICHOW

HUNAN

Yuan

Siang

KIANGSI

FUKIEN

Foochow

Taipei

TAIWAN

BHUTAN

Brahmaputra

INDIA

Ganges

BANGLADESH
Dacca

Calcutta

Kin sha

YUNNAN

KWANGSI

Hongshui

KWANGTUNG
Canton

Hong Kong

Irrawaddy

Salween

Lantsang

Mandalay

BURMA

BAY OF BENGAL

Rangoon

Hong (Red)

Hanoi

GULF OF TONKIN

Hainan

SOUTH CHINA SEA

VIETNAM

LAOS

Vientiane

Mekong

THAILAND

MOUNTAINS OF THE MIDDLE KINGDOM

SCALE

Excluding Detail (upper left)
of the central Himalaya:

0 100 200 300 400 500 KILOMETERS
0 100 200 300 400 500 MILES

M. LIVINGSTON DELT.

Note on Chinese Names

I have decided not to use the new Pinyin system of romanizing Chinese names dictated by the government of the People's Republic of China. Many writers and publications have chosen the opposite course, changing "Peking" to "Beijing," and "Chou En-lai" to "Zhou Enlai." They have done so in accordance with the consummate desire of the United States to maintain friendly relations with China, not out of logic. Simply because media dependent on keeping staff in China have kowtowed to the dictate of that government does not mean that I as an independent writer need do so.

We Americans have not changed how we say or write "Germany" because that government calls its nation "Deutschland." We would never allow our government to change our heritage in a comparable way: in Pinyin, "George Washington" would become "Zhorz Huaxington."

Because tonal variations are as important as the sounds themselves in Chinese, the language can never be correctly rendered in roman letters. The Pinyin system, which does not address this problem, is a well-intentioned attempt to improve English spellings by assigning new sounds to certain letters. For example, "q" is pronounced "ch," "x" is "sh," "ei" is "ay." If every English-speaking person had daily dealings with Chinese names, such a new system might have a chance of working. But since only a small percentage of our population will ever have a chance to do so, I believe that Pinyin only serves to confuse us until it goes the way of Esperanto, "a fine, doomed idea."

There are already contradictions among the most avid American users of Pinyin. The *Washington Post* may use datelines from "Beijing," but do they ever print a headline about "Qina" instead of China? No, because major place names have a special permanence and correctness about them as they appear on a printed page. I believe minor names also have such a feeling about them, and that both place and personal names should be spelled in the classical style we already know.

I have changed the spelling of several names where I personally found local usage to be different from classic spellings; for example, I have decided to use "Anye Machin" instead of either the classic "Amni Machen" or the Pinyin "Anyemaqen."

Kongur, 25,325 feet, highest of
the Mustagh Ata group.

PART ONE: MUSTAGH ATA

Modern camel caravan in the Pamirs near the ancient Silk Road.

Chapter 1: The Father of Adventure Travel

He was eighteen that summer, crossing the Pamir steppes in a caravan. His father and uncle were traders on their second journey to China, traveling through a no-man's-land between Muscovy and Imperial China. The youth had no concept of being an explorer. Indeed, their strings of camels plodded along a timeworn track. He had been on the trail for the better part of two years, a considerable portion of his formative years. Brief flurries of camp activity punctuated the monotony of constant travel as he passed into manhood on the back of a camel.

The youth kept a journal with detailed notes on his travels. The pastures that he knew in Europe were artificial spots cleared of rock and scrub. Here they spread for miles, flat as lakes, green as spring leaves, and no less natural. Such valleys had given the surrounding mountains their name. He wrote, "This plain, whose name is Pamir, extends fully twelve days' journey. In all these twelve days there is no habitation or shelter, but travelers must take their provisions with them. . . . Because of the height and cold . . . fire is not so bright here nor of the same colour as elsewhere, and food does not cook well."

When the caravan passed beneath a mountain swathed with a dozen glaciers, the youth wrote, "This is said to be the highest place in the world . . . a plain between two mountains with a lake from which flows a very fine river." Mustagh Ata, called the Father of Ice Mountains, rose from a landscape grand beyond human sense of scale. Here, sand dunes began two miles above the sea and climbed thousands of feet toward the heavens, still not touching the eternal snows of the peaks. The youth described "the best pasturage in the world," with grass so lush "that a lean beast will fatten to your heart's content in ten days." Here, "wild game of every sort abounds. There are great quantities of wild sheep of huge size. Their horns grow to as much as six palms in length."

As long as the youth could remember, his life had been tenuous. When he was six, his father had left for China to trade jewels, hoping to return a rich man. Years passed with no word; then his mother died. Even greater uncertainty came into his life at fifteen, when his father returned with an unquenchable sense of mission. China's ruler, the "Great Khan," wanted a hundred learned emissaries of Christianity to come to his kingdom "at the ends of the earth in an east-northeasterly direction." The Great Khan also wanted proof of the power of the faith in the form of oil from a lamp of eternal flame on Christ's tomb in Jerusalem. The youth was excited to be invited on such an important journey, but at first it did not live up to his expectations.

Instead of a hundred emissaries, the pope sent two. Both quit early in the journey. All that remained of Christianity for the Great Khan was a camel load of crystal vessels, holy oil, and letters from the pope. When the youth fell sick for many months in this strange part of the world, neither his Christian father nor the religion of the Islamic "idolaters" was able to do anything for him. He cured himself by going "to the mountain tops," where he found air "so pure and so salubrious" that just a few days' stay banished his malady forever.

From the very center of the Christian world, where that faith was universal and all-powerful, the youth had come through the Middle East, where many faiths coexisted and a Hebrew poet had once written, "I will lift up mine eyes unto the hills." Farther from the center of the faith he had found no Christians; the hills themselves had healed him. He was far from his world now, in a totally different one, where his old faith had no power. Without a single emissary from the pope, his father's caravan was unlikely to spread the Christian faith into the empire of the Great Khan.

The Khan's Mongol Empire was rapidly shrinking. Just twenty-odd years before, it had stretched from the edge of Hungary and Poland across most of Russia, Persia, China, and Afghanistan to the edges of the Pacific and Indian oceans. Now it was less than half that size, with an indistinct western boundary just where they were traveling through the Pamir Range (straddling the spot where modern China, the Soviet Union, and Afghanistan come together).

Here on the high, treeless plain were herds of yaks and sheep tended by Kirghiz nomads living in round tents shaped like the snow peaks around them. These unique dome tents of Central Asia, called yurts, consisted of a willow framework about fifteen feet in diameter and covered with felt, often dyed in colorful patterns. The Kirghiz lived in their yurts all year, surviving –40° F. nights around fires of yak dung. These people were so much a part of the land that they defined the steppes—level highlands inhabited by nomads and their animals—that stretched from Siberia to the Himalaya.

Traffic was slow on the trade route, and for weeks the boy saw no other caravan. For centuries, luxury and privation had been bed partners on this "Silk Road" linking the Mediterranean with China. Luxuries were kept on the backs of camels; privation was the life of a trader. One created the other, for the almost magical value of a luxury came from the misery that men suffered to transport it over a vast distance.

The youth's father and uncle were among the very few traders who had made the journey over the entire Silk Road. Normal caravans moved just a section of the six-thousand-mile track at a time, trading as they went, passing goods into the next territory, then returning home. So the youth had an unusual view of the whole process, of silk moving inevitably toward Europe, where it was worth its weight in gold to royalty—the only ones who could afford it. People at either end of the road had no contact with each other, and were almost unaware of the existence of each other's race.

The secret of silk manufacture was China's key to trade. For thousands of years, spies, pirates, and every manner of experimenter had failed to bring the simple truth of the silkworm to the Western world. The Chinese had long used silk as a form of currency both in their own country and for trade. Taxes were collected in silk bales. When the Mongols, now led by the Great Khan, had invaded Imperial China, they demanded five million bales of silk from the conquered emperor's court. Silk was traded for ivory, diamonds, horses, gold, and musk. The value of these treasures was not just intrinsic, but derived in great part from the man-years of labor required to move them from their sources. Being exotic was the basic definition of a luxury.

Years later the youth, now a middle-aged man, returned to Europe with a new form of exotica: twenty-four years of field notes. At first they brought him nothing but contempt. No one in Italy believed his tales of rocks that burned like wood (coal), cloth that blocked fire (asbestos), giant cows (yaks); nor, most of all, that silk—which touched the flesh of royalty—originated at the back end of a worm.

Two years after his return, in the midst of one of the civil wars that swept through Europe during the Crusades, he was imprisoned in Genoa. The year was A.D. 1298. In prison he befriended a romance writer, Rustichello of Pisa, who helped him turn his notes into a book, *The Travels of Marco Polo*. Although the work was widely read, it was just as widely discredited.

The lure of trade with China grew as precious silk dribbled lot by lot into Europe. Later generations sought to discover the source. Two centuries after Marco Polo's journey a man from Genoa filled the margins of a copy of *Travels* with his

The Gez Defile, meeting place of ice and desert.

Eric Shipton, 1947.

own notes. He planned a journey to China, but by sea. When he reached a land with strange dark-skinned natives, Christopher Columbus, remembering Marco Polo's descriptions of such a place south of China, called the people "Indians."

The fame of Marco Polo did not arise out of his being first at anything. His father and uncle had made the journey to China before him, but by a partially different route that went to the north of the Pamirs. A Franciscan missionary, William von Rubruck, had skirted the Pamirs by this northerly route in 1252, a decade before the elder Polo's first journey. Von Rubruck visited the great Kublai Khan and noted in his journal mountain sheep similar to those that were later to be given Marco Polo's name.

Two factors prevented von Rubruck's journey from becoming known to the world. Unlike Polo, he never reached China, since the Khan's headquarters were not yet established there. And unlike Polo, he made no fortuitous connection with a man of letters who could transform his field notes into a highly readable book.

Marco Polo took his place among the most famous travelers of all time simply because he took the time to describe the peoples and places he saw, and to share that information with the world. His was not a chronicle of his own quest, nor was it the stylized legendry that the Chinese wrote of their homeland. It was something new; if history wants to label him as first at anything, his passive participation on a trip planned by others, laborious note-taking, and publication of a heavily rewritten manuscript qualify him as the father of all adventure-travel writers.

For nearly six centuries after Marco Polo, the great wild sheep of the Pamirs were not described by any European visitor. The Italian writer's stock rose considerably in 1841, though, when a British naval lieutenant, John Wood, delivered a paper to the Royal Geographical Society in London describing the sheep and other key features of the Pamirs. The lieutenant had just returned from a winter journey up frozen rivers to discover the source of the Oxus, the great river that begins in the snows of the Pamirs. (This was the strategic but then unknown region where Afghanistan joined Chinese Turkestan and held apart the expanding empires of Russia and British India.)

The Marco Polo sheep, *Ovis ammon poli*, has the longest horns of any wild sheep in the world: up to six feet on each side. Considered the ultimate trophy by later generations of British officers stationed in India, this sheep was already a symbol of the powerful and the wild. Tibetans worshiped a god of the earth in the form of a giant ram. This god, *Nyan*, was called by the same name that they used for the Tibetan argali, a cousin of the Marco Polo.

Even Rudyard Kipling brought the great sheep into his poetry: "With a trusty, nimble tracker that I know / I have sworn an oath, to keep it on the Horns of Ovis Poli . . . and I must go!" During the 1890s scores of British and Russian officers crossed the Pamir frontier, pleasantly engaged in sport hunting, military intelligence work, and often both. Then came an anomaly, Sven Hedin, a Swedish explorer with a great mind for scientific detail. This latter-day Marco Polo painstakingly mapped every region through which he passed on the long route overland from Europe to Tibet. Geology, meteorology, botany, and glaciology were his primary interests, but the idea of climbing a high mountain stopped him in the Pamirs at their intersection with the Kun Lun Range. He was attracted to Mustagh Ata, the same Father of Ice Mountains seen by Marco Polo. The peak was on the then-undemarcated frontier between Russia and China, just seventy miles north of Afghanistan.

Hedin attempted to climb Mustagh Ata four times in 1894. He thought it was one of the world's highest peaks after surveying it at 25,600 feet. At 24,757 feet, Mustagh Ata is, in fact, barely in the top fifty. Hedin's style of mountaineering anticipated his failure to complete a high-altitude ascent. He claimed to have discovered how to avoid debility at high altitude. "The secret," he informed the world, "lies in avoiding bodily exertion as far as possible."

To accomplish this end, Hedin tried to ride a yak to the summit of Mustagh Ata. At first he marveled at his relative briskness compared to his Kirghiz guides on foot. Every so often he dismounted to take a temperature reading or insert a rod into the ice to measure glacial movements. At the outflow of the Yambulak Glacier, for example, Hedin measured a stream 33¾ feet wide, 13¾ inches deep, with a velocity of 7¼ feet per second, and a temperature of 42.2° F. Of considerably more interest is his note: "The slight exertion of remounting the animal gave me violent palpitation of the heart, and I was almost choked by breathlessness." Hedin and yak gave up together at his measured altitude of 20,600 feet (it was probably not more than 19,500 feet).

No one climbed higher on Mustagh Ata until after World War II. Eric Shipton, one of the greatest Himalayan explorers, was then British consul of Kashgar, a major city on

Kirghiz extended family at
14,000 feet under Mustagh Ata.

7

LEFT *Baby in a hammock.*

RIGHT *Inside a Kirghiz yurt.*

the Silk Road just 120 miles from the mountain. The walled Moslem town was ancient and in most ways still locked in the Middle Ages. The consulate sat on a bluff at the edge of the Taklimakan Desert, from where on clear mornings the consul could "look back across the purple-shadowed plain to the Pamirs, sparkling in the early sunlight. In those two hours before breakfast I held daily communion with this antique land, its outward appearance unaltered since the days of Marco Polo."

During the summer of 1947 Shipton had a visitor who also gazed reverently at the Pamirs on clear mornings. Bill Tilman was Shipton's old climbing partner from their years in Kenya and later on Himalayan expeditions. Both men had led attempts on Mt. Everest through Tibet and were considered among the best of the world's high-altitude climbers. One morning they set off with Mrs. Shipton, two camels, a Sherpa servant who had climbed on Everest, a local Uygur (pronounced wee-grr) coolie, and a knicker-clad coolie wearing a homburg and sun goggles who had worked for Sir Aurel Stein, a turn-of-the-century explorer.

At the base of Mustagh Ata they arranged for Mrs. Shipton to stay with a Kirghiz family in a yurt. The two gentlemen felt it was perfectly safe to leave the woman with these Kirghiz nomads, who had a well-deserved reputation for hospitality. Here in Chinese Turkestan they were isolated from the heartland of Islam, and their religious customs were very relaxed. Women went without veils, and unbelievers were welcome in homes.

Physically, however, the Kirghiz's connections with the Mediterranean end of the Silk Road were apparent: hints of Egyptian high foreheads, Arabian chestnut skin, and Caucasian noses. Beyond these was something especially powerful about a Kirghiz face, a look unlike any other people in the world, for set into those features from the West were incredibly upthrust cheekbones and eyes with Mongol folds. Anthropologists disagreed about their descent, but Shipton subscribed to the theory that they had intermingled with Siberians, acquiring not only physical features but also the distinctly arctic lifestyle that allowed them to survive on the freezing steppes of the high Pamirs.

The Kirghiz lived on flat grasslands that met desert as abruptly as a Las Vegas lawn but extended as far as the eye could see. The many glaciers of Mustagh Ata and neighboring Kongur funneled their meltwater through porous moraines into a hidden groundwater reservoir beneath a Pleisto-cene lake bed. Within a couple of vertical feet the thick green carpet gave way to parched earth.

Shipton and Tilman, being well acquainted with Hedin's attempt on a yak, traded their animals for one of these beasts. Well below the snow the yak "very sensibly struck and sat down at the very first hint of what was expected of him." The men transferred the loads to their own backs and began to climb, marveling at "how much better they did these things in Sven Hedin's time."

After a bivouac near 20,000 feet, they headed for the summit. The upper mountain was a very gentle slope, but an obstacle unlike any the men had faced before. Steep terrain they could handle, but bottomless deep powder was an unforeseen adversary. "Whenever we dared to look up," Tilman wrote, "our eyes met the same unbroken snow horizon, maintaining its unconquerably rigid distance of two or three hundred feet."

Somewhere around 24,000 feet they gave up. As Tilman later commented, "The perversity of inanimate objects is always a force to be reckoned with." Shipton's toes became inanimate objects, much to his surprise. They turned black from frostbite the following morning and, although he did not lose any of them, he was still hobbling on crutches to formal dinners at his consulate two months later. Tilman attributed the failure to overconfidence, unexpected cold, and bad snow conditions, summing up the trip by stating, "We live and learn, and big mountains are stern teachers."

Shipton was the last British consul of Kashgar. In October 1948 he closed the doors of his beloved "castellated mansion"

Shipton's consular mansion in Kashgar, 1980.

When Shipton came to Kashgar in 1940, the British saw neither India nor China as the major threat; the Sinkiang region of western China was a police state run along Stalinist lines by a warlord, and it seemed on the verge of being taken over by the Soviets. Shipton left Kashgar with the realization that "I might well be the last westerner for many decades to travel in the Tarim Basin . . . for it was all too clear from the way events were shaping in China that sweeping change could not be long delayed."

Chairman Mao soon got his way. The rebel leaders of Sinkiang were invited to negotiate in Peking during the founding of the People's Republic in 1949. Their plane mysteriously crashed, killing all aboard. Subsequently, Sinkiang was easily included in the umbra of Mao's government, although periodic rebellions occurred.

The strength of the new unified China surprised the world. The Soviets became its allies. When the Moslems of Sinkiang did fight against Chinese rule, the propaganda sent to Peking and the outside world intimated that they were really rebelling against their feudal landlords in keeping with the Communist system. China's claims to Sinkiang were thus ultimately respected, and the Great Game for control of Central Asia ended for the time being.

The city wall of Kashgar was torn down. A statue of Mao was erected high above the town square with a symbolic hand upstretched over his subjects. Poplar trees were planted on both sides of the roads leading into town. The people, however, continued to wear their traditional bright-colored cottons, ride their donkey carts to the mosques in town, and pray to Allah as usual.

In the Soviet sector of this region is a cluster of high Pamir peaks. By the early fifties Russian mountaineers had climbed them. But the two highest summits were in China, a hundred miles to the east where the Kun Lun begin an eastward arc longer than that of the Great Himalaya. Mustagh Ata (24,757 feet) and Kongur (25,325 feet) were finally in a defined nation (although geographers continued to dispute whether the peaks were actually in the Pamirs or the Kun Lun). The Russians were eager to climb them, too, and an agreement was made for a joint expedition to Mustagh Ata in 1956.

A Russian mountaineer, Comrade E. A. Beletsky, led the expedition. A full month was spent in the Soviet sector training and acclimatizing before going to Mustagh Ata. Nineteen Soviets and twelve Chinese reached the summit

Eric Shipton (center) as British consul in Kashgar.

and considered emigrating to New Zealand, far from the political dark clouds that shrouded Asia. Other members of the British raj were simultaneously departing from their posts all across the frontiers of India and China.

Kipling had written, "The responsibility for governing India has been placed by the inscrutable design of providence upon the shoulders of the British race." History was proving him wrong. Inscrutability was a trait often attributed to the Chinese, and providence was about to shine on the grand design of Mao Tse-tung. While Communist armies fought the American-backed Nationalist forces of Chiang Kai-shek and won, India was collapsing upon itself. In the strangest birth of a democratic nation the world has yet witnessed, the British officially departed from old India in August 1947. The country was divided into a weaker independent India and the openly hostile new nation of Pakistan, created from two disconnected parts of the old Indian heartland. Millions were dying in open battle along the borders while both new nations laid claim to the Kashgar consulate.

after a long siege that included placing four camps up to 22,300 feet and returning all members to base camp.

Details of this first successful Chinese high-altitude climb were translated into heroic propagandese by the Foreign Languages Press of Peking. Every step became a deed for Chairman Mao. The climbers of Mustagh Ata, however, experienced the same private joy of high places that motivates mountaineers elsewhere. Politics were surely not as important to them as the press reports indicated, but politics were more closely associated with the ascent than any of them could have guessed. After the 1962 split between China and Russia, the ascent of Mustagh Ata was virtually wiped from Chinese annals of mountaineering. No mention of the ascent was made either in Chinese chronicles of mountain conquests or in descriptions of Mustagh Ata written up to the present day.

In 1958 the Chinese Mountaineering Association was founded with the official purpose of "making mountaineering serve the economic construction, national defense, and high-altitude scientific investigation" of the young nation. A more immediate purpose was to create a national team strong enough to make the first ascent of the Tibetan side of Mt. Everest.

Among those recruited into the CMA was a twenty-four-year-old woodsman from Yunnan Province, Chu Yin-hua, who had never climbed a mountain in his life. He enjoyed rambling great distances across rugged terrain, and his endurance was legendary among his peers. When he showed up for training, he found four distinct "species" of would-be climbers.

The first group were Hans (the ethnic majority in China), far taller than average and possessed with the cautious affectations of nobility. These were the future leaders, already selected from the common people by their very size, masculinity, and birth. They were, or were soon to be, members of the Central Communist Party, a privilege accorded only 2 percent of the population. In every field of endeavor a similar hierarchy was evolving. Discrimination against leadership by the old landlord or bourgeois classes was leading to an unplanned selection process of its own. With concrete criteria for leadership removed, more primitive aspects common to all higher forms of life took over: males of greater size or greater manipulative ability took over positions of control.

The second group of climbers were of Tibetan descent.

Their birthright at extreme altitude gave them an edge in endurance for high climbing. With few exceptions, whenever a Han climber was equal to a Tibetan, his physical training had far exceeded that of the Tibetan. Emotionally as well as physically the Tibetans were natural mountaineers with a special sense of how to move and how to live in snow and cold.

The third group was composed of women, strong women who loved the outdoors and had proven themselves in other activities. Some of them were national-class volleyball players; others were Tibetans. The Chinese government saw women's accomplishments as a relatively easy way to set world records and gain recognition, since women in the West had not yet reached extreme altitudes. If even one woman could reach the top of Mustagh Ata, then China could claim her first world altitude record.

The fourth group was comprised of Hans with special abilities, including doctors and scientists. Chu Yin-hua felt a part of this group because of his knowledge of the woods and the fact that he didn't belong to any of the other three. A robust, plain-featured man of average height, he lacked the stage presence of his Group One companions, but more than made up for it with an unself-consciousness that brought out a quiet strength much like that of the Tibetans. At meetings in the city, Chu was all but invisible—small, shy, unmemorable; on a mountain he turned into a bold and charismatic man in firm control of his surroundings. Mustagh Ata was his first high-altitude climb.

The mountain has a southwest slope more gentle than that of any other major peak, making it a perfect proving ground. Base camp was pitched in a level meadow, which was inset between the moraines of the Yambulak Glacier and the first thrust of the mountain. More than fifty people camped on the few acres of grass for a week before venturing upward.

Chu carried a gun, as he had always done in the woods to live off the land. He found marmots, chukars, snow cocks, and a band of Marco Polo sheep at 16,000 feet. Every night the group feasted on wild mutton or bird. Camps were fixed on the peak, but the group descended again to eat well and lie about in the wildflowers and tall grass before the final push for the summit.

Since some of the climbers had been to the top with the Soviets in 1956, the route was known. On July 2 they began to move up the peak, en masse. Using the four camps of the earlier assault, they positioned thirty-three climbers—twenty-five men and eight women—just a thousand feet below the top. All went to the summit in a single wave on July 7, 1959.

On the summit that day were representatives of the four informal groups of mountaineers, and at least one from each group would stand on the top of Everest in the years to come.

All that time a peculiar ideology was emerging; a form of fundamentalism not unlike that of certain strict Christians who deny dates older than those in the Bible. Across China, Mao's followers had begun to erase evidence and memories of what went on before 1949. "Since Liberation . . ." became like saying, "Since the beginning of history." Success in anything needed to follow "correct" political thinking. When Russia and China went their separate ways in 1962, it was no longer correct thinking to trace the success of Chinese mountaineers to earlier contact with the tainted Soviets.

So the thirty-three who stood on top of Mustagh Ata in 1959 became, like the signers of our Declaration of Independence, hallowed founders of their movement. They would find preferred places on the expeditions of the future and, if they were Han and Communist Party members, in the hierarchy of the Chinese Mountaineering Association for decades to come.

Kirghiz elder and son.

Mustagh Ata from the west,
reflected in the waters of Little
Karakul.

14

Chapter 2: The Father of Ice Mountains

In July 1980 Chu Yin-hua rode a donkey across the highest meadow just beneath the peak of Mustagh Ata. Twenty-one years had passed since his successful climb. A rifle was slung over his shoulder. With his eyes alert for movement, he stopped, dismounted, and walked over to a pair of sheep horns lying in the grass. He stared at them for a long while, looking up every so often for the motion that would never come.

Long-forgotten odors came to mind. The stench of urine on the rocks of the sterile moraine above camp, of gunpowder at the moment of the kill, of moist air and spices as gamey meat boiled for hours in the pot.

The grass seemed so short and sparse. Was it his memory? The season? Or was the land really different now? His eyes scanned the hillsides and saw many new trails, cross-hatched webs that told of the mass passage of herds. The domestic goats that grazed by the thousands in the lush pastures miles below must have been here too. Were there so many goats now that the Kirghiz needed to graze them this high?

Chu had no answers. He knew only that there were no Marco Polo sheep, and that thousands of hooved creatures had come to this place at 15,000 feet, where like locusts they could devour the entire winter range of the wild sheep in a matter of days.

Chu walked with a limp, like an old Han woman whose feet had been bound as a child. Each step was a purposeful effort to keep his weight centered. He was more aware of it here than in the city, where he could hide the effort behind a slow pace. His limping through the meadow clashed with memories of bounding through the grass with his fellow climbers in 1959.

Ever since he had returned from the summit of Mt. Everest in 1960, Chu's life had been radically different. He was a national hero now. But his renown for being the first to climb Everest from Tibet had a dark side, a sense of failure, of being an incomplete man for life. All ten of his toes were gone, cut off flush with his feet after frostbite from climbing the Second Step at 28,000 feet on Everest in his stocking feet.

He often wondered if his gain had matched his loss, especially because China was so different now. The values of his childhood were deeply ingrained in his culture, but no longer taught. Before Liberation in 1949, schoolchildren memorized the dictums of filial piety, including "the body, the hair, and the skin are received from one's parents and must not be injured." Tsengtse, a great disciple of Confucius, died saying, "Examine my hands! Examine my feet!" Confucius himself said, "A man does not travel to distant places when his parents are living."

A latter-day Confucius named Lin Yutang even singled out mountain climbing as the antithesis of filial piety: "The filial son does not climb high, and does not tread on dangerous places. There is therefore not a single filial son in the Alpine Club."

Lin Yutang's "Alpine Club" was only metaphorical when he wrote those words in 1935. The Chinese Mountaineering Association's first season of activity coincided with Chu's climb of Mustagh Ata in 1959. Now his visit to the same mountain coincided with yet another first season for the CMA, which had become a government agency for mountain tourism rather than a national alpine club like that of Western nations. Foreign visitors were at last being allowed into China's mountain areas, but only under its auspices.

Chu was the liaison officer assigned to the first American expedition permitted to climb in the People's Republic of China. I was a member of this six-person team, led by Ned Gillette, who had succeeded in obtaining the first Chinese permit where scores of other American expeditions had failed in the past. He succeeded by doing the right things in the right place at the right time.

The right things began with sharing an expertise with the Chinese. Ned had once been a member of the U.S. Olympic Cross-Country Ski Team, and the Chinese invited him to ski with them and share his knowledge. The right place was on Chinese soil, even though he jokingly described his time in the rolling hills of Manchuria "like traveling ten thousand miles to ski in Iowa." The right time was February 1980, when the CMA was announcing to the world the opening of eight peaks, the first tourism of any kind allowed in Chinese wilderness.

After uneventful skiing but highly successful cultural exchange, Ned visited the CMA and inquired if there were any high peaks in China that could be skied from summit to base.

Shih Chan Chun, the director of the CMA, replied, "You are a very lucky man. Not only are you here just as we open our mountains, but also one of our eight permitted peaks is perfect for expert skiers. I know because I climbed it myself. The name of this peak is Mustagh Ata. Apply for it following our regulations, and I will personally see that you are granted a permit for this year."

With Ned was Jan Reynolds, a young woman who directed ski touring for Trapp Family Lodge (of *Sound of Music* fame) in Vermont and regularly competed in ski marathons. Jan was also interested in skiing the peak.

When Ned asked me to go in June—just three months away—I was skeptical. During the previous five years I had been on the roster of four prospective China expeditions, each with contacts at high levels in both the U.S. and Chinese governments. All had come to naught. Besides, Ned and I were leaving within the month for the most serious ski expedition of our lives, which had my first priority. We were leaving in mid-March on an unsupported ski traverse of the Karakoram Himalaya, not expecting to return until May. He had nothing in writing from the Chinese.

Ned's attentions became impossibly divided between obligations from already-completed adventures and future ones in the Karakoram and China. My living room became the preliminary base camp for the Karakoram, and my friend, Jo Sanders, generously came to our rescue. Her organizational abilities, honed by years in the adventure-travel business, so impressed Ned that he invited her to come to Mustagh Ata if she would handle the written permit, fund raising, and other necessities in our absence.

We returned after a successful Karakoram trip to find the planning for Mustagh Ata on the home stretch. A permit was in hand, potential backers had been approached, and the team was complete with two more members: Cameron Bangs, an Oregon physician who frequently lectured on mountain medicine, and Dick Dorworth, a writer and mountaineer who had once held the world's speed record on skis.

We arrived in base camp on July 9, and only then did a degree of normalcy return to our efforts. Finally we had left behind the bizarre combinations of buses, camels, boxes, barrels, and donkeys that have so little of the natural dignity of caravans of old. Many of the scenes gave our serious project the distressingly funny look of a fine show dog with tin cans tied to its tail. Camels moved in timeless fashion across the Pamir steppes—with brand new skis on their backs. In the middle of a 12,000-foot meadow filled with buttercups and clover was our Chinese bus—rented at $7 per mile plus $120-per-day parking fee. Our Chinese interpreter wore dark glasses, a Budweiser cap, and a Harold's Club T-shirt. Chu, the great mountaineer and hunter, rode to base camp on a small donkey, brandishing a rifle and wearing new Nike running shoes.

On the morning of July 11 our string of camels set off with five 220-pound loads of food and equipment. At 17,000 feet the scree slopes began to be covered with snow. Loads were cached and the camels turned back. Using camels in-

ABOVE *Chu Yin-hua.*

OPPOSITE *Kirghiz crossing a glacial stream.* © *National Geographic Society*

17

stead of high-altitude porters seemed novel to us, but long ago when the Silk Road was in use countless camel caravans had traveled even higher, en route to India from Kashgar over 18,200-foot Karakoram Pass.

We were all fascinated by the Kirghiz people who lived at the base of Mustagh Ata, and we wanted more spontaneous encounters with them than the kind we had in the presence of our Chinese interpreter and liaison officer. We sought them out repeatedly before and after the climb. One incident stands out from all the rest.

On the day that we were leaving for the roadhead I deviously obtained permission for Jo and me to wander and take photographs—so long as we rejoined the group by evening. As the others headed downhill toward the plains, we made a beeline across meadows and canyons until we looked down into a valley I had spotted earlier from high on the mountain. Below us were twelve yurts pitched by a stream, a scene as idyllic as a picture in a child's book. Hundreds of sheep grazed a sunlit hill, tended by a little girl in a red dress. Smoke rose from the tops of two yurts. Not an adult was in sight.

The hillsides were a patchwork of green and tan, barren except where meltwater from the eternal snows of the mountain had seeped into the ground. In the distance was a far larger patchwork of similar colors, created by hidden corridors of groundwater flowing into the vivid green valley below, set into a desert that geographers liken to Nevada's. Our base camp was set in another of these oases at the edge of the glacier itself.

We felt a little intimidated by the prospect of walking unannounced into a community where the inhabitants might never have seen a foreigner. We spoke no common language. As soon as we neared, people began to pour out of the yurts and surround us. They stared at our bare legs and the strange bright bags strapped to our shoulders. Several people cornered me and stroked my hairy arms with the unself-consciousness of children.

We were ushered into one of the felt-covered domes, seated on red quilts, and fed fresh yogurt with hot bread. Some twenty-odd people crowded into a room about fifteen feet across, staring and laughing. Someone produced a jar of *kumiss*, an alcoholic brew made from fermented mare's milk. Nothing about the scene indicated the influence of the Communist system. In every way these Kirghiz seemed to be the same nomadic pastoralists as in Sven Hedin's day.

Our vision of Kirghiz families at home in their mountain fastness clashed with published accounts of Communist oppression. The nomads of Central Asia and their extended-family units were, according to George Mosely's *A Sino-Soviet Cultural Frontier*, "tossed on history's rubbish heap." The individual was supposedly dispossessed from traditional ways. "His liberation . . . was to be total: not only were his social values to be squeezed out of him, but he also had to be made into a Chinese."

What Mosely wrote and what I saw were both the truth; the difference was that we were reporting on different times. Much had changed for the Kirghiz since his book was published in 1966.

Our later visits to other Kirghiz yurts with our interpreter were slightly less spontaneous, but far better in terms of learning experiences. We listened closely as Turdi Beg, a fifty-five-year-old village elder who had been an adult at the time of the Communist Liberation, told us how it had affected his people. Before that time they were nomads (not the popular misconception of people who wander like gypsies, but temporary residents who move from fixed summer pastures into a communal winter camp). The entire area around Mustagh Ata had been controlled by three wealthy landowners who exacted high taxes for use of the pastures.

When Mao took over control in 1949, minority people were guaranteed equal rights and the freedom to "develop their dialects and languages, to preserve their traditions, customs, and religious beliefs." The first "lower cooperatives" did not interfere with the extended family, and the people were happy to have a higher standard of living through greater productivity and equal sharing.

A big change came in 1956 when the Central Communist Party decreed policies to break the power of Islam in the Autonomous Region of Sinkiang. The alphabet was changed from Arabic to Russian. This was supposed to be for the purpose of improving education, but the real reason was to isolate future generations from the Arabic teachings of Islam. Finally, the introduction of full-fledged communes in 1958 brought widespread rebellion. The Kirghiz and other nomadic minorities did not take to living in adobe-walled complexes with great dining halls. One such complex was built at Bulunkol, now the commune headquarters for the Mustagh Ata Kirghiz.

Chinese troops were called in to suppress rebellions throughout Sinkiang in 1959. More than sixty thousand peo-

*Riders beneath giant sand dune
at 12,000 feet in the Pamirs.*

Man in a window, Id Kah Mosque, Kashgar.

ple fled to the Soviet Union with the aid of visas that were bought for two dollars at the Russian consulate in Kashgar. After Sino-Soviet relations deteriorated in 1962, Soviet broadcasts promised Islamic minorities in China the freedom to keep their languages and traditions if they defected.

Tension along the Soviet border and the heavy presence of Chinese soldiers continued throughout the Cultural Revolution of 1966 to 1976. After the fall of the Gang of Four, policies toward minorities were liberalized. A 1978 constitution guaranteed the minorities freedom to choose languages, customs, and local officials. In 1979 the Communist Party of Sinkiang allowed minorities to become property owners in a limited way. Up to fifteen sheep, two horses, and three yaks per person could be privately owned.

In 1980 the opening of limited tourism brought more money and freedoms into the system. We were among the very first foreign visitors to the minority regions around Kashgar and Mustagh Ata. The money from our purchases of staples and souvenirs, as well as the social contacts with people from the West, were part of another step toward liberalization.

The Communist system had not advanced the Kirghiz in the sense that Mao envisioned. The Kirghiz were finally permitted to live traditionally after the planned unification of all the Chinese peoples failed. The same extended families that had previously grazed valleys were "ordered" to graze them again by their elected commune leaders. In winter they gathered together as in the old days, but in a far more comfortable central complex than the old circle of yurts pitted against the icy winds of the Pamirs. Increased productivity, equal economic sharing, health care, and education gave them the best of both worlds.

Although we were allowed at least three weeks' time on the mountain, both Ned and I were eager to finish early so that we could investigate more of the region and its culture. Dick Dorworth was adamant about spending at least a week acclimatizing at base camp before beginning the actual climb. Ned wanted immediately to move up to the new Camel Camp, where we could ski and shake down our equipment while we acclimatized.

Dick and Ned had had opposite experiences with high altitude. Ned had once climbed in Alaska from 10,000 to 20,000 feet in a single day just three days after leaving sea level. He had suffered no ill effects. Dick had had a close bout with cerebral edema at 15,000 feet on the same peak—the very elevation of our present base. The elevations below 17,000 feet are the most critical for acclimatization.

I put in a word for a compromise: three or four days at base camp followed by three or four more at Camel Camp. There the matter rested. The next day was a lazy one, but the morning after that I was awakened by Ned, urging me to pack up and move. I declined. So did Dick and Jo. Ned agreed to stay, but said he wanted to talk to the group.

After another lazy morning, Jo and I set off at three in the afternoon for a walk on the Tergam Bulak Glacier next to camp. When we returned, base camp was strangely empty. Dick ran to meet us with concern written on his brow: "Five minutes after you two left, Ned, Jan, and Cam began packing. At first I didn't know what they were doing. They left for the mountain without even leaving us a list of what they have up there and what they're taking. If we follow, we won't even know whether to bring a stove or toilet paper or anything else. Chu's been sitting by himself over there on the hill just staring."

"There's no sense chasing them," I replied. "I've got a cough I'd like to get rid of, and we all want more time to acclimatize."

"I don't know about you," Dick said, "but I'm staying here for several days more, and if they head for the summit without me, that's a risk I'm willing to take."

Three days passed. Storms moved through, alternating rain and snow, cloud and clearing. I spent most of one day searching the region for wildlife signs. It was mid-July now, and our Kirghiz camel drivers had told me that a few Marco Polo sheep lived here from early winter until May.

At the top of a knoll above camp, I found a series of rounded depressions surrounded by old sheep droppings, tracks, and the bones of a lamb. The depressions were day-beds, and the age of the sign confirmed what the Kirghiz had told me. This herd's winter range at an unusually high 16,000 feet was in a place where wind kept the snow depth far less than in the lower valleys.

I had combed the lower valleys too. There were no signs of other large mammals except for an occasional fox. Marmot holes were everywhere, but none had that battlefield look indicating the presence of brown bears. The wolves seen by Shipton and Hedin were gone, victims, like the grass missing from the high meadows, of domestic grazing. As the Kirghiz expanded their herds to meet Chinese goals of increased productivity, odds began to stack against the wolf.

Habitat destruction and hunting decimated the Marco Polo sheep, the main item of the wolf's winter menu after the snows buried its summer diet of marmot and pika. Domestic herds became the wolves' targets, and in turn they became the target of the Kirghiz.

Sven Hedin reported what the Kirghiz did if they found a wolf near their flock. When possible, they would capture one alive, "tie a heavy pole to his neck and a piece of wood between his jaws, and wind ropes about him. Then they would let the wolf loose, torture him with whips and scourges, blind him with glowing coals, and stuff his mouth with dry snuff."

I can only speculate on the Kirghiz's solution to the wolf problem today. I do know that Kirghiz and wildlife continue to coexist in other parts of the Pamirs outside of China, such as in the Aksu Valley, situated where the Pamirs reach into both Afghanistan and the USSR. A 1974 United Nations research project studied a group of 380 Marco Polo sheep in the Afghan sector. Scientists found a balance between Kirghiz pastoralists, wolves, and wild sheep. The large Marco Polo herds were under "the healthy influence of wolf predation" with an annual kill of 8 percent. Overlap between the winter ranges of the Marco Polo and domestic sheep was present, and there was evidence "that the closeness of humans caused considerable disturbance to and disruption of wildlife grazing and habitat utilization." But the end result, unlike that in the Mustagh Ata area, was a mountain region with its original range of wild species relatively intact.

As Dick and I climbed from base camp to Camel Camp after three extra days of acclimatizing, we passed the skull and horns of a Marco Polo just below the snowline. It symbolized our sense of aloneness. Even though we could now look up and watch the others skiing down perfect snow next to camp, we were prepared, if need be, for a self-sufficient two-man climb. Jo, who had hoped to at least visit Camel Camp and Camp I, stayed behind because of the uncertainty. She had little mountaineering experience, and, without knowing whether there would be, among other things, an extra stove and extra food for her, she didn't want to risk the possibility of staying alone at such altitudes.

After we reached camp late in the day, I joined the others for a ski run. Later we set up our tent as if nothing had happened in the past three days. Any attempt at a discussion would certainly have ended in a confrontation, so we purposefully avoided the subject.

The next day we moved the rocky Camel Camp to solid snow at 18,000 feet. A storm moved in, pinning us in camp for several days and preempting discussion of the need for further acclimatization. On the third morning I wrote the following diary entry: "20° F. at 10:00 A.M. Winds gusting to 40 knots. Clearing under stratus layer with snow down to about 13,000. Eight inches of new snow. Dick left the tent this morning at five for the doctor's. He feels weak, nauseous, and his head aches. I took his pulse yesterday at 64 and today at 88. Something's wrong, but his lungs are clear and he has no fever. . . . I know he's really hurting."

Dick wanted to go down. Ned and Cam helped him to the snowline, from where he walked on to base camp by himself. I expected Dick to recover from his bout with the altitude and join us, possibly for a second summit bid, a few days after ours.

Waiting out a storm at high altitude is usually depressing, but we kept a remarkably positive attitude by relishing the thought that when it stopped we would be skiing in two feet of new powder. When the clearing came, we were off to climb the peak as quickly as possible. On the first day we carried sixty-pound loads to Camp II at 20,200 feet, using skis with climbing skins the entire way. Obstacles we had seen from below—crevasses, ice cliffs, slopes of bare ice—all could be avoided by routes that we could manage with our skis on.

We planned to climb the remaining forty-five hundred feet in a single day, then ski back to Camp II for the night. The rationale for such a big summit day was not only that upward progress would be easier with light daypacks instead of the heavy loads needed to set another camp, but also that the safety and enjoyment of our downhill run would be enhanced without great weights on our backs. We did want to have at least a little fun on what would be, at fifty thousand dollars for three people, one of the more costly single ski runs in history. (We were down to three now because Cameron, who did not have our experience skiing with a pack, decided to wait out our summit bid in high camp.)

The next morning we skirted the last ice cliffs and entered the realm of deep snow and receding horizons that had defeated Shipton and Tilman. When we took off our skis to rest, we instantly sank to our thighs; with them on, our progress was as rapid as walking up hard snow. Although a rope connected the three of us in case we broke into a hidden crevasse, we were alone in our thoughts. Gasping for breath

Kirghiz family, Subashi.

Climbing Mustagh Ata on skis.

I took over breaking trail, and Ned dropped back to be with Jan. After a while she left her pack, and the pace appeared to pick up. Then evening was upon us. Our planned 8:00 P.M. turn-around time came before the summit was in sight. Odds for getting to the top and skiing down to camp seemed slim. Jan was tired and dehydrated from vomiting, but otherwise all right. I gave her my water bottle and headed on alone, deciding to give the mountain my best shot before giving up.

An hour later I reached a strange windblown knob that dropped off radically to the south. Although I had a feeling of well-being without oxygen at nearly 25,000 feet, my thought processes were not at their best. It took me quite awhile to deduce that I was on top. Then I took a requisite summit photograph that I thought showed my face with the Soviet Pamirs behind me. The evening light was perfect, and the shot was used full page in *National Geographic* for its oddity. It showed no mountains whatsoever, and my face was unidentifiable behind an ice-caked mask, which I forgot to take off.

I stayed on top for half an hour, recording the temperature at exactly 0° F. and taking photographs in all directions, especially toward the Karakoram Himalaya through which Ned and I had skied just two months before. We were only about a hundred miles away, yet politics had led us to travel fully around the world to get here. From Pakistan we had flown west and crossed the Atlantic, obtained special mountaineering visas through the Chinese Embassy in the United States, flown across the Pacific to Peking for protocol, then across the breadth of China to Kashgar.

My strongest memory of the summit is the simple sense of freedom I felt in getting back on skis and moving so quickly downward at such an altitude. Contrary to popular belief, no mountaineer discovers the meaning of life—or even lesser insights—at the top of a peak. As with other events in a person's life, reflection comes later when the excitement is gone. Only then do summit moments take on meanings beyond the obvious.

Like ingredients of a recipe, impressions of a climb lose their individual flavor and become part of a whole, with a taste indescribable to those who have not sampled similar fare. The efforts of the news media in this regard fail entirely, because, in their search for facts, they focus on the individual ingredients.

The idea that I was embarking on the highest complete

at 24,000 feet while climbing upward is hardly conducive to spirited conversation. The rope made us move at the same pace but not with the same effort—whoever was breaking trail had the hardest job. Ned was the strongest and best acclimatized, so he broke for the entire morning. In the afternoon Jan and I took over for shorter stretches. I did not feel as well acclimatized, and I feared that extra effort might do me in. Jan seemed very strong until at about fifteen hundred feet below the summit she doubled up in her tracks and vomited. A few minutes later it happened again. Altitude and fatigue were taking their toll.

ski descent from the summit of a mountain was not in my mind, although it dominated press coverage. What intrigued me most was how easy the skiing had been. I speculated that Shipton and Tilman would have reached the summit in 1947 had they had skis.

As I descended, I met Jan and Ned on their way up. Waiting, I watched Jan crest the top of her first real mountain. Not a climber, she was setting a world altitude record for women on skis. For her, everything was new except the skis on her feet, which she had worn since she could walk. For Ned, everything was familiar; the summit was merely the high point of his recent career of skiing expeditions around the world. For me—not a lifetime skier—I doubted I would ever ski as high a peak again, since the higher peaks of the world are all far more difficult.

Beneath these outward experiences were deep feelings that would coalesce later. For the next two hours we were spellbound by the fascination of carving wide turns in perfect powder as the sun turned the snow to gold. We raced the sunset, plunging to meet the rising shadow of darkness. Staying near our uphill tracks, we skied unroped—separate and free. Night caught up with us just as we reached our two tents beneath an ice cliff.

Another long day of skiing with our homes on our backs took us to Camp I, and the following morning we straggled into base camp. Jo met me on the way down and decorated all of us with garlands of wildflowers. Dick was gone. He had been evacuated to Kashgar when his altitude sickness, later diagnosed as cerebral edema, failed to get better.

Only then, in the meadows of base camp, did I have the luxury to reflect on my experience. What stood out the most was not any particular difficulty, but simply the time that I had spent alone on the summit plateau.

Why was time alone on a mountain so inestimably precious to me? I thought about wild creatures and the fact that those we humans admire most are solitary. Herd animals simply don't hold the esteem we accord to the eagle, the bear, or the lone bighorn ram. Yet in our own lives we are all herd animals, living almost totally in relations with our own species. In mountain climbing I find a world apart from the human herd. No description of just climbing or adventure will describe the whole of this other world in which I sometimes live. Poets have come the closest.

Soon after I began climbing as a teenager, I discovered that the other world I entered through mountain solitude was starkly outlined by these words from Robinson Jeffers: "Integrity is wholeness . . . the wholeness of life and things . . . Love that, not man apart from that, or else you will share man's pitiful confusions."

Walking up mountains with a group never gave me the same feeling of wholeness, of directly experiencing the earth. The feeling was there when I climbed alone, and it was there on technical ascents where the alternation of leading and following gave me time to contemplate away from my partner.

Moving roped together on Mustagh Ata was not conducive to that feeling. But alone at the summit, even with the altitude and my preoccupations, I moved into another world. The sensation of starting to ski down Mustagh Ata gave me the same feeling of soaring above the present concerns of humanity that Jeffers so vividly describes through the flight of an eagle:

> And Lenin has lived and Jehovah died: while the mother-eagle
> Hunts her same hills, crying the same beautiful and lonely cry
>   and is never tired; dreams the same dreams,
> And hears at night the rock-slides rattle and thunder in the
>   throats of these living mountains.
>   It is good for man
> To try all changes, progress and corruption, powers, peace
>   and anguish, not to go down the dinosaur's way
> Until all his capacities have been explored: and it is good
>   for him
> To know that his needs and nature are no more changed in fact
>   in ten thousand years than the beaks of eagles.

His words are a rationale of my quest for wildness, solitude, and occasional risk. They also explain some of the other rewards of remote expeditions to Asia. To see wild creatures and native cultures is to see the "living mountains" that have recently undergone "changes, progress and corruption, powers, peace." The wholeness of my experience was rooted in understanding the entire natural and cultural realm, not just the sterile snows of the high summits.

Mountaineering is my personal ticket to experiencing the earth, but I hold no fancy that it is unique in this regard. I know that naturalists and sailors accomplish similar journeys of the mind, each in his own way. I was not, however, prepared to find out later when we returned to Kashgar that during the eighteenth century a Uygur woman of that re-

mote city had seen more of the wilds and splendors of China than any of us.

Uygur women are a double minority, lower in status than either their Moslem husbands or the dominant Han Chinese. Although there are six million Uygurs in Sinkiang, only one Uygur woman appears anywhere in Chinese historical records.

Kashgar is a medieval city with the exception of a few paved streets, vehicles, and government buildings. The high mud-walled homes, mosques, black-veiled women, and white-capped men give much more an impression of being in the Middle East than in China. One afternoon we were shown what appeared to be a huge mosque. Inside was a single, domed room with a ceiling over a hundred feet high. Our guide said that it was the largest building in the province, built by the Ching dynasty emperor, Chien-lung, for his favorite concubine.

Hsiang Fei had been taken from Sinkiang to Peking by the emperor's assistants because she was the most beautiful girl in Turkestan. According to local legend, she refused to go unless several promises were met, among them that if she died while in Peking, her body would be taken back to Kash-

gar and buried in a special tomb. Although she was the emperor's favorite, legend has it that she never succumbed to his advances and carried a sharp weapon at all times. A special Moslem quarter with a Turkish bath was built for her inside the palace grounds. When she died, her body was hand-carried over the Silk Road back to Kashgar. The journey took three and one-half years.

The Concubine's Tomb of Kashgar houses not only the body of Hsiang Fei, but also eighty-four of her relatives and the wooden palanquin in which she came. Rays of light beamed onto the caskets through high windows. Never before had I visited a place of burial so inspiring. For an hour we entered the time-sense of an era in which the travel we do by jet in part of a day required a commitment to leave one's home and family for years.

The city of Kashgar was still officially closed to tourism. Everywhere we walked we were surrounded by throngs of people. When an old woman approached us with tears running down her cheeks, we thought that somehow we might have offended local customs. She clung to Jo's arm while I asked the interpreter to find out her problem. Tears came to his eyes as he gave us her answer, "I am one hundred years old, exactly one hundred. I have never seen a foreign woman before, and I am deeply moved."

These cultural "first ascents" were even more gratifying than those in the mountains, but they did have their drawbacks. One morning as I vainly tried to take photos in a cluster of thousands of curious Kashgarians, Dick said, "Now you know what it feels like to be Bob Dylan for a day."

Dick had been walking the streets of Kashgar the past few days with Chris Bonington, Britain's best-known mountaineer, who was on his way back from a reconnaissance of Mt. Kongur next to Mustagh Ata. Bonington found a different kind of fame in Kashgar: the locals thought that with his black beard and European features he bore an uncanny resemblance to one of the faces above the town square. Dick also shared this resemblance. They earned the nicknames Marx 1 and Marx 2. Once Bonington suffered a far worse indignity. Uygur men favor short haircuts. A group of well-intentioned spectators began to laugh when they saw him, commenting within earshot of his interpreter, "My, foreign women have long beards!"

The crowds of onlookers didn't threaten me in the least because they seemed so honestly curious about us. Not once did I feel a hint of hostility. Our Chinese hosts told us how

Uzbek man of Kashgar.

East Brigade Street, Kashgar.

well integrated into the system the people of Kashgar had become, but in town I met an English-speaking dissident who had an entirely different side to present.

"Years ago I spoke up for my rights," he said, "but the Chinese have no character in their dictionary for human rights. I was sent to work in a coal mine for twelve dollars a month, and they even made me buy my own coal pick. The people of Kashgar look westward. Toward the Middle East they see the spread of their own people. Toward Peking they do not see their own kind or their values. While you were in the mountains, four Chinese PLA [People's Liberation Army] soldiers were beaten to death in front of a mosque by an angry Uygur mob because they had not shown respect for Islam. I'm not really sure how it started. The soldiers are not allowed to shoot back at minority peoples without special permission, so the survivors returned to headquarters, and more soldiers returned with guns and shot into the crowd. Many Uygurs were killed. But this is only road news. You will never read of it in a Chinese publication. It is our real history."

At dawn the next morning I walked down East Brigade Street toward the center of town. The Lombardy poplars rustled in the breeze, forming a straight corridor aimed at a giant statue of Mao that rose above the old town. I had the feeling that I was witnessing the end of an era. This part of Central Asia was ever more removed from contact with the rest of the Islamic world to the west. Whether Mao would replace Mecca I couldn't guess, but I saw irony in the fact that visitors like myself—the first Westerners in recent decades—were arriving from the East, from Peking where regu-

lations of the CMA required us to enter the country. Traveling to Kashgar through Peking made about as much sense as a foreign visitor to San Francisco being required to pass through Washington, D.C., first, but in a larger sense I could see why the Chinese might want to have representatives of exotic lands come from Peking rather than through India, Nepal, or Pakistan.

To have traveled such a circuitous route to Mustagh Ata, though, gave me a valuable perspective I otherwise would have missed. In our minds the visions of Kashgar, the Kirghiz, and the geography of the mountains together overpowered by far the significance of our climb itself; yet, as we were toasted at banquets at each point on our homeward traverse of the country, our travels were cast into the single mold of *conquest*. Our ski ascent of the mountain was taken from its context of mountain experience for its own sake and changed into an attainment that fulfilled the wishes of China, America, and our commercial sponsors. We, no less than the Chinese of 1959, had climbed for goals other than our own.

In Peking the night before we left for home, I looked at Chu enduring yet another banquet, and I remembered his random wanderings through meadows and over glaciers despite the handicap of his feet. His eyes met mine in silent communication of his inner self. Under the skin of our bodies—despite different nationalities—was the same knowledge of the other world we had independently discovered. That moment was a more powerful conclusion to my journey than any of the glossy words passed back and forth at the formal celebrations before we jetted home.

Heavenly Pool and Bogda Feng.

PART TWO: TIAN SHAN

Badlands at the foot of the
Tian Shan.

Chapter 3: Through the Dusts of Sinkiang

IN THE SUMMER OF '42, a 1934 Ford truck chugged its way from Kashgar to Urumchi. A Union Jack was mounted on the bumper, yellow dust long since having obscured its vivid red, white, and blue hues. The truck was also yellow with dust. Its inhabitants were yellow. The air and the ground were yellow.

The distance between the two cities was a thousand miles by road, a road that had come into being seven years before for this very truck. In 1935 Sir Eric Teichman had used it to cross Central Asia from Peking. He started off with two trucks, but only one survived the journey, later to be abandoned in Kashgar as a donation to the British consulate. Now the consul himself, Eric Earle Shipton, was using it on official business. In no way did Shipton resemble a representative of His Majesty's Government. He was a slender, boyish thirty-five, and his one patrician feature, his massive eyebrows, were entirely buried under two avalanches of yellow dust, which clung to his forehead at a steeper angle than snows to the Himalaya.

Shipton had long wanted to visit Urumchi, capital of the provincial government of Sinkiang. Now, since he was being replaced as consul, he was going there to pick up his successor, Michael Gillett, who was simultaneously en route to Urumchi from central China.

The road traced an arc along the northern edge of the Taklimakan Desert, a no-man's-land where every river disappears into the sands. At this boundary of desert and mountain, barren lands fingered into the ridges and valleys of the Tian Shan like fjords on the coast of Norway. Along this lifeline caravans could follow gentle slopes and find occasional water where streams came down from the peaks and glaciers. Nowhere else was travel feasible.

Shipton's driving strategy was to go "as fast and as far each day as the machine and the human frame would stand." On this journey he found the terrain "so spectacular, so varied, and so strange that not even the hideous discomfort of motor travel could wholly spoil its enchantment."

On most days the sky was filled with the legendary dusts of Sinkiang. Even when the air was completely still, a veil of fine particles remained suspended, defying gravity until a rain or a great wind bore them away. Much of the soil of central and western China is this wind-borne sediment called "loess." The explorer Baron von Richthofen was the first to point out that the dusty yellow air, the fertile yellow soils, and the soft yellow rocks were all accumulations of loess particles blown from deserts and vegetation-free highlands, which had been exposed by the melting ice sheets of the last Pleistocene glaciation.

Rivers that flow through loess also become yellow. The largest of these is the Huang Ho, or Yellow River. It empties into a sea that in turn becomes discolored: the Yellow Sea. This sea lies between China and Korea, lands of yellow people.

The yellow consul motored eastward, sometimes going more than a hundred miles at a stretch without a trickle of water for his radiator. Sands blowing across the road often forced him to lay planks for his rear wheels; in one particularly bad spot he made just a few hundred yards in an hour. But that same evening he drove through scrub jungle where wild pheasants nested, and water lay in pools, flowed in streams, and filled the night air with mist. The road followed a line of giant willow trees into the oasis town of Aksu. Here he washed off his yellow veneer and attended a banquet held in his honor by local dignitaries. After considerable lubrication with rice wine and brandy, he lapsed into deep sleep.

Before dawn Shipton was on the road again. He had to wake the night watchman to open the massive gates of the walled town. Then he drove through mists blanketing rice fields while "night still clung to the loess cliffs which towered above us on our right. Straight ahead, floating above the mists, yet with their capture of the earliest light the only clearly defined objects in view, were the great ice-peaks of the central Tien Shan. I had not seen them before."

Most travelers went days and weeks next to these mountains without the curtain of loess lifting. When the curtain did rise, it exposed a miraculous sight: mountain peaks appeared to be floating on the clouds of heaven. The entire twelve-hundred-mile-long range borders loess lands, and became known as the Tian Shan, the "Celestial Mountains."

Shipton saw the great rock and snow faces of Khan Tengri, 22,949 feet, long thought to be the highest peak of the Tian Shan. Not until four years after his journey in 1946 did a party of Soviet climbers discover a much higher mountain just ten miles behind it, hidden from the world for at least three hundred days a year by loess dust. A 1931 Soviet expedition had made the first ascent of Khan Tengri, which lay on the border with China. They had no inkling that a higher mountain was so close. That peak, named Peak Pobeda by the Soviets and Mt. Tomur by the Chinese, also straddled the border. At 24,392 feet it is the second highest in the Soviet Union. A large Soviet expedition led by the legendary climber Vitaly Abalakov made the first ascent in 1956. The Chinese repeated the ascent in 1977.

The day before Shipton arrived in Urumchi he crested a grade at 6,000 feet and peered into a desert basin surrounded by mountains on all sides. This was the Turfan Depression, 505 feet below sea level, the lowest point in China. Like Death Valley in the United States, this desert basin roasts in 120° F. summer temperatures; unlike Death Valley it has supported habitation for over two thousand years. The ancient city of Jiaohe was an important post on the Silk Road across Central Asia, and Shipton passed by its decaying walls en route to the modern town of Turfan.

On the floor of the valley lay a long ridge, sculpted by the elements into a spiny pattern like the backbone of a prehistoric monster. This is the "Mountain of Flames," rising in contoured sandstone with alternate layers of white silica and the Tertiary red beds that color desert badlands the world over. So hot was this place that a Chinese poet of the Tang dynasty wrote: "Fire clouds over the mountain never dispel/ Birds dare not approach within a thousand *li*."

But in the midst of this furnace agriculture was thriving. Loess soil deposited by eons of winds is extremely fertile, and though the place looked absolutely dry, groundwater from streams out of the Tian Shan was running about sixty feet below the surface. Wheat, cotton, fruit, and even rice and vegetables flourished during a growing season of 220 days per year.

Shipton arrived in Urumchi just six and one-half days after leaving Kashgar, breaking the previous driving record by a full five days. His reward was a treeless city with bazaars of "unspeakable squalor." Kashgar had been a fantasy town for Shipton, an ideal vision of the pastoral life of times long past in Europe—Urumchi was a monstrosity. The soft loess dust of the south side of the Tian Shan was here replaced by the coal dust of an increasingly industrial society.

Cosmopolitan elements were intermingled with the old poverty. Up from the traditional mud-brick buildings rose the massive Bank of China, which had the stolid look of Leningrad with tall Corinthian columns and sheer facades of stone. The Russians maintained a mysterious presence in a vast consulate hidden behind high walls. The American consular buildings were inactive and on a side street near the outskirts of town. The British had no office in Urumchi, so Shipton stayed in the quarters of the Sinkiang Foreign Affairs Department.

This international juxtaposition in Urumchi had strong correlations with the politics to come. Chinese presence was

Kazak horses in a Tian Shan meadow.

35

Oasis in the desert, Kashgar.

ever stronger, Russian less certain, American and British weak.

Throughout its history Urumchi had frequently switched allegiance to one wave after another of conquering hordes. During the first and second centuries A.D. Huns plunged through on their way to Europe. In the ninth century the Uygurs set up a kingdom around Urumchi from a base in Mongolia. The Uygurs are a Turkish people who settled in Mongolia before taking on the Islamic faith. As they expanded their realm, much of Central Asia became the kingdom of "Turkestan," a name that is still in use today. In the twelfth century the Uygurs were conquered by the Kara Kitay, a branch of the Liao dynasty that blended Mongol, Turkic, and Tangul blood with Chinese. Less than a century later the Mongol hordes of Genghis Khan took over, and in the fifteenth century the Chinese subdued the Mongols. By the seventeenth century Dzungarian Mongols had retaken the region, only to be annihilated by Manchus from the north in the eighteenth century.

Like the American West and Australia, these barren lands were often pioneered by people who were fleeing the laws of the civilized world. In 1864, during a rebellion of Tungan Moslems and immigrated outlaws, 130,000 Manchus and Han Chinese were killed. Anarchy prevailed for seventeen years until Chinese troops decisively won on both sides of the Tian Shan and organized the region into Sinkiang Province in 1881.

Violence and bloodshed were still everyday events in Urumchi at the time of Shipton's visit. One evening the provincial government invited him to the local opera—a traditional Chinese dance-drama. During a violent war dance the head of a giant spear accidentally flew off into the audience, striking a girl in the front row fully in the face. As blood gushed from her wounds and she slumped in her seat, the crowd applauded and roared with laughter. The dance continued.

Shipton and Gillett, the new consul, were scheduled to spend several weeks in Urumchi as guests of the government before driving back to Kashgar. With time available they leapt at an invitation to trek into the Bogda Ola Mountains behind the city. Not unexpectedly the two diplomats were given a large armed escort. Their destination was Tianchi, the "Heavenly Pool," a mountain lake set into a forest of fir and spruce at 6,600 feet beneath the ice-capped peak of Bogda Feng.

The usual path to Tianchi was blocked by floods, so the entourage headed into the forest instead. In the evening they spotted a group of *akois*, the tents of Kazak herdsmen, felt-covered domes almost identical to the Kirghiz yurts that Shipton had seen in the Pamirs. All were invited inside to sit around a fire and drink bowls of *kumiss*, the fermented mare's milk liquor of Central Asia. A sheep was killed in their honor for a banquet that lasted well into the night.

Shipton found the Kazaks "more truculent and less amenable to control" than the Kirghiz, whose way of life was very similar, but "on this occasion their hospitality left nothing to be desired." Setting off the next morning into the fresh, damp, pungent forest was sheer delight for a man who had just spent two years in the deserts of southern Sinkiang. Nearing the lake beneath green forests and white snow he felt "a thousand miles, instead of a bare twenty, from the vast, barren steppes of Central Asia."

They arrived the next day at the Heavenly Pool and spent the next night in a lakeside monastery inhabited by Taoist monks. The blue bricks and dark tiles of the monastery blended with the natural scene. Here also was the modest temple of Fu Shou, a place of blessing and longevity next to the Heavenly Pool.

Shipton's *Survey of India* map showed no high peaks in the area, yet Bogda Feng appeared very steep and formidable. A German geologist, Groeber, surveyed the peak as 21,626 feet in 1903; *The Times Atlas* marked it 22,770 feet. Gillett and Shipton walked by themselves until the firs gave way to grass slopes, and they kept going for hours more to the top of a rock pyramid where they came face to face with Bogda's highest peak swirling in the clouds. Ice-falls and hanging glaciers clung to its sides. As the two watched in awe, they heard a noise close by. Peeking over the crest they looked down onto fifteen ibex—giant wild goats—grazing totally unaware less than a hundred feet away.

Shipton left Urumchi for the duration of World War II, his memory of the Bogda region heightened by "the curious sense of unreality that I feel for all Central Asian country when I am not there." After the war, in 1947, Shipton visited Heavenly Pool again with his wife. He was still recovering from the frostbite he suffered during an attempt to climb Mustagh Ata with H. W. Tilman a few months before. Before Tilman left for England, they vowed to attempt Bogda Feng together the following summer. Now Shipton had a chance to reconnoiter the problems they would face.

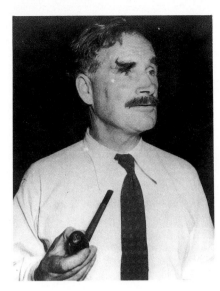

H. W. Tilman, 1951.

He was reasonably convinced that the peak was somewhere around 18,000 feet, as Sven Hedin had surveyed it from a distance in 1932. This accounted for the usually precise *Survey of India* not showing anything high here, because in Himalayan parlance an eighteen-thousander is a hillock. Peaks were far snowier at forty-four degrees north latitude than at twenty-eight (where Mt. Everest lay). He realized that it would be "difficult to adjust ourselves to the idea that a mountain of 18,000 feet could present a really tough proposition." Yet in front of him were the steep walls of the north face rising 7,000 vertical feet from the glaciers. "All I could predict with reasonable certainty," he noted, "was that the rock would be good and the climb would be of a high order."

Shipton and Tilman arrived at the foot of the mountain in early July 1948. With them were two native helpers. One was a Sherpa named Lakhpa who had climbed to Camp VI on Everest and accompanied Shipton to Kashgar, where he acquired both a Uygur wife and a fat belly. The other was a young Marco Polo sheep hunter from Hunza nicknamed Hill Billy, who had no climbing experience but had always lived in the mountains.

One day Tilman was exploring alone when a Kazak with a rifle accosted him, took note of his field glasses and ice ax, then motioned for his shirt. Tilman took a puff on his pipe and walked away, later writing, "It wasn't a very good shirt, but it was the only one I had." The Kazak tried a second time, but Tilman walked uphill faster than the native, who gave up without firing a shot. Some days later he learned that the Kazaks thought he was a Russian; when they learned he was British their attitude softened to some degree.

After two weeks in the area, Shipton and Tilman had circled much of the broad massif, and they decided to ascend the east ridge of the south face. They cut steps up steep blue ice for hundreds of feet and camped on a narrow ridge. But from there they could see that the rest of the climb was beyond their capabilities. They climbed to the top of an "incident" on the ridge that they judged to be 16,500 feet, then retreated to Urumchi.

The schedule called for Shipton and Tilman to leave for Kashgar, but their truck—the same 1934 Ford—was in the shop with a cracked cylinder that would take at least another week to repair. On a pretense of gathering ice from the glaciers for the consulate cocktail glasses, they returned to the mountains in an official American vehicle together with the consul, Lakhpa, Hill Billy, a White Russian mechanic and his wife, an American woman visitor, and a journalist. They stopped en route to shoot at several herds of gazelles, but failed to bring one down.

The climbing party separated from the ice-gatherers and headed toward the heights, only to walk into a three-day snow storm. The upper mountain emerged on the fourth day definitely out of condition for climbing. They climbed to about 15,000 feet on a subsidiary ridge and looked at the northeast ridge of the peak, certain that they could climb the upper part in one day of good weather in better conditions—but just as certain they didn't have time to wait for those conditions now.

"How much of the pleasure of mountaineering," Shipton later wrote, "lies in all the varied experience of the Attempt; how much depends on the garnish of Success? We like to think that success is not essential to our maximum enjoyment, which should derive from our knowledge and experience of mountains. The men who eventually reach the top of Everest will not know the mountain as Mallory knew it. Had we in the beginning tried the North-east ridge and succeeded, we should not have experienced Bogda as we did."

On the return they walked along an isolated ridge 8,000 feet above the plains, looking down into the green valley of Heavenly Pool. Wildflowers covered the slopes, and they surprised several herds of fifteen to twenty ibex within a stone's throw. The descent brought them into willows and scrub already tinted with the reds and golds of autumn toward a river sparkling in the sunlight.

That evening they reached a Kazak camp at dark. "They gave us yoghourt but no horses," Tilman explained. "In order to explain ourselves we said we were walking to Urumchi for fun, to which the Kazaks coolly replied that in that case we might as well prolong our fun by walking for two more days until we reached Urumchi."

The two attempts in two weeks by Shipton and Tilman were singular in the mountain's history. No one had ever given Bogda a serious try before. No one would again for decades, until foreign mountaineers were once again permitted to climb in China.

The Tian Shan in summer from the air.

Aerial view of the Bogda Range.

Chapter 4: Ice Mountains of the Flaming Desert

THE RUSSIAN ILYUSHIN I-16 cruised at eye level with Mt. Bogda as I gazed out the window, letting the journal in which I had been writing fall to the floor. What I saw seemed not to be China, but Salt Lake City and the Wasatch Front; through the haze the blurred details of the land seemed identical. Desert ran headlong into a mountain escarpment with snowy summits. A city of at least half a million sat on the edge of the plain, with nearby smokestacks pouring murk into the sky.

But the scene was more immense than the one where Brigham Young halted his Mormon flock by saying, "This is the place." The desert floor in Utah was at 4,000 feet below the 13,500-foot peaks of the Uintas, a giant escarpment by North American standards. The Tian Shan summit out my window was 17,864 feet with a desert floor of under 3,000 feet, creating true Himalayan proportions rising out of Central Asian desert. While the city looked about the right size for my Salt Lake analogue, instead of two hundred thousand people it contained nearly one million. Smoke billowed from coal-fired electric plants instead of the giant copper smelter by Salt Lake City, but I wondered why a town situated so near the obvious hydroelectric potential of mountain rivers chose to smother itself in coal dust.

The people of Sinkiang had no choice. Neither the central nor the provincial government had the funds to invest in hydro or a whole range of other things that would improve the quality of life.

When my journal fell to the floor, I was writing impressions—not about the Tian Shan—based on what I had seen from the air en route from Peking:

For a thousand miles I have seen barely a spade of ground unturned. Human presence has modified this land again and again. No matter what the political philosophy of one billion people, they can never catch up to America living here. Their resources are used up and not awaiting new generations. They may find oil or uranium some day in tremendous quantities, but they will never find the precious ingredients of the *quality* of life. The land will only recover in a time frame beyond my frame of reference. There is no wilderness, no virgin forest, no land that gives the feeling of being created by the current of evolution instead of human modification.

The Sherpas of Nepal turned toward the West at just the right time to save their culture, when the door to Tibet was closing. The People's Republic turned westward toward technology and machines when the old ways were endangered, like wildlife, by sheer loss of habitat. It may be too late. Sinkiang is one billion

Statue of Mao leading his troops.

acres of dust. People who live on the verge of social and economic chaos are not apt to do technical mountaineering in their spare time or to concern themselves with the welfare of wild animals or the environment.

Remembering Sinkiang's history of armed Moslem rebels terrorizing the countryside, I expected the worst as the plane descended toward Urumchi for a three-day stopover en route to Mustagh Ata in the far west of the province.

In the Welcome Guest House about five miles from town I asked for a room key. "You do not need a key," our local interpreter said. "No one locks hotel rooms here in Urumchi. There is no crime."

I later learned that Urumchi has six hundred police officers, but all of them go off duty at 8:00 P.M. Much of what a police officer does in the United States is outside the realm of these men. If a traffic accident occurs at any time of day or night, a crowd gathers immediately and witnesses argue over who was wrong. The crowd pronounces the judgment.

Rather than some higher form of law, this system of justice is actually tradition asserting itself in the absence of law. China has a minimal legal system, especially in the area of international law, where business is normally conducted on a handshake. While we were in Urumchi, Professor Duanmu Zheng, chairman of the law department of Sun Yat Sen University, told Americans that he followed the *Harvard Law Review* and the *American Journal of International Law*. His latest edition was 1951.

Throughout China few things were as they were reported to be by the Chinese media or interpreters. Mostly it was a case, as with the law books, of telling the truth but not the whole truth. For example, according to Chinese sources the irrigation of the desert around Urumchi was a seemingly magical process dating from antiquity. Aqueducts called *karez* ran underground for hundreds of miles all over the hot desert, carrying water unexposed to evaporation to points where it mystically surfaced without pumps and irrigated the loess soil into rich farmland. With a wise nod of the head we were told that the system was two thousand years old, reinforcement of the idea that the Chinese invented everything before we Westerners did.

In reality the ingenious *karez* were imported from Persia in the eighteenth century by the Uygurs, a Moslem minority bearing no love for the Chinese. *Karez* were made by drilling a well to groundwater about sixty feet below the surface, then drilling slightly shallower wells in a line descending into low ground such as the Turfan Depression. By connecting them with a horizontal flume, water would surface by gravity in the area where irrigation was needed.

Before 1949 only 5 percent of the population of Sinkiang Province was Han Chinese. Now Hans comprise 45 percent. The Uygurs' practice of Islam has been curtailed, accompanied by an official rationale of greater freedom. Jack Chen explains why in his sympathetic book, *The Sinkiang Story*:

The feudal landlords and nobility, khodjas and khans were at the same time rulers and religious dignitaries. . . . They used religious dogma and their religious prerogatives to force their dictates . . . of land tenure and of marriage, the subordinate position of women, how the people should amuse themselves, dress, and so on. . . . The history of Sinkiang was made hideous and bloody by their intolerance. . . . Ending the privilege of such religious feudal lords was a prerequisite of true freedom of religious belief.

Although our hotel was well out of town, we were free to roam. If we desired motor travel we had only to request it, and a van, interpreter, and liaison officer would take us, choosing a route through the best parts of town. There are no taxis.

One afternoon I donned running shorts and headed out for a fifteen-mile loop through parts of town where our drivers had not ventured. Starting on pavement, I soon switched to gravel, then dirt, then cross-country over a hill with no trail onto railroad tracks that led toward cement plants, coal-fired electric generators, and assorted factories. Some people stared, but many ignored my presence because of my strange, nearly naked appearance. When we passed in vehicles or walked fully dressed, all smiled and waved.

I followed a dirt path into a housing area that had seemingly no planning. Several attempts to penetrate the maze failed, and I ran into a group of children in a cul-de-sac. I gestured in the direction I wished to go, and the ragtag dozen set off with me to show the way. We ran at considerable speed across a Harlem basketball court, past a Delhi mud wall, and out through a Detroit of shattered glass and concrete into the fields.

The smells were even more varied than the sights: the sweetness of ripe melons, the pungence of donkeys, the special nausea of human excrement, then finally the aroma of wet sagebrush and desert earth after a rain.

Three boys of twelve to fourteen kept running with me for half an hour, smiling and sharing in my wonder. They stopped only when I reached the main highway, where I entered and won a new competition with a donkey cart, to the cheers of two old men. A bicyclist came up from behind and took up the challenge; I sped up and beat him up a hill, only to have him come by laughing triumphantly on the downslope. The people were so much more spontaneous here than in Peking, and for the first time I felt like a participant in China rather than a spectator or a side show. It was a joy to return to my unlocked room, shower, and have a warm beer before dinner.

My glimpses into Uygur life in Urumchi were broadened by a later visit to a private home in Kashgar with our interpreter. We asked to see how an average worker lived, and although the Chinese swore that the family was not out of the ordinary, it was immediately apparent that the building into which we were escorted was larger, cleaner, and better decorated than the surrounding mud-walled hovels. Mutton was roasting on an open fire, and a singer sat cross-legged in the main room accompanying himself with jangling discords on a mandolinlike *datar*.

On the surface we appeared to be at a Chinese version of a Sunday barbecue in the suburbs. Ned Gillette described the scene for a commissioned article in *National Geographic*:

One morning we sit on worn carpets in Aziz Aysa's five-room house. Seven years old, it is flat-roofed and made of sun-dried mud bricks reinforced with straw—adequate, since only about three inches of rain fall a year. Aziz works at a large commune east of Kashi that grows more than fifty kinds of fruit—melons, pears, apricots, peaches, pomegranates, plums, and *aq alma*—huge white apples. He owns his house. His bicycle, which cost 179 yuan ($112), stands outside. He wears a watch.

His family has lived here for generations. He has six children: Minorities are not subject to the birth-control regulations that encourage Han couples to have only one child.

Another reality here was beyond the scope of the *National Geographic* or the simple statements we all made in lectures afterwards in America. Aziz is no doubt a generous, kind man. He smiled a lot. He seemed to like us. But he did not invite us into his home. The Ministry of Foreign Affairs asked him to do it. Every once in a while he let his guard down and I saw a look that I had seen in America many times. Genuine hosts don't ever lapse into momentary unfocused stares that border on contempt. I had watched American Indians and blacks do the same thing to uninvited guests from the ruling class. There were three races in our little room. One was in control, one was visiting, and one just lived there. What we saw was analogous to a Chinese delegation being shown how well a black family lived in their two-hundred-thousand-dollar-ranch-house in Watts.

Also in Kashgar we visited a cotton factory with thirty-two hundred workers and seemingly equal decibels. The director proudly showed us his fine cotton products—corduroy, muslin, and the gaily colored plaids favored by the Uygur women. He wore polyester.

The duality of the Uygurs goes to the roots of their being. In one light they seem pure Turkish; in another, Oriental. Their religion conforms neither to that of their rulers nor to that practiced by their strict Islamic kinfolk. They appear easy-going, but their history is rife with violence. Ellsworth Huntington wrote in *Pulse of Asia* that the Uygurs' good qualities are "gentleness, good temper, hospitality, courtesy, patience, contentment, democracy, religious tolerance, and industry." Then he listed their bad ones: "timidity, dishonesty, stupidity, provincialism, childishness, lack of initiative, lack of curiosity, indifference to suffering, and immorality."

Our interpreter, Wang Wei-ping, put things more gently: "The Uygurs are like the wheat they sow. Winds blow them one way and then the other, but their roots are firmly in the ground."

When a van drove us to Heavenly Pool in the Tian Shan, we went from Uygur to Kazak territory. The Kazaks are also active Moslems, but as different from the Uygurs as they are from the Chinese. Descended from Uzbek stock of Genghis Khan's Golden Horde, they emerged as an ethnic group in the sixteenth century. Most of them live across the Soviet border, better known to the Western world as "Cossacks," the legendary horsemen of Central Asia.

In northern Sinkiang Province these very flexible people often live in communes with Buddhist Mongolians who raise pigs, while they raise horses. The Kazaks reap the monetary rewards of utilizing the same land for both animals even though their Moslem faith doesn't allow them to touch pork.

We started into the mountains before dawn, hoping to see Bogda at sunrise across the lake. Rounding a large curve in the road, desert suddenly joined with alpine terrain. Meadows flowed through open forests, draping north-facing slopes in solid green. Distant peaks glistened with snow, and the haze over the desert was pink with the dawn.

Soon we came to a spruce-girt pasture filled with horses. The sight gave me an unexpected rush, and I thought of the Buddhist saying that horses were put on earth to make lands beautiful. Next to the pasture were two *akois*. A woman with surprisingly Oriental features was bringing a pail of water from the stream with two boisterous children.

This was the first of many similar scenes that day. These Kazaks live in a storybook world, herding sheep, goats, horses, cattle, and camels. They are a happy, healthy race without the plethora of small ailments that often plague China's lowlanders. Their energy, enthusiasm, and hospitality match the elevation of their homes. How could I refuse the invitation of a family which blocked my way with smiles, took my hand, led me to their *akois*, and sat me down? Inside the round dome things were very different than in a Kirghiz yurt, where modern fabrics were made into traditional quilts and clothes. The Kazaks seemed to love all things bright and shiny and off the shelf. They had little or no appreciation for their own traditions. I sat in an aluminum folding chair with a polypropylene cushion, ate boiled eggs out of a plastic bowl on an imitation wood table with a machine-made purple tablecloth. The rugs on the wall had the bright and varied colors of a Los Angeles flea market. Yet the basic dwelling was beautifully hand-built from willow wands and natural-colored felt.

We found no monastery, no Taoist monks. A small inn bustled with Chinese tourists who come up from Urumchi on rare holidays. Through the interpreter I asked about wildlife in the region, remembering Tilman and Shipton's dozens of encounters with gazelles and ibex. No one had personally seen large mammals in recent years, but I was assured that "way back up in the mountains" wolves, gazelles, and wild goats still gamboled.

The deep blue lake looked as if it belonged in western Canada. The forests, however, were broken by grass that was too smooth and green to be natural. Everywhere I looked, overgrazed slopes stretched toward the snowline, a grim reminder that since Liberation the province has tripled its livestock industry with no emphasis on range management. Wildflowers were beginning to bloom all over this altered ground. I found edelweiss, but none of the special lilies that the locals once prized for herbal medicine. An amateur botanist with a later party found over fifty varieties of flowering plants in the region.

Modern Chinese publications list a plethora of wildlife in the Bogda area: bears, wolves, ibex, gazelles, marmots, deer, elk, ermine, fox, plus in other parts of the Tian Shan, snow leopards, lynx, sika deer, roe deer, and otters. I could not find anyone who had seen a large mammal in person in recent years. (This total lack of wildlife in the Bogda area was later confirmed when seven Americans, four Dutch, three Germans, and three Chinese spent eight days trekking in the Bogda Range. In their 120-man-days of searching, not a single wild thing was seen except birds, rodents, and spiders.)

When it was time for us to leave Heavenly Pool, Jan Reynolds and I decided to run down the dirt road and have the bus pick us up. We wanted some exercise, and we wanted a more intimate view of the terrain. We expected to go a mile or two, but because of the normal hurry-up-and-wait delays of Chinese tourism, we ran ten miles through Kazak encampments next to rushing streams, a fitting end for what had been a slightly depressing visit to the hidden alpine paradise described by Shipton and Tilman.

Another environmental change at lower elevations around the Tian Shan was an eerie confirmation of my comparison of the region to the Great Basin of Utah and Nevada. Locals told me that something strange was happening in Devil Mountain behind Urumchi. At first I thought their use of English was incorrect; they must have meant "on" the mountain. No, they said. The mountain was off limits to citizens, hollowed out inside, and set up with large cooling fans on top. Did I know what was going on?

Cabbage harvest in a Uygur vegetable commune.

46   *Interior of a Uygur home.*

I answered no, and the topic changed to the convoys of trucks that drove at night through the Turfan Depression into nowhere. Seven drivers were used for one truck for one day, each taking a small leg of the journey without being told where the truck came from or where it was going. Each driver was a Communist party member.

My informers were not absolutely sure what was going on, and in typical Chinese fashion they provided only hints. I remembered some facts from researching an article on the bizarre CIA plan to plant a nuclear-powered sensing device on top of Nanda Devi in the Himalaya to monitor Chinese missile and bomb testing in Sinkiang during the sixties. "Lop Nor," I said, watching eyebrows raise around me. "Atomic testing."

"That is what we think too. We hear all about the movements of heavy crates by the road news, our word-of-mouth telegraph. Some things come by airplane to Yuli by the river that runs out to Lop Nor, the salt lake. Heavy things come by rail and then by truck. At Lake Aydingkol, the lowest point of Turfan, they have a place to assemble these things before they move them in the dead of night. We used to see many flashes when the night sky became bright as dawn. That doesn't happen very often these days, but when it does it is always just after the trucks have been driving into the desert."

Next to Lake Aydingkol is the legendary Mountain of Flames. The words of the Tang dynasty poet took on a new meaning:

Fire clouds over the mountain never dispel
Birds dare not approach within a thousand li.

*The main Sherpa trade route into
Tibet enters by this great gap in
the Himalayan crest, the
Nangpa La.*

PART THREE: INNER TIBET

*Pilgrims lining up to worship in
the Jokhang Temple, Lhasa.*

Chapter 5: Into Tibet

SINCE HIS YOUTH Heinrich Harrer had dreamed of going to the Himalaya. Now the dream had come true, but with a harsh reality beyond his wildest imagination. He was walking briskly through monsoon jungle, lusting for the holy Ganges with the intensity of a zealous pilgrim. Like such a pilgrim, he was clothed in rags and brown of skin, for his distinctly European features were hidden beneath permanganate stain and grease.

Later he would reflect, "For a man who was neither British nor wealthy there was only one way" to get to the Himalaya: doing "something which made it impossible for one's claims to be passed over." After becoming a downhill racer on the 1936 Austrian Olympic Team, he made the first ascent of the most legendary north face of the Alps—the Eigerwand—in 1938. Despite his accomplishments and his longing for the Himalaya, he was almost passed over for the 1939 German Nanga Parbat expedition. He was invited just four days before departure.

Five years had passed since that expedition. From India the war in Europe seemed far away, but it affected his life as if he were home. When he returned to civilization in 1939 after the long expedition, the war had begun and he was imprisoned at Dehra Dun by the British.

Harrer had twice escaped from the British POW camp; twice he had been caught. The third time he laid the groundwork more carefully.

Dehra Dun, the largest camp in India, contained over two thousand prisoners of war and a library of books on Asian languages and exploration. Before escaping this third time Harrer taught himself Tibetan and Hindi, made notes and maps on Tibet, and exercised for hours each day, even in the monsoon rains.

Harrer's destination was considered impossible even by the British, who were free to travel in India. He had dedicated his life to doing the impossible, and to him it seemed logical to break out of prison and walk a thousand miles to Lhasa—in the heart of forbidden Tibet. To be caught en route would at the very least give him free days in his beloved Himalaya, instead of boredom behind barbed wire.

Tibet's most successful defense against visitors from the outside was not well-guarded borders, but cultural and legal inhibitions against villagers supplying food or lodging to foreigners. Anyone who tried to bring enough goods for the entire journey was instantly suspect; subsistence living on the barren, two-mile-high Tibetan Plateau was all but impossible.

To penetrate Tibet without a small army required the constitution of an athlete, the pretense of an actor, and the knowledge of a scholar. Harrer had already failed on his earlier breakout attempts with men who did not meet the first two of these standards. The third standard was equally important. Understanding medieval Europe helped considerably. Lhasa was Tibet's Vatican, the Dalai Lama its pope. Tibet was still a feudal theocracy with an all-pervading religion. One-fifth of the populace dedicated their entire lives to the church.

On May 17, 1944, Harrer entered Tibet over a 17,200-foot pass, the Tsangchok La. With him now were three other escapees from Dehra Dun, who had traveled separately to the Ganges. Among them was Peter Aufschnaiter, his partner both in prison and on the Nanga Parbat expedition.

In the first village, Kasapuling, the starving men were refused food. Calling the bluff, they threatened to take a goat by force if they could not buy one. They were sold the oldest billy goat for an exorbitant price, and they slaughtered it in a nearby stable. At each successive village they bluffed their

Heinrich Harrer in Tibet.
© *National Geographic Society*

52

way, sometimes obtaining legal travel permits for short distances, other times moving under cover.

During the first six months in Tibet, two of the men decided to take their chances elsewhere rather than continue with the daily uncertainties. One set off for India, the other for Nepal. This left only Aufschnaiter and Harrer, who were by now poorer than the average Tibetan in both lifestyle and appearance. In some places it took them months to patiently negotiate or deviously plan their further travels.

In the village of Tsaparang they searched in vain for evidence of a Christian church built in 1625 by two Portuguese missionaries, Antonio de Andrade and Manuel Marques, the first known Europeans in Tibet. Another missionary, Johann Grueber, who had smuggled his way into Lhasa in 1661, was a particular inspiration to them because after all his hardship and intrigue, he had been very hospitably received in the holy city.

The landscape became indelibly impressed on them. One particular vision contained the universal essence of their dreams of Tibet. Mt. Kailas was the holiest peak in Tibet for both Buddhists and Hindu pilgrims from India. It rose elegantly, layered with ancient sediments and ice, above the waters of the great Lake Manasarovar. To Harrer it was "certainly one of the loveliest spots on earth," surrounded by barren plateau, clouds, and glaciers flowing from the higher, but less holy heights of 25,355-foot Gurla Mandhata. In the midst of this splendor was a unique geographical occurrence. Near Lake Manasarovar were the sources of two of the greatest rivers of Asia, the Indus and the Brahmaputra. Because their courses predated the geologically recent uplift of the Himalaya, they actually cut through the main Himalaya (something as improbable as if the Mississippi crossed the Continental Divide in America), then flowed through separate nations before emptying into the Indian Ocean fifteen hundred miles apart.

As they passed across Tibet, Harrer and Aufschnaiter saw other high peaks rarely glimpsed by even the greatest explorers. Shisha Pangma—unclimbed, unattempted, the highest peak wholly in Tibet—rose to 26,291 feet above the deep blue lake of Pelgu Tso. Later came Cho Oyu, slightly higher at 26,750 feet, on the border of Nepal set behind the level plains of Tingri.

Wildlife was plentiful. Herds of Tibetan gazelle grazed the banks of the Tsangpo River, which is known as the Brahmaputra in India. In the hills were blue sheep, which

Tingri, a trading village high on the Tibetan Plateau.

Peter Aufschnaiter with a Tibetan woman. © *National Geographic Society*

they hunted to add wild mutton to their diet of *tsampa* (Tibetan barley). Brown bears virtually identical with the American grizzly crossed their path at close range, striking fear into their hearts. The most impressive animal of all was the *kiang*, a wild ass the color of a palomino and the size of a mule. Harrer described it as elegant, curious, graceful, and enchanting. "Since I first saw them these untamed beautiful beasts have seemed a symbol of freedom."

Another symbol of freedom was the monastery at Longda built by the beloved Tibetan saint and poet, Milarepa, in the eleventh century. Like Harrer and Aufschnaiter, but for totally different reasons, Milarepa had left his comfortable life and family to travel in rags across Tibet, discovering the same sort of inner strength that the two fugitives were finding within themselves:

I have the superiority of indifference
My audacity knows no obstacles
Diseases, evil spirits, sins, wretchedness
Adorn the hermit who I am.

Milarepa embodied many of the dualities of Tibetan existence. He was born of a noble family, yet forced to work like a slave. He was first a lusty, hard-drinking youth, then an ascetic holy man. He was a black magician who struck dead his enemies from afar; but he came to be known as the most loved Tibetan poet, wizard, and saint. Other societies have such dualities in their folklore, but the Tibetans are unique in their honest exposition of human nature.

Lamas were not the counterpart of priests; nor were they intermediaries between men and their gods. Fosco Maraini, an Italian anthropologist who visited Tibet a few years after Harrer, described the lama as "a selected soldier, not an exorcist or a possessor of secrets."

Legend has it that Milarepa learned the miracle of levitation, of exploring the deepest abysses and most giddying heights while his body glowed with power. But the lamas Harrer met claimed no supernatural powers beyond their own enlightenment. Years later he wrote: "The Tibetan monk, or lama, makes do with two eyes just like any other man, and when he wants to fly in the air he uses an ordinary aeroplane for the purpose."

Harrer found much of what had been written about Tibetans "wretchedly irresponsible pseudo-literature." Scholars had recorded in seriousness what Tibetans said for the childish pleasure of "pulling other people's legs, particularly learned ones." He felt that the tenets of Tibetan Buddhism could not be summarized like those of other faiths, because they were regarded as the "fundamental treasure of each individual," different for different peoples and regions, and "therefore something about which it was impossible to generalize."

He could concisely describe how Tibetans worshiped, but not what or why. This, then, was the real mystery of Tibet, not the hidden secrets of mystical beings, but the unknowability of ordinary men who had no need to explain the creation of the world as a whole nor to unify their beliefs with those of their neighbors in the next valley.

Tibetan culture is full of what appear to be paradoxes. The land itself has extreme alternations of season, and a rugged appearance with a most fragile dusting of soil. Village life sets the bright exterior splendor of nature against the dark interior worlds of the home and the monastery. Individuals display opposite personality traits, which would be deemed contradictory in the logic-ridden Western world: extreme generosity and extreme cruelty, spontaneous laughter and mystical ritual, orthodoxy and tolerance, superstition and sagacity.

Tibetan Buddhism exemplifies these dualities through celestial Buddhas appearing in both beatific and wrathful forms. Unlike Christianity, their tradition does not hold most immoral acts as religious violations. Even a lama's actions are not always expected to agree with his words.

Coming from the soil of another civilization, ancient India, Buddhism became patently dualistic as soon as it was overlaid upon Tibetan culture in the eighth century. Paintings on monastery walls depict sea monsters and dragons out of a dark Indian jungle densely populated with snakes, unbelievers, elephants, tigers, and unspoken forces. This imagery clashes with pastoral Tibetan shepherds, yaks, open space, and also with the sterile, snowy peaks—abodes of the gods.

The best Tibetologists do not speak of the merger of India and Tibet. They accept the dual nature of the culture. Fosco Maraini, who accompanied the Italian scholar Giuseppe Tucci into Tibet, states: "Tibet is like a living museum. In the darkness of Tibetan temples there still survives the India which was transplanted there more than a thousand years ago. It is an invisible jungle of the spirit, invisibly fossilized among the ice."

From the Indian myth that Himalayan snows are the home of *vidyahara*, supermen invested with magic and special knowledge, comes what R. A. Stein calls "the popular European picture of Tibet as the dwelling place of immortal sages guarding the ultimate secrets."

Until the 1860s, Tibet was little more than a geographical curiosity to the Western world. The Russians considered expansion of their empire into Tibet while the nervous British had virtually no knowledge of the northern approaches to their own Indian empire through a land totally closed to foreigners. The British believed that no Caucasian could penetrate the Tibetan cultural blockade, but they came up with a highly imaginative counterforce.

At Dehra Dun, where Harrer later escaped from his POW camp, British officers of the Great Trigonometrical Survey of India trained dark-skinned Indians for a Mission Impossible-style task. They were briefed on the use of the compass, sextant, and celestial navigation, supplied with gadgetry such as false-bottomed luggage and prayer wheels with hidden note pads, then disguised as traders or pilgrims for the duration of their mission. The British called these clandestine operatives "pundit explorers." Their immediate goal was to acquire enough information to produce the first accurate map of Tibet.

After two years of training, the British launched the first pundit, Nain Singh. He walked into the heart of Tibet repeating mantras like a true pilgrim—in reality his own findings set to verse—so that they could be memorized by repetition, like prayers. Having perfected a uniform stride, he measured distance by dropping a prayer bead from a special rosary with 100, instead of the usual 108, beads after a certain number of steps.

Nearly a year later he reached Lhasa, where his observations of the sun and stars enabled him to plot the exact latitude and longitude of the place for the first time. By measuring the boiling point of water he found Lhasa's elevation to be 11,699 feet.

Caravan under Chomolhari, 1941.

55

Another pundit, named Kintup, embarked on an 1880 mission to put marked logs into the Tsangpo River in Tibet at 10,000 feet, to ascertain whether it was the same as the Brahmaputra River of India at just 500 feet on the other side of the Himalaya. Only 120 miles of the river had defied exploration. Kintup was disguised as the servant of a real Mongolian lama, who was privy to the project. The lama became discouraged when the going became rough in an impassable gorge, and he not only deserted Kintup, but also sold him as a slave. Kintup escaped and later contrived his own sale to the head lama of Marpung near where he planned to release the logs. He worked as a slave, gained his new master's confidence, appealed for leave to make a pilgrimage to Lhasa, sent a message to India from Lhasa telling the exact date the logs would be released, returned to his master, worked nine more months, released the logs at the appointed time, escaped to India, and arrived home four years after he began. Unfortunately, his message never reached India, and the logs floated unseen into the Bay of Bengal.

The most famous of the pundits became the model for a Kipling character in *Kim*. Sarat Chandra Das was in a key position as headmaster of a boarding school for Tibetan immigrants in Darjeeling before he was recruited. He stayed with the school, carefully selecting students for training at Dehra Dun, thus adding an invaluable element of ethnic identity to the pundit formula.

Das became an active pundit himself after he managed to negotiate permission from the Panchen Lama (who, with the Dalai Lama, comprised the political leadership of central Tibet) for a six-month visit to the Tashilhunpo Monastery. As the house guest of the lama's first minister, Das gained invaluable information on the political situation in Tibet. He correctly assessed the surprising degree of Chinese influence in Tibetan affairs that came after the Chinese army helped Tibet win a war against invading Gurkhas in 1792. Das discovered that the Tibetans erroneously believed that the British had supported the Gurkhas.

The Tibetans had a deep-seated fear of the British. From a private trading venture in 1600, the British East India Company had spread its power until His Majesty's Government took over direct control of India in 1858 "to be in closer touch with Indian opinion." However more fair the rule of the British raj than that of the old maharajahs, the Tibetans wanted no contact with it whatsoever.

The British failed to recognize a concept fundamental to all future dealings with Tibet, one that would have quieted their fear of a Tibetan alliance with Russia. It explained the xenophobia that walled out Harrer and other explorers. It explained much of the country's legendary mystery. It explained why Tibet avoided at all costs treaties with world powers who could have ultimately saved it from the Communist Chinese.

Beneath the glitter and ritual of Tibetan lamaism was the greatest paradox of all, the Achilles heel of this feudal society. Harrer, an enthusiastic admirer of Tibetan culture, explained this concept gently:

They [lamas] are clever enough not to believe that their power is limitless, but they punish anyone who suggests it is not. Our behavior, which remained uninfluenced by any of their superstitions, must have given the Tibetans something to think about. We used to go by night into the forests without being molested by demons, we climbed mountains without lighting sacrificial fires; and still nothing happened to us.

Henry Savage Landor, one of the few Englishmen not in the service of the British raj ever to reach Lhasa, also remarked on the lamas:

These lamas . . . are very clever in many ways, and have a great hold over the entire country. They are, 90 percent of them, unscrupulous scamps, depraved in every way, and given to every sort of vice. So are the women Lamas. They live and sponge on the credulity and ignorance of the crowds; and it is to maintain this ignorance, upon which their luxurious life depends, that foreign influence of every kind is strictly kept out of the country.

Landor's second illegal journey into Tibet came just after Colonel Francis Younghusband's military excursion to Lhasa in 1904. He saw no justification for his soon-to-be-knighted countryman's actions "butchering thousands of helpless and defenceless natives in a manner most repulsive to any man who is a man, and of which we can but be ashamed."

After Landor wrote his outspoken thoughts in two books, British scholars waged a campaign to discredit his two journeys entirely. A cloud of doubt hung over his explorations for the rest of his life. Only decades later were his descriptions of previously unknown parts of Tibet shown to be true. His accounts of the integrity of lamas were not characteristic for all of Tibet, but only for Lhasa, where political intrigue was a constant complication of monastic life.

Because of a rumor that the Dalai Lama was negotiating with the czar of Russia through a Mongolian lama named

Women on the road at dawn,
Shigatse.

Staff of the 1904 Younghusband expedition in Tibet.

plus an assortment of 3,451 yaks, camels, mules, ponies, and zebrules—donkey-zebra hybrids so unruly that they were never used by the British again.

Not unexpectedly, the British got in a fight. Younghusband met three high lamas sent from Lhasa and confronted them with the issue of Russian influence. The lamas denied that anything like that existed, and repeated over and over again that since their religion had to be preserved, no European could ever be permitted on their soil. Younghusband matched the lamas' intransigence by calling their belief that their religion was in danger "irrational."

As the small army continued to move across a plain near the town of Guru, it came face to face with several thousand Tibetan soldiers armed with ancient muzzleloaders and broadswords. Not a shot was fired. Younghusband did not want bloodshed, but he wanted his men to stand their ground. The Tibetans had apparently been ordered not to shoot or resist; sensing this, the feisty Sikh soldiers began to disarm them. The Tibetan general watched in humiliation for long minutes, then blew off the jaw of an Indian soldier with his revolver. All hell broke loose. Few Tibetans ever fired their muzzleloaders, and the plains were quickly strewn with wave after wave of bodies. Six hundred Tibetans died; just six British were wounded. Even the British Parliament labeled it "a massacre of unarmed men."

General Macdonald did not want to continue, but obeyed orders from Curzon, the viceroy of India. In Gyantse the British forces successfully sieged a fort held by five thousand Tibetans for seven weeks, and continued toward Lhasa.

The British action forced the Dalai Lama to flee to Mongolia, and he left with the very lama, Dorjieff, who was supposed to be the agent of Russian imperialism. The twenty-eight-year-old ruler, who had never been away from the luxury of his holy court, spent months on the road and four long years in exile before returning. The experience helped mold this thirteenth reincarnation into one of the two strongest leaders in Tibetan history. (He can hardly be blamed for later rigidly declaring freedom from China, Russia, and Britain, thus virtually assuring Chinese intervention after his death.)

Younghusband forced a treaty with the ranking regent in Lhasa, but it was not signed by the Chinese *amban*. The Chinese had been nominal overlords of Tibet since 1720. Just the act of making a treaty upset age-old balances. The Chinese denied the validity of an Anglo-Tibetan agreement

Dorjieff, Younghusband and two hundred soldiers entered a Tibetan border town as an official mission from British India to discuss future relations. The Tibetans refused to negotiate. The British waited in vain for five months for permission to go to Lhasa. Younghusband was then granted permission from London to advance as far as Gyantse in central Tibet.

Younghusband was a Sandhurst graduate and a veteran of past Russian intrigues in both Hunza and the Pamirs. The viceroy of India told him that the Tibet mission must be a success, making an aggressive advance a near-certain contingency. The British raj would never have settled for the only other alternative: a meek retreat from the first town. The Tibetan government had always refused to negotiate; the British had no reason to expect a change.

To help negotiate in Gyantse, Younghusband brought with him General J. R. L. Macdonald, 532 British warrant officers, the Seventh Mountain Battery of the Royal Artillery, a Maxim gun detachment from the Norfolk Regiment, half a company of the Second Sappers, six companies and two guns from the Eighth Gurkhas, eight companies of the Twenty-third Sikh Pioneers, an ammunition detail, and a field hospital. Transportation was provided by 1,450 coolies signed without them, and denounced the Dalai Lama's title. Two years later an Anglo-Chinese treaty guaranteed China's sovereignty of Tibet, and a year after that an Anglo-Russian treaty also confirmed it. The Dalai Lama now had no choice but to deal with Peking if he ever wanted to reign in Lhasa again.

The Dalai Lama went to Peking and was rebuffed in attempts to address the dowager empress without going through an *amban*. The American minister in Peking, William W. Rockhill, was an expert on Tibet and a prophetic diplomat. He wrote an official note to President Roosevelt warning that the Dalai Lama's "pride has suffered terribly while here, and he leaves with his dislike for the Chinese intensified. . . . Serious trouble may yet be in store."

Shortly before his death in December 1933, the Thirteenth Dalai Lama wrote in his will: "Unless we can guard our own country, it will happen that the Dalai Lama and Panchen Lama, the Father and the Son, the Holder of the Faith, the Glorious Rebirth, will be broken down and left without a name."

The Dalai Lama was destined to be reborn within a couple of years. A delegation from Lhasa set out to find the new incarnation in the northeast, because the Great Thirteenth had turned his head in that direction inside his coffin. The entire northeast part of old Tibet had become Chinghai Province of China, but this did not deter the search. In October 1937 in the town of Tengster near the Kumbum Monastery a two-year-old boy named Tenzing Gyatso surprised a disguised member of the delegation by calling him a lama from Lhasa, and identifying objects belonging to the last incarnation. The child came to Lhasa as the new Dalai Lama in September 1939, the same month that Harrer and Aufschnaiter's incarceration in India occurred, pointing them, too, in the direction of Lhasa.

On January 15, 1946, two scruffy men in torn sheepskin coats approached the head lama of the village nearest to Lhasa. Their thick beards showed them not to be Tibetan, but their scaly sun-blackened faces didn't seem European. Claiming to be the advance guard of the large entourage of an arriving dignitary, Harrer and Aufschnaiter were given a donkey and driver. After two years on the trail, they were escorted into Lhasa, where to the best of their knowledge no European had ever arrived without a permit.

On the way into town they passed the white buildings of the Drepung Monastery, sprawled at the base of barren hills like a city of ancient Greece. More than eight thousand monks lived in this largest of the world's monasteries, but it was not nearly so impressive as the Potala, the winter palace of the Dalai Lama.

They found the Potala Palace more than a Tibetan acropolis. The Potala did not sit on a hilltop; it *was* the hilltop. Totally dominating Lhasa on a seven-hundred-foot hill in the center of town, its golden roofs sparkled against the fresh snow of distant 18,000-foot peaks. Broad steps led toward the clouds. The Potala was not a single architectural entity like St. Paul's Cathedral; its cluster of walls and buttresses were more like an exquisite group of mountains, each separate yet unified by a design beyond the power of mortal men. The first castle was built in the seventh century, but the majority of the structure was completed during the reign of the Great Fifth Dalai Lama a thousand years later. Besides a palace, the complex housed government offices, warehouses, a school, a monastery, and a prison.

The Potala housed most of the incarnations of Chenrezi, the bodies of the Dalai Lamas. One was ten years old and living; the others were embalmed in tombs decorated with rubies, sapphires, and gold. Over one hundred thousand ounces of gold had been used just in the tomb of the Great Thirteenth, but the acquisition of gold was another of the many Tibetan dichotomies. Tibetans believed that Padmasambhava, an Indian saint who introduced Tantric Buddhism to Tibet in the ninth century, made their soil fertile by endowing it with gold. For a mortal to dig up the gold would ruin the land.

According to myth, some gold came to the surface from the diggings of giant ants. This account came back through the pundit explorers, confirming the Greek historian Herodotus who wrote in the fifth century B.C. of a desert north of India where great ants dug up gold and fierce tribesmen rushed in to gather it.

The most logical explanation for the tale of the ants is that it was a cover story meant to keep would-be miners from where other Tibetans really were digging gold. Viewed from a distance out on the plains, bent figures scratching the ground with antelope horns could be passed off as dangerous killer ants, thus the necessary gold could be collected for projects such as the Potala.

In the heart of Lhasa, surrounded by so many buildings that it was impossible to see as a whole, Harrer and Aufschnaiter came upon the Jokhang Temple. It seemed unim-

The golden roofs of Tashil-hunpo, the best preserved monastery in Tibet.

pressive compared to the huge Drepung or the stately Potala, yet its dark corridors were the holiest of all Tibet. The Jokhang, built in the seventh century, housed an image of Buddha brought to Lhasa by a Chinese princess who married King Srongtsen-gampo. Queen Wen Cheng and another queen, a Nepalese, succeeded in converting the king—and eventually all of Tibet—to Buddhism.

Pilgrims from all over Tibet poured into the Jokhang. Hundreds of prayer wheels in a great courtyard began to spin by the power of devout hands as soon as the sun rose. A rumbling sound, audible from the street, continued throughout the day until the last pilgrims left at dusk.

Harrer and Aufschnaiter's arrival caused only a brief commotion. They were soon taken in by a noble family, and eventually given permission to stay. "It is probable that no other country in the world," Harrer wrote, "would welcome two poor fugitives as Tibet welcomed us. Our parcel of clothes, the gift of the government, had arrived with apologies for delay caused by the fact that we were taller than the average Tibetan and there were no ready-made clothes to fit us."

He was even received cordially by the British legation in Lhasa, until he chanced to discuss the subject of mountain climbing with their doctor, an enthusiastic mountain hiker who volunteered his opinion that "extreme" climbing such as the north face of the Eiger was the sign of a diseased mind. Harrer was unaware of the extent of anti-Nazi fervor that the Eiger climb had aroused. In both America and Britain it had become a classic example of Nazi nationalism, the perfect acting-out of Hitler's superman concept.

No longer able to contain himself, Harrer volunteered that he had made the first and only successful Eiger climb. "Obviously no one believed a word I had said. After all, why should this Mr. Harrer, who by rights ought to be a POW in India, not have suffered some damage to his mind as well as the lumbar pains he had acquired during the ordeal of his escape? A superior, tolerant smile was still on their faces when I took my leave."

During the next several years Harrer and Aufschnaiter worked in Lhasa and made summer excursions to climb nearly all the peaks of 17,000 to 19,000 feet in the region. They received frequent world news, sometimes even firsthand, as in the case of Tsepun Shakabpa, who traveled to Europe and the United States in 1948. The other end of the earth for this Lhasa noble was the bewildering bridges and

Hundreds of lamas in the Jokhang Temple.

cable cars of San Francisco, which he reached by train from the East Coast.

Harrer became a jack-of-all-trades in Lhasa. One of his jobs was to build the Dalai Lama a movie projection room in the Norbulingka, his summer palace. He was given an especially large and powerful Tibetan for an assistant, not only to build the theater, but also to make the films. This giant carted heavy camera paraphernalia while parting crowds with his forbidding appearance. The Dalai Lama wanted Harrer to film the normal life of his country that he as a sheltered ruler couldn't experience.

In the Norbulingka garden was a zoo. The Buddhist faith prohibits killing, so over the years injured and baby animals had been brought to this sanctuary, along with exotic creatures from other lands. One day there was a tremendous commotion in the garden. A wild snow leopard had found its way inside. A crowd cornered the animal and someone shot it in the foot. No one dared approach the enraged cat, until Harrer's attendant went for it alone with his bare hands, wrestled it to the ground, and held it until it could be put into a sack. The attendant was badly clawed, but otherwise unharmed; the leopard died soon after in the Dalai Lama's zoo.

In 1949 the Dalai Lama broke precedence by inviting Lowell Thomas and his son to Lhasa with free rein to broadcast and photograph; in trade, of course, for a worldwide publicity campaign in favor of Tibetan independence just when the Chinese were making threatening gestures toward Tibet. The Thomases were most surprised to meet the young

61

The two wear purple robes, eat Tibetan food and speak the language like natives. The Tibetans are fond of them. They in turn like the Tibetans. So it seems to be an exceedingly satisfactory combination—so much so that both Peter and Henry plan to remain residents of Tibet for the rest of their lives.

When the Thomases returned home in October 1949, Communist troops were invading Chamdo in eastern Tibet. The Chinese *amban* in Lhasa was expelled by the Tibetan government. In Peking Mao Tse-tung swore that he would "liberate" the people of Tibet. By late 1950 the situation worsened. On October 7 the Chinese attacked the Tibetan frontier in six places. As the armies descended on Lhasa, Harrer and Aufschnaiter fled yet another country, this time in the company of its ruler.

On January 20, 1951, an Associated Press story shocked the world:

The flight of the young Dalai Lama from his capital in Communist-invaded Tibet was one of the strangest journeys ever made by a monarch, an aide indicated today. The aide and *two European technicians* [emphasis added], who accompanied the Dalai Lama, said the Red Chinese flag already was flying over the old Chinese residency in Lhasa, the capital, when plans were started on December 17 to save the sixteen-year-old ruler from the Reds.

Plans for the Dalai Lama's dramatic trip over a perilous icy trail were made in the utmost secrecy, as Peiping emissaries in Lhasa reported by radio to Communist field headquarters every known move made by the Tibetans. . . . Stars glowed with winter brilliance as the Dalai Lama made his way from the palace alone about 2:00 A.M. the next morning. . . .

Ten miles from Lhasa the boy king descended from the palanquin (covered chair) and gazed back at the white mass of Potala Palace lighted by the first rays of the morning sun. . . . It was apparent from questions he asked that he was uncertain where his travels would end.

ruler's two Austrian confidants. Aufschnaiter worked as an engineer on a small hydroelectric plant and the construction of new canals. Harrer was revising maps for the Tibetan foreign bureau and personally tutoring the Dalai Lama. Lowell Thomas, Jr., reported on their lifestyle:

Old lama in the courtyard of Drepung, Lhasa.

The lush valley of the Tsangpo
River, a respite from the arid
steppes.

Chapter 6: At the End of the Rainbow

SPRING IN LHASA. Snow dusted the high peaks, but only blossoms were falling in the warm valley of the Tsangpo. A sea of smiles and waving hands confronted me as I walked through the town bazaar. The joyous crowd retreated in rhythm with my steps as if I were viewing the scene from the front row of a theater. My companion, Harold Knutson, turned to me and said, "These people seem so unbelievably friendly and happy that I wonder if this isn't some kind of mass spectacle set up for our benefit by the Chinese."

Both Harold and I had traveled extensively through Asia and the Himalaya. Harold had spent years working with Tibetans as a geologist assigned by the king of Nepal to map resources in disputed border regions. Both of us agreed that Lhasa conveys a feeling of well-being unlike any other Asian city. Even the dogs showed it. An assortment of sleek, fleshy animals lay sprawled on the sidewalks with their eyes closed, confident that no harm would come to them. We talked about the Asian cities where dogs are cowering bone-racks, and worse places, where there are no dogs at all.

For most of its history, Lhasa operated in total geographical isolation. Tibetans lived simple lives, inhabitants of a desert island cut off from the temporal concerns of the world. All that was changed now. Tibetans and Chinese have been at each others' throats. As we stood on the hallowed ground of Lhasa, I knew one thing for certain: what I had read had not prepared me for understanding Tibet.

I was humbled that my preconceptions were wrong. It was simply impossible to solve what had gone on here like a TV mystery. Tibetans accepted contradictions as a way of life. The country had been invaded, and its people were second-class citizens in their homeland. On the other hand, Communism had replaced feudalism and brought progress plus a measure of equality in its wake.

As an American I was hardly a detached observer. My CIA had supplied the Tibetans modern weapons and secret mountain-warfare training in Colorado during the sixties. My president, Richard Nixon, whose career was launched on anti-Communism, had begun our love affair with Communist China in the seventies. And in the eighties, the era of politics by mass journalism, *Reader's Digest* was matching the most shameless anti-American Chinese propaganda of old with the words of Pulitzer Prize-winner Harrison Salisbury: "Today, the golden city of Lhasa, goal of explorers and mystics, is a dismal slum—a cesspool of filth and run-down streets filled with beggars, cripples, and hungry children." In reality the Chinese had introduced modern sewers, garbage collection, and health care. Tibetans were far healthier than other Asians. We saw no cesspools, no beggars, no hungry children, and fewer cripples than in Pleasantville, New York.

In fact, *National Geographic* ran an extremely accurate 1980 cover story on Tibet that was seen by forty million people—seen but not read. The magazine's old tradition of minimizing world controversy has kept its readership looking just at pretty pictures long after new editorial blood began to focus on the real issues. Only two of the fifteen Americans in my group (who had paid over six thousand dollars to come here) had read the text, although all had seen the issue of the magazine. Most Americans don't know where Tibet is, or that it was annexed by China.

To really understand Tibet requires entering Harold's geological time frame as well as that of modern events. The world had crashed in on Tibet through both realms, one measured in eons, the other in days and months. Tibet is a sea of frozen land crested with frozen waves of mountains; Lhasa is literally an ocean basin where a belt of rocks called ophiolites indicates where the ancient Tethys Sea held apart India and China, much as the whole of Tibet does today.

Forty million years ago India crashed into Eurasia so powerfully that the inertia of the collision has continued to change the face of the land under the eye of the evolving human race. Every year the old lowlands of India slide an additional fraction of an inch underneath the old lowlands of China, raising some parts of the Himalaya as much as three feet in a century.

Two million years ago, when men with brains much like our own already walked the earth, Lhasa was a lush plain just 3,000 feet above the sea instead of its present 12,000 feet. The rising Himalaya and expanding Tibetan Plateau began to block moist air movement from the south. Tibet became high desert.

Twenty years ago Mao's rising star forced Tibet into the Chinese empire, blocking age-old cultural connections with India and Nepal to the south. Tibet became a spiritual desert; the practice of Buddhism was prohibited by law. Of the twenty-seven thousand monasteries active in 1959, only eleven were in operation at the time of our visit in May 1981; all, not by coincidence, in the few areas where we were allowed to travel.

One of these was the Jokhang Temple in Lhasa, which I entered on a weekday morning with considerable skepticism.

Accounts from Tibetan exiles indicated that this holiest of all temples had been ravaged by the Chinese during the 1959 rebellion: Chinese troops had been quartered inside, Buddhist images wantonly destroyed. In the courtyard of the Jokhang I saw hundreds of worshipers waiting in line to enter the inner sanctum and prostrate themselves before great Buddha effigies in the flickering light of yak-butter lamps.

A few steps had taken me from the bright streets of modern Lhasa into the darkness of the Middle Ages. The only light was dimly reflected from the flagstones of a courtyard into alcoves walled with the deep reds and golds of Buddhist art. Pilgrims' faces seemed to glow with a warm, clear light I had seen only in Renaissance paintings. Reverent calm replaced the broad smiles and waving arms that had greeted me on the streets. Oblivious to those around them, these devout pilgrims repeated their mantras, clutched their rosaries, and spun their prayer wheels while waiting to enter the shrine. Here was a Tibetan counterpart of Rembrandt's "Nightwatch," a vision to symbolize an entire culture. Light alone was not responsible for the glow. Part of it really did come from within, from the realization of pious dreams.

City folk from Lhasa in cottons and tennis shoes mingled with country folk in traditional *chubas*, long-sleeved coats whose various lengths, fabrics, patterns, and colors bespoke their owners' origins and lifestyles.

On this early May morning a number of locals wore blue summer *chubas* that hung below their knees. A swarthy man with wild, wiry hair was swathed in a sheepskin winter *chuba* that was short-waisted for rugged use and sooty as a fireplace. One sleeve was extra long so both hands could be stuffed together out of the perpetual winds on the plains. On his feet were red woolen boots with turned-up soles of thick yak hide. Once traditional throughout Tibet, these are quickly disappearing in favor of store-bought Chinese shoes.

A young woman in a patterned silk blouse chatted with an older woman in a blue-striped *chuba*. Most striking of all was a leather-faced woman whose thinly braided hair and black *chuba* with rainbow hems are customary in the Kokonor region of Chinghai, a thousand miles away.

It was hard to believe that these same people, these wonderful, gentle Tibetan peasants and traders, had been led by the Chinese Red Guard during the Cultural Revolution of 1966 to 1976 into a frenzy of destruction of their own monasteries. Tibetans in exile frequently deny this, but witnesses have confirmed it beyond a doubt.

LEFT *Trader with a parasol,*
Shigatse.

RIGHT *Baby with a parasol,*
Norbulingka.

*Cho Oyu rising to 26,750 feet
above the Tibetan Plateau.*

Even the *Tibetan Review*, published by Tibetan refugees in India, admitted that the Red Guard had mobilized the population. Tibetans between fifteen and twenty-five "were assigned the task of destroying monuments reflecting the obsolete lifestyle." The Jokhang had been stormed, its prayer wheels totally destroyed, its walls defaced, and many of its images defiled. Thankfully, the holiest image of all Tibet survived untouched, but not by a miracle. This ancient Buddha figure, Jowo Rimpoche, was brought from China by Queen Wen Cheng during the seventh century. The Red Guard alone would have destroyed it; witnesses to the storming of the Jokhang say that the presence of Tibetans who could not bring themselves to commit so final an act saved the image for the pilgrims of today. We, however, were not permitted by the lamas to go into the deepest inner sanctum where the image is kept.

I was in Tibet as the leader of the first group of American trekkers ever permitted to visit the backcountry. Lhasa was on our way to the base of Mt. Everest, but for each of us this summit of Tibetan Buddhism was as important a goal as the mountain itself. When Tibet opened to limited tourism in 1979, only an estimated 1,200 foreigners had ever seen Lhasa, 623 of them members of the Younghusband "expedition" of 1904. Just 800 tourists a year were now permitted, 600 to the environs of Lhasa, and 200 on expeditions and treks.

The first tourists paid $300 per day to stay in Lhasa. We were charged a flat fee of $150 per person per day for accommodations that would cost less than $15 a day in neighboring Nepal or India. Just being in Lhasa was dazzling enough to hold back most complaints about service or cost. As leader, however, I was soon deluged with an inverse proportion of problems to cost. I had to divide a group that had paid equally into one room for six and four doubles. Many had to wait five hours for rooms booked a year in advance. The hot water was out. There was not even running water for toilets between 6:00 P.M. and 10:00 A.M. the next morning, precisely the time of most use. The door locks were broken. A fifty-dollar camera accessory was stolen during dinner.

Our Chinese guide informed us that we were indeed lucky people, for on our return from the mountains we would celebrate the "thirtieth anniversary of the peaceful liberation of Tibet" on May 23, 1981. A sudden recognition kindled inside me, the same kind of "aha!" response that always comes when a difficult concept finally implants itself in one's mind. This Chinese version of peaceful liberation and happy Tibetans coincided exactly with our so-called "trip of a lifetime" to mysterious Lhasa. Lhasa was no less dazzling because of our petty lodging hassles. But Tibetans were no less liberated from prior feudalism because some of them died or fled and their culture had been turned upside down. In both cases a traditional Chinese cloak of pageantry, more venerable than either Tibetan Buddhism or our Christian heritage, concealed facts, feelings, ethics, morals, and the contents of human souls.

During the dynasties of Imperial China, prostitutes went through finishing schools. Beautiful peasant girls learned to read, draw, dress, and give their guests the most delectable experiences. They were taught that lust was an inevitable human condition. No matter how cruel and deplorable, it needed to be attended, like death, by rituals of grace, dignity, and beauty. The life work of a prostitute was to cloak lust in pageantry.

We had lusted for Tibet, and we were paying for it. The Tibetans had lusted to hold onto their feudal theocracy, and they had paid a far higher price. Neither our simple dream or that of the Tibetans would ever come true, and to explain why required the deepest baring of human souls.

Part of my "peaceful liberation" was my recognition of the Chinese cloak of pageantry. The fact that reported Chinese actions conflicted with Tibetan eyewitness accounts no longer bothered me; I had seen under the cloak. The Chinese had indeed liberated Tibet. While the young Dalai Lama fled in 1951, the People's Liberation Army came in gently, with virtually no fighting, proceeding with restraint. Religion was little affected except for the political regime of the high lamas; PLA soldiers even bowed to Buddhist images. The Chinese wanted military control of Tibet to safeguard their new Communist government. Their stated intention was nothing more than to recreate the security they had enjoyed for centuries with a recognized Chinese representative in Lhasa and an impenetrable geographical buffer between China and India. They signed an agreement with Tibetan nobles in the absence of the Dalai Lama; China would handle Tibet's external politics, while allowing internal autonomy to continue.

The Dalai Lama returned a few months later. Chinese roads and airfields were built. Tibet became a colonial outpost of China in which the natives were second-class citizens.

LEFT *Face of the seventy-foot-high image of Chamba, Buddha of the Future, in Tashilhunpo.*

RIGHT *Women waiting in line to pray, Jokhang Temple, Lhasa.*

The lamas saw the old way of life in which the masses supported them endangered. To build anti-Chinese sentiment they told peasants that trucks, never seen before in rural Tibet, ran off the blood of little children.

The Chinese introduced land reforms. Monasteries and nobles owned 95 percent of the arable land, yet only 30 percent of the harvest went to the peasants. The twenty-seven thousand monasteries used one-third of all the butter produced in the country to light their eternal lamps; the Jokhang alone burned four thousand pounds a day. To reduce the power of the church, the Chinese issued orders preventing boys from entering monastic life.

Serfs who became landowners were shocked by the Chinese taxes levied to support the socialist system. The concept of Marxist dialectical materialism that Mao used to win over the Chinese peasantry made little impression on the Tibetans. The old Buddhist policies were as unquestioned as the icy winds and barren plains into which they had been born. No one could convince them that lamas and nobles constituted a ruling class that needed to be abolished in the name of equality.

The Dalai Lama was invited to Peking in 1954, where he met the rulers of neighboring nations for the first time: Mao, Khrushchev, Bulganin, and Nehru. Peace reigned in central Tibet, but by 1956 an all-out war against the Chinese began among the Khampa nomads of northeastern Tibet and their Golok cousins in Chinghai Province of China, immediately to the north. The Chinese categorically denied rumors of what was becoming the greatest revolt against Communism in history. The *London Times* received accurate reports from secret correspondents in Tibet and on May 6, 1956, printed a shrewd, almost oracular prediction of events three years in the future:

It is in the present unrest in the eastern provinces that Tibetans see the most immediate danger both to the Dalai Lama's personal position and to their hopes of retaining a certain degree of national individuality within a Chinese framework. The recent Golok rebellion was, according to all reports, entirely spontaneous, and is deplored in Lhasa as both dangerous and untimely. At the best it is certain to lead to the Chinese further tightening their military and political hold on the country for an indefinite period; at worst it could lead them to revise their whole policy of according limited autonomy.

What became known to the world as the Tibetan Rebellion occurred in 1959. It indeed resulted in the total military and political subjugation of Tibet, the permanent exile of the Dalai Lama, the deaths of over one hundred thousand people, and the destruction of an entire culture unparalleled in modern history. Tibetans in exile appealed to the United Nations, but in the typically rigid fashion that doomed their cause from the beginning. Instead of asking for a simple censure of Chinese aggression, they asked for recognition of an independent Tibetan nation. Not a single world power supported them, both because of the history of Sino-Tibetan ties, and the compelling fact that the United Nations-recognized Nationalist Chinese government on Taiwan also claimed sovereignty over Tibet.

The tragedy beyond immediate Chinese aggression was the deeper issue, as stated by Tibetologist R. A. Stein, "of a civilization under threat of death for not having been able to adapt itself gradually to the changes taking place around it." Lamaistic Buddhism was an all-pervading religion with no vehicle for change. In its web were all the country's politics, economics, and education as well as spiritual concerns.

When the Chinese "freed Tibet from feudal serfdom" by destroying Buddhism, they took away the context in which all social judgments were previously made. The Tibetan people were rudely thrust from isolation into contact with the modern world, and it is little wonder that their impressions of those old days, lived without comparison at the time, are often far from accurate. The falsehoods in *Reader's Digest* about modern Lhasa stem from the writer's good intention: "Let the Tibetans tell their story. They tell it best. They lived it."

An equally important reason for the contradictions in Tibet's oral history—part of human nature the world over—applies to all situations where facts must be gleaned from anecdotal evidence. Just as the Chinese hid certain truths of the Tibetan "Liberation" behind pageantry, the Tibetans themselves concealed others behind this subtle device that I call "Powell's Law." Doug Powell, a University of California geographer who traveled with me to the Tibetan Plateau, told me years earlier about a theory that gives him an uncanny ability to explain broad-reaching controversies. In his studies of climatology he developed a keen sense of how to judge the accuracy of eyewitness accounts. At the heart of his method is the realization that in memory "the extreme becomes the norm." Asked how cold the winters get, a farmer would answer "fifty below," even though that extreme occurred once in his lifetime. If Doug asked a native of any region how much it snowed there, the man was likely to hold his hand at the deepest level he had ever seen. The level of the hand itself was deceptive where childhood recollections were involved: chest-deep snow is not the same for an adult and a three-year-old.

Powell's Law helps me understand why today's Tibetan refugees living in India, Switzerland, and the United States knowingly relate how good things were before the Chinese came. When British journalist Chris Mullin visited Tibet and wrote a balanced article for *China Now* that clearly took the Chinese to task, the *Tibetan Review* took him to task for hinting that the Chinese improved the lot of the masses. Mullin countered with examples "of the kind of exaggeration that has damaged the case of Tibetans in exile."

The political history of Tibet is considerably more clear than the cultural history, although compelling "evidence" supports both Chinese and Tibetan claims to sovereignty. China's claims begin as far back as the seventh century. During the Yuan dynasty in the thirteenth century, Tibet paid homage to Kublai Khan. In 1720 a Chinese army invaded Lhasa, turned the Kokonor region of Tibet into

Chinese police prevent a woman from praying on the steps of the Norbulingka, the Dalai Lama's summer palace.

Chinghai Province of China, and set up a protectorate over Lhasa that lasted until 1912. China defended Tibet against foreign invasions, including the Gurkha War of 1788 to 1792, and set up the right to oversee the choice of both new Dalai and Panchen lamas. Only after revolution weakened China in 1912 did the Dalai Lama proclaim Tibet's sovereignty. China didn't try to regain its authority in Tibet until immediately after Mao solidified the nation in 1949.

The present Dalai Lama counters these claims with a simple statement of Tibetan *de facto* independence based upon "a separate language, culture, borders, money, and world acceptance of Tibet as a country." David Snellgrove, the West's most respected Tibetan scholar, discounts China's claims on Tibet with a powerful analogy:

China's only claim rests upon asserted rights of possession of Tibet as a dependent territory, rights which ceased to have any de facto validity in 1912, and which no one would be prepared to admit nowadays in the case of any western imperialist power. By the same argument Britain should still be ruling the whole of Ireland, not to mention India as well, and France still in control of all her former North African territories.

The rigid Communism of China's Cultural Revolution softened after the fall of the Gang of Four in 1976. In October 1979 a delegation of Tibetan exiles sent by the Dalai Lama was allowed to officially inspect Tibet for the first time; during the next year two other delegations followed. Some of the information they brought back fit Powell's Law, contrasting current "abject poverty and suffering" with the good old days that they remembered from thirty years before.

Other data, however, led to inescapable conclusions. The Chinese spoke of advances in higher education, four colleges in Tibet, two thousand Tibetans studying in China. But the second delegation asked their Chinese hosts, who proclaimed equal treatment of all "national minorities," why not one of the fifty-five thousand students sent to the United States by China was a Tibetan.

The Chinese veil had hidden the realities of Tibet even from the leadership in Peking. After extensive comment on Tibet in the world press, Hu Yaobang, general secretary of the Central Communist Party, went to Tibet to see for himself. This bold man read the riot act to several Chinese officials in Tibet and publicly admitted the failure of Chinese policies. After he returned to Peking, massive reforms for

Three pilgrims in the Jokhang Temple.

Tibet were announced in April 1980, including opening of trade with neighboring countries, a two-year moratorium on agricultural taxes, abolition of state grain quotas, increased private ownership of plots and livestock, the right to operate small businesses without employees, and the exodus of the majority of the 120,000 Chinese personnel over a two-year period.

Pema Gyalpo, sister of the Dalai Lama, traveled eight thousand surface miles in Tibet on the third delegation in 1980. "I wanted to photograph the wildlife, which I remembered as plentiful. In three months of extensive traveling in Tibet, I did not see any wild animals."

During the same year, the distinguished field zoologist George Schaller traveled some of the same route with a scientific delegation. (His fascination with Tibet and its wildlife began in the early fifties when his partner on the first ascent of Mt. Drum in Alaska was a visiting lecturer named Heinrich Harrer.) Shortly after his return Schaller wrote me about his trip, confirming Pema Gyalpo's impressions: "I have been talking to the Chinese about establishing wildlife reserves in Tibet, but have no information. I spent two weeks in southern Tibet, from Lhasa down to the latitude of Kathmandu, but there is little wildlife: too many people, too much livestock. Scenically lovely but the trip was rather depressing . . ."

By 1981, when I arrived in Lhasa, the townspeople were used to seeing foreigners. On a sunny May afternoon I attended the festival celebrating the thirtieth anniversary of the peaceful liberation of Tibet. Draped with Nikons, I walked through thousands of picnickers in the garden of the Norbulingka, the Dalai Lama's old summer palace. A young Tibetan man addressed me in perfect English: "Come here! Sit down and have some *chang* [rice beer]."

I was led to a place between his Japanese portable stereo and his pretty Tibetan girlfriend dressed in Western-style Kashmir woolens. Only the man's face was Tibetan, and even it lacked the characteristic leathery appearance. Tight slacks clung to his chunky legs, and a Swiss watch flashed from his wrist. A broad comb hung in thick, black hair carefully slicked behind his ears.

"Where did you learn English?" I asked.

"In Kathmandu in Nepal. I was born in Lhasa, but my family went there when I was a boy."

"What made you leave Nepal?"

"I wanted to find out what Lhasa was like. I'd heard about it all my life. Last year I came on a visit, and I liked it.

Especially the weather. It's so much nicer than Kathmandu. Not so much rain or humidity. So I went home, got my things, and started a tea shop in Lhasa. I'm much happier here."

"You don't ever want to go back?"

"Not to live. I'll visit my parents and my friends, but unless things change I'll stay here forever."

Mr. Chen, the Chinese tourist officer in the town of Shigatse, had different aspirations. A genteel, energetic man in his late thirties, he seemed very much at home as he guided my group through Tashilhunpo Monastery with a deep respect for Buddhist traditions. "How long have you lived here?" I asked.

"Five years."

"Are you going to stay here permanently?"

"Oh my, no!"

"Why? Don't you like it in Tibet?"

"Tibet is a very beautiful place, but I do not want to be here. I do not like the cold and the wind. I love my family very much. My wife and children have waited for me these five years in Peking."

Perhaps the Chinese government had purposely chosen a man whose interest lay outside of Tibet to show off Tashilhunpo, the crown jewel, the best preserved of all the monasteries. It had been spared during the Cultural Revolution for several reasons, not the least that its chief, the Panchen Lama, second only to the Dalai Lama, was a puppet of the Chinese government living in Peking.

The vast halls of Tashilhunpo, empty while Buddhism was forbidden, housed six hundred monks after 1978 under freshly painted walls and golden pagoda roofs. We saw many craftsmen engaged in the restoration of vandalized art and decaying woodwork. One scene overpowered the rest. Inside a dark chamber an image of Chamba, the Buddha of the Future, sat on a lotus flower with hand raised and thumb and forefinger held in a circle. A man standing on this thumb with his own hand raised would barely be able to touch the next finger.

This largest of Tibetan Buddhas is superlative in every way—nine stories high, cast from one hundred tons of bronze, gilded with eight thousand ounces of gold, and studded with over three hundred precious stones. It is so holy that photography was strictly forbidden—unless the monks were paid fifty dollars by each photographer. Such tactics on a far larger scale had built this entire monastery as well as every other one in Tibet. The lamas themselves said that one hundred million ounces of gold had been "given" by the people to construct the Potala.

Although we were far more able to pay than the poor Tibetan nomads, peasants, and traders, I felt a clear sense of being ripped off. Such an emotion had been absent in past situations where I had respected religious restrictions imposed by Moslems, American Indians, and those benevolent Tibetan transplants, the Sherpas of Nepal. But my experience here was no different than that of Father della Penna, an eighteenth-century missionary who had written of the lamas, "They are greedy of money . . . arrogant and proud . . . given to lust . . . inclined to vindictiveness," or of the first British journalist into Lhasa, Percival Landon, who reported in the *London Times* at the turn of the century, "No priestly caste in the history of religion has ever preyed upon . . . its flock with the systematic brigandage of the lamas."

Today's tourists, coming passively to look, were enchanted by the monks' quaintness and were typically unaware that their avarice was as unchanged as their appearance. Because the Chinese had outlawed the religious training of youth before the 1959 rebellion, there has been little opportunity for progressive change in Lamaistic Buddhism. Even though I was able to admire the edifices of the faith, my own conclusion was that it is doomed by its own contradictions.

The Dalai Lama, no longer the naive teenager who fled Lhasa in 1951, has become one of the world's most astute political observers, well aware of the sad reality that no country in the modern world, whether subjugated or totally free, has ever successfully reverted to a past society, much less a theocracy. He and his representatives have simply declared that he will only return to an independent Tibet.

The challenge of the Dalai Lama is not to bring back the old religion to Tibet, but, now that there is a missing generation of lamas, to change it so that it can withstand the tests of these times, not those of the past.

Apart from the lamas, I have no doubt that the Tibetan people will regain their dignity. I remember especially one ten-year-old boy I met on the street outside Tashilhunpo. In one hand he held a worn school book and in the other a makeshift leash attached to a wiggly puppy. We walked together for an hour, sharing smiles, a few words of mutual language, and curiosity that knew no bounds. In his gentle, unaffected character were the roots of the best traditions; and I saw, once again, the contented dogs on the sidewalks of Lhasa, the joyous crowds that we had at first thought were phony, and the majesty of devotion in the Jokhang Temple.

At moments like this Tibetan living seemed as pastoral as that of the yaks I saw grazing in the fields under mountain and cloud. But the yaks, too, were far more involved in the world around them than they appeared. Their butter lights the lamps of monasteries; their wool carpets floors, blankets beds, tents homes, clothes bodies; their milk and cheese nourish children; their skins raft people across great rivers, sole tender feet; their dung warms homes, cooks their own meat.

When the explorer P. K. Kozloff returned to Russia in 1901, he began the narrative of his adventures with a comparison of two incompatible races he had met in Central Asia: the Chinese Mongols and the Tibetans. The desert Chinese were as much People of the Camel (for which Kozloff developed quite an affinity), as the Tibetans were People of the Yak. He learned never to mix these two cultures:

In the mountains and high tablelands of Tibet exist tribes as different in their manners and customs from the Chinese Mongols as their fierce and obstinate yaks are from camels. On the word "tsok tsok" and a gentle pulling of the lead rope, the camel lies down to be loaded. The bull yak is always looking for an opportunity to gore his neighbor. Some of them will lie down to be loaded, but others plunge about, and having broken away from their attendants, never rest until they have thrown their loads.

On the eve of our departure from Lhasa, I set off into the fields while the group went to dinner. On a hunch I chased a weak rainbow I had seen hovering just above the horizon. The end of a rainbow is set by one's own perspective, and I jogged along a dirt path to move mine where I wanted it. Forces beyond my control came to my aid to lengthen and brighten it against a black sky. A hole opened in the clouds, aiming sunbeams on one spot: the Potala Palace. The rainbow rose magically from the golden rooftops of this summit of Buddhism as if some power in the palace were its source.

Rainbow over the Potala Palace, Lhasa.

Winds of over one hundred miles per hour blow plumes of snow off the north face of Chomolungma.

PART FOUR: CHOMOLUNGMA

Tibetan chariot approaching
Shekar.

Chapter 7: Quest of the British Raj

DAWN CAME CALM, CLEAR, AND COLD. Eight Englishmen shuffled about the courtyard of a small village, trying to keep warm as they directed coolies and yak drivers in the loading of a tremendous array of boxes, food tins, ropes, and oxygen bottles. The men wore wool knickers, knee socks, and tweed sport coats. The leader, Lieutenant Colonel C. K. Howard-Bury, had a tie; the other climbers wore open-necked shirts and sweaters beneath their tweeds. A ninth man watched from a litter, dull-eyed, quiet, and disheveled.

It was the spring of 1921, and these were the first climbers permitted into Tibet. They were British because the British under Colonel Francis Younghusband had invaded Tibet seventeen years earlier. Sir Charles Bell, political officer for Bhutan, Sikkim, and Tibet, had become a friend of the Thirteenth Dalai Lama, and he successfully negotiated for the first permission to climb Mt. Everest at the behest of the Royal Geographical Society, whose new president was none other than Sir Francis Younghusband.

In the late nineteenth century, literary critic and Alpine Club president Sir Leslie Stephen wrote without a grain of doubt, "Mountaineering as a sport was the invention of . . . cultured and imaginative Englishmen." The group of men in the Tibetan courtyard were the embodiment of such elitism.

George Leigh Mallory moved across the courtyard with distinctive grace, a long-limbed, slender man with a firm body developed through years of gymnastics and vigorous weekends on the cliffs of Wales. Even in his midthirties he retained a teenager's complexion, made all the more obvious because he shaved on the trail while his companions let their beards grow. Mallory's Cambridge affectations were reinforced by the artistic allusions he liberally sprinkled into conversations, a legacy of his career as a schoolmaster.

But only on the surface was Mallory a dandy of British society. He was actually quite unpretentious, and known for forever doing the unexpected. He had gone to Cambridge, for example, only after deliberately flunking his exams for the Royal Military Academy. His preoccupation with appearance had little to do with his upbringing, for he had been an unruly and untidy child, the son of an unruly, untidy mother and a minister. His boyish good looks contributed to his patrician air. Large, long-lashed eyes with the drooping lids of British royalty sparkled out of a long Nordic face with a long, yet almost delicate nose.

Mallory had already become one of the greatest names in British climbing, more because of whom he knew and his future promise than for what he had done. That fire burning within him had been so obvious as an undergraduate that

Lytton Strachey, a member of the Cambridge intelligentsia and an open homosexual, had written his secret thoughts to Virginia Woolf: "George Mallory! . . . he's six foot high, with the body of an athlete by Praxiteles, and a face—oh incredible—the mystery of Botticelli, the refinement of a Chinese print, the youth and piquancy of an unimaginable English boy . . . his intelligence is not remarkable. What's the need?"

Perhaps because of the ease of his acceptance at a literary tea party or climber's pub, Mallory was a drifter who waited for life to take its course rather than to shape events himself. Yet he did not admire the prominent people in authority who catered to him as much as he did the mavericks, whom he so often chose as partners in the mountains. The man who lay now on a litter on the road to Khampa Dzong, Dr. A. M. Kellas, was one. Before Kellas fell ill with dysentery, Mallory wrote to his wife:

Kellas I love already. He is beyond description Scotch and un-couth in his speech—altogether uncouth. . . . His appearance would form an admirable model to the stage for a farcical repre-sentation of an alchemist. He is very slight in build, short, thin, stooping and narrow chested. . . . He is an absolutely devoted and disinterested man.

These were kind words from a man who could be very judgmental. He found Tibet "a hateful country inhabited by hateful people." The expedition was "a fraud from be-ginning to end, invented by the wild enthusiasm of one man, Younghusband; puffed up by the would-be wisdom of cer-tain pundits in the Alpine Club." Of its leader he wrote, "Relations with Bury have not been easy . . . he is a queer customer."

Dr. Kellas had the most Himalayan experience of the group. He had been on seven long journeys and made several ascents above 22,000 feet. In 1907 he had recruited porters from Darjeeling for his first trip and discovered a group of immigrants from Nepal who performed far better than any of the other men. These were Sherpas, people from eastern Tibet who had migrated to the Nepal side of Mt. Everest roughly four hundred years earlier. At Kellas's insistence, Sherpas were along on this expedition.

As the group neared Khampa Dzong, Mallory began to appreciate the countryside: "One comes to bless the absolute bareness, feeling that here is a pure beauty of form, a kind of ultimate harmony." Out of this moonscape, Mt. Everest came into view for the first time, a scene Mallory compared to "a prodigious white fang excrescent from the jaw of the world." Kellas never saw it. He arrived in Khampa Dzong dead on his litter. Though too ill to ride a pony, Kellas had been cheery that morning; no one in the party thought his condition to be anything more than temporary. Weakened and dehydrated by the long bout with dysentery, he expired on a high pass from which three of the peaks he had ascended for the first time were in view. He was buried on a hill with-in sight of Everest, and the party moved on.

"We're just about to walk off the map," Mallory wrote home. The last leg of the route to Everest was unknown but had been anticipated on an earlier journey by a daring young British captain. In 1913, disguised as a Moslem trader, John B. L. Noel had tried to reach Everest from Darjeeling. He managed to get within forty miles of the mountain before Tibetan soldiers gently but firmly turned him around. World War I interrupted Noel's plans, but in 1919, lecturing before the Royal Geographical Society, he insisted, "Now that the poles have been reached . . . the next and equally important task is the exploration and mapping of Mt. Everest." He had heard of a valley with an easy trail that led to Tibet's highest monastery under a great peak. Noel was reasonably certain that the peak must be Everest, which the Tibetans called Chomolungma.

Another mountain impressed the 1921 climbers almost as much as Everest itself. As they rose out of a gorge cut into ancient conglomerates, they came face to face with what Noel described as "the fantastic dream castle of Shekar-Dzong—'The Shining Crystal Monastery'." Four hundred monks in innumerable buildings lived on a brown shark's tooth of a peak that rose 1,500 feet above the town of Shekar. *Dzong* is Tibetan for fort; Shekar-Dzong was the name of both the monastery perched on the middle of the cliff and the Gothic-appearing fortress that sat on the very top of the mountain.

Inside the monastery were a gilded Buddha over fifty feet high and an incarnate lama of indeterminate age who had been there for sixty-six years. The lama wore a robe of gold brocade with exquisite turquoise, and had one tooth in his mouth. Howard-Bury made a photograph of him and gave away copies in other villages. These prints proved to be better passports than the permit from the Dalai Lama; re-cipients put them into shrines, burnt incense in front of them, and prayed.

The 1921 expedition found more wildlife than they had expected. The people of these remote highlands were very strict about not taking anything from the earth. Rocks were not to be removed even as geological samples, nor were wild animals to be killed. It was quite all right, however, for domestic animals to be killed and eaten. A few avid sportsmen on the expedition viewed this as duplicitous, but the majority recognized the logic of reaping only what had been sown, whether plant or animal.

Herds of wild asses roamed the plains, often coming to the outskirts of their camps. Wolves and foxes were usually seen at dawn or dusk silhouetted on the horizon. Tibetan antelopes pranced in small bands, sporting single, spiraled horns that had led an early missionary to report the discovery of unicorns in Tibet in the eighteenth century.

The grandest visions of wild animals were near Tingri, an important trading center for Sherpas from Nepal. Here a fertile plain over twenty miles wide and 15,000 feet in elevation lay at the foot of Mt. Everest and a host of other mountains. The plain was a high-altitude counterpart of East Africa where wild asses, gazelle, antelope, blue sheep, and Tibetan argali—with horns up to a foot in diameter—grazed in sight of peaks far higher and more rugged than Kilimanjaro.

As they walked up the gradual Rongbuk Valley, Everest came into view at close range. Perfectly aligned with the valley, it filled the southern sky. Perspective had eliminated the high satellite peaks nearby, leaving only the one grand pyramid. Mallory wrote in his journal, "A grim spectacle most unlike the long, gentle slopes suggested by photos . . . a tougher job than I bargained for."

Sixteen miles from the peak, at a place that seemed virtually underneath the giant mountain, the expedition reached Rongbuk Monastery. Here at 16,500 feet pilgrims spun prayer wheels and hundreds of lamas meditated in a cluster of brightly painted buildings and open courtyards walled off from the winds. Just beyond the buildings the expedition set up a base camp. Howard-Bury noted, "Every animal in this valley that we saw was extraordinarily tame." Blue sheep came down to the lamas' quarters in the early morning. The region's most timid creature seemed to be the head lama himself, who refused to show his face because he was in a long retreat.

The monks of Rongbuk were not at all happy to have their meditations interrupted. It took the expedition party days to gain their confidence. The climbers were told the legend of a pass that had been used to go directly into the Khumbu Valley of Nepal until the head lama forbade the traffic. Mallory and another climber investigated and found two cols that dropped radically into steep ice or rock, one now known as the Lho La. A trade route could never have existed over either of them. But Mallory thus became the first foreigner to look at the Nepal side of Everest, and the first to scan the South Col route. He wrote, "We have seen this western glacier and are not sorry we have not to go up it. . . . It was not a very likely chance that the gap [the South Col] between Everest and the South Peak could be reached from the west . . . I do not much fancy it would be possible." Yet thirty-two years later a British expedition did just that; Hillary and Tenzing made the first ascent by this very route on the Nepalese side.

Months of reconnaissance passed without finding a suitable route to the summit from Tibet. The expedition found that the Kama Valley on the east side of Everest had a climate quite unlike the barren Rongbuk Valley. The Arun River penetrated the crest from Nepal, bringing with it monsoon moisture to nourish forests of silver fir, giant rhododendron, spruce, pine, juniper, larch, and also tremendous glaciers that hung menacingly from the east face of the mountain. While crossing a pass at 20,000 feet their Sherpas found tracks of Metokhangmi, "the abominable snowman." Most of the climbers thought they were melted-out fox tracks.

Mallory led the search for a route to the North Col, which he rightly judged to be the key to the easiest ascent from Tibet. But in looking for the col, he wrongly judged the course of the glacier that descended from it; the glacier wasn't found on the Kharta side, nor was it in the main Rongbuk Valley. His climbing partner, Bullock, deduced that this glacier must flow into the Rongbuk somewhere. Finally the expedition surveyor, Major Oliver Wheeler, produced a map showing the correct but confusing course position of the East Rongbuk Glacier, which flowed east from the North Col, then into a sharp bend that took it north to the main Rongbuk.

Too proud to admit that he had wasted months by failing to locate the glacier in a side valley just above the terminus of the Rongbuk, Mallory labeled Wheeler's map as "very rough . . . notably wrong in some respects," although it was generally quite accurate. Saving face, Mallory forced a route to the North Col from Kharta over the 22,200-foot Lhakpa

George Leigh Mallory, 1923.

83

The 1921 Everest expedition.

leader, who retorted, "Mallory, you know the one good thing the Bolsheviks have done in Russia? They've obliterated the intelligentsia."

A veteran of travels in all the major parts of the Himalaya, Bruce was as shrewd as he was funny. The incarnate lama of Rongbuk, just out of a year's seclusion, wanted to know exactly why the expedition had come to his holy place. Bruce said that his men had come on a pilgrimage. They belonged to a sect in England that worshiped mountains, he revealed, and they wanted to worship the highest mountain in the world.

The lama, a large, handsome man of sixty, broke into a broad smile. With infinite wisdom and dignity he made his requests for preserving the holiness of the region. No animals were to be killed in the entire valley. No rocks were to be removed. Contributions would be accepted at the door.

Bruce had met his match. One of his team said the lama was "either the holiest saint or the greatest actor in the world." When the lama asked Bruce to partake of Tibetan tea, made as usual with rancid butter, Bruce solemnly answered that he would have to decline because he had sworn off butter for the duration of his pilgrimage.

Over the next month four camps were established to the North Col. The East Rongbuk Glacier, which Mallory had misjudged in 1921, was followed for the first time. Within a few miles the climbers entered a sea of ice pinnacles, sparkling white in the light, blue in the shadows. Some were two hundred feet high, etched by the sun for eons. Traversing directly through this ice jumble would have been impossible, but some force—unknown to them and akin to the parting of the Red Sea—had opened a smooth and narrow path paved with rock for the entire ten miles of the glacier.

Later glaciologists explained the miracle highway. The same differential melting that had created the ice pinnacles in this arid, sunny region had also allowed the rocks of a medial moraine to melt their way through the ice until they formed a flat area on top of it.

The men of the expedition were at greater heights than any mountaineers in history. Without oxygen Mallory reached 26,985 feet along with Major Edward F. Norton and Dr. Howard Somervell. After this feat two of the expedition's weaker mountaineers, Captain George Finch and Geoffrey Bruce, reached 27,235 feet with four-cylinder oxygen systems that weighed thirty-three pounds each. Finch had been rejected from the 1921 expedition after two

La (a pass). It made little difference, however, since there was by then no hope of climbing the mountain. The climbing party was reduced by illness and Kellas's death to three—Bullock, Wheeler, and Mallory.

As winter cold descended on the mountain, the three together with three Sherpas reached the North Col on September 24. They had cut more than five hundred steps in ice on a steep headwall broken by seracs and crevasses. On top of the 23,000-foot col icy winds removed all desire to climb higher. Mallory looked up toward a "flat edge ascending at no very steep angle—easy rocks and snow all the way to the northeast crest."

During the long journey back, Mallory wrote home, "I wouldn't go again next year for all the gold in Arabia!"

But on April 30, 1922, he was in Rongbuk again, this time with a thirteen-member expedition and an elaborate oxygen apparatus that utilized four tanks per climber. Mallory viewed the use of oxygen as unsporting and un-British, but being a team player he went along with the decision to use it. His constant philosophizing about everything from oxygen to Shakespeare clashed with the swashbuckling, practical style of General Charles Bruce, the expedition

Tingri—a fertile plain over twenty miles wide and 15,000 feet in elevation, a high-altitude counterpart of East Africa at the foot of Mt. Everest.

Andrew Irvine. © *Mount Everest Foundation*

separate doctors reported him to be anemic, sallow, and underweight yet flabby. Bruce, the leader's nephew, was a hiker with no mountaineering experience; he had been given a crash course in use of the rope only as they started up the climb.

The most difficult climbing had not been at these higher altitudes, but on the way to the North Col up a steep wall of ice and snow. On June 7 Mallory led seventeen people toward the col for yet another attempt for the summit. At 1:30 P.M. in deep snow, a sound like a rifle shot took them by surprise. The entire group began to slide backwards.

The avalanche partially buried the three British, but carried many of the Sherpas over a cliff into a deep crevasse that filled with snow. Seven Sherpas died. The expedition was over.

The head lama of Rongbuk was deeply sympathetic. Although he had sent an earlier message urging the party to quit climbing because he had had a vision of an accident on the mountain, he blessed the survivors and fixed no blame. He believed that the men who died had been sacrificed to the mountain god, and that this kind of thing simply happened to those who were at a particular spot at a particular time.

But he was concerned if more men were to try the same path. A new fresco appeared on a wall of Rongbuk, depicting a wrathful goddess encircled by angry snow leopards and hoofed demons spearing men off a mountainside. At the bottom was the body of a naked white man, violated with many spears.

Mallory returned home devastated, taking the full blame upon himself. Never having seen an avalanche in the Himalaya, he had convinced himself that the snow on Mt. Everest evaporated rather than slid. He returned to no job and a family to support.

He was now internationally renowned, however, and he ventured to the United States on a lecture tour. In America he discovered an intellectual vacuum. No one seemed to understand or care about classical references or concern for ethics. In Washington, D.C., he found "the most unresponsive crowd I ever talked to." New York City to him was "a splendid gesture against a background of emptiness." American journalists kept pushing for simple answers to complex questions. When asked in Philadelphia why he wanted to climb Everest, Mallory flashed his well-bred grin and said, "Because it is there."

These words became the most famous in the history of mountaineering, uttered by world leaders, analyzed by philosophers, repeated from the pulpits of every faith as inspiration to mankind. Robertson, Mallory's biographer (and son-in-law), wrote: "Those who knew Mallory best have treated *Because it is there* less seriously—the utterance of a tired man, not naturally patient, on hearing for the *n*th time a question that could be answered illuminatingly only if at considerable length."

In his writings Mallory offered a much stronger explanation of the motivation to climb:

Our case is not unlike that of one who has, for instance, a gift for music. There may be inconvenience, and even damage, to be sustained in devoting time to music; but the greatest danger is in not devoting enough, for music is this man's adventure. . . . To refuse the adventure is to run the risk of drying up like a pea in its shell.

When Mallory wrote that "a day well spent in the Alps is like some great symphony," he was speaking only for himself. Not everyone who ventured there would hear the symphony. His intensely personal philosophy comes through in his second-most-famous quotation: "Have we vanquished an enemy? None but ourselves!"

Mallory tended to intellectualize climbing to the point where risk took a back seat to self-discovery and artistic metaphor. In contrast to Tibetan fatalism about death on a mountain, Mallory audaciously predicted the kind of man who would die:

There have been great climbers who have grown so confident that they . . . have undertaken for pleasure the climbing of places which no human being could climb with safety, and added so a fresh element of risk by pushing our sport beyond its natural limits. Condemn them if you like, but not those of us who don't do those things and don't get killed . . .

In 1924 Mallory returned to Everest for the third time on an expedition led by Colonel Norton. On June 8 he set off before dawn toward the summit from Camp VI at 26,800 feet. With him was Andrew Irvine, a twenty-two-year-old Cambridge undergraduate with little mountaineering experience but who had done a fine job pulling a sled in the Arctic the previous summer. Just four days earlier Norton had reached 28,125 feet without oxygen. His companion, Somervell, had gone almost as high. With oxygen Mallory knew the summit was his. He had sent messages down with a

Sherpa: "Perfect weather for the job. . . . It won't be too early to start looking for us either crossing the rock band or going up the skyline at 8:00 A.M."

At 12:50 P.M. Noel Odell looked up from 26,000 feet to see the clouds part over the final peak of Everest. "I noticed far away on a snow slope leading up to what seemed to me to be the last step but one from the base of the final pyramid, a tiny object moving. . . . A second object followed, and then the first climbed to the top of the step. As I stood intently watching this dramatic appearance, the scene became enveloped in cloud once more."

Mallory and Irvine were never seen alive again. They disappeared into thin air, the cold thin air of the worst spring season in thirty years.

Noel Odell, a geologist who hadn't acclimatized quickly, moved about the mountain alone and without oxygen as no man had ever done. The day before Mallory and Irvine disappeared he left the North Col at 23,000 feet, climbed to Camp V at 25,500, and spent the night alone. The day after the disappearance he climbed to 27,000 feet in search of the missing men, then descended that evening all the way back to the North Col. The following day he began yet another climb back to Camp VI to investigate the tragedy.

Odell, the only eyewitness to see the climbers on their summit bid, was also the only member of the expedition who staunchly maintained that they had had a strong probability of success. In history the disappearance of the two men became not so much a great tragedy as a great mystery. Unquestionably the men had given their lives for Everest—but had they made it?

Back in Britain the Everesters regrouped for yet another attempt at "their mountain." The Dalai Lama, however, refused to permit future expeditions because of deaths on the three previous attempts. His Buddhist beliefs convinced him that the others who ventured into this realm of the gods would meet the same fate, an opinion no less logical than that of Britain's most respected mountain writer, GeoffreyWinthrop Young, who summarized his case for success with the words, "the peak was first climbed because Mallory was Mallory."

Shortly before the death of the Thirteenth Dalai Lama, permission was granted for a 1933 expedition. Another British team, with fourteen climbers, set out determined to climb the peak without oxygen. Most of the members were men in their twenties who had not the slightest doubt that they could climb higher, farther, and faster than the others in the party, an assortment of geologists, surveyors, and middle-aged men who by their own admission were in various stages of unfitness. Two of the Sherpas suffered surprising amnesia from the effects of altitude. One man was firmly convinced he was dead. He wouldn't move, since he argued with perfect logic that dead men couldn't walk.

Wyn Harris and Lawrence Wager reached this expedition's high point, running out of strength and time at precisely the same height as Norton did in 1922: 28,125 feet. As they were traversing toward the First Step on the summit ridge at about 27,600 feet, they came across an ice ax lying on gently angled slabs. It was of a brand supplied to all members of the 1924 expedition.

The mystery of Mallory and Irvine deepened. Was the ax dropped from the ridge above? Did it mark the site of a fatal fall? Were the men roped together? Were they on the ascent or the descent?

There were no sure answers.

A year later an ex-captain of the British army attempted to climb Everest alone. World War I had left Maurice Wilson a mental casualty like some Vietnam veterans today. He was depressed by life in general, yet overcome with a divine faith that he believed would solve the world's problems if only he could convince people of it. His chosen method of convincing was to use his faith to perform an impossible task.

He knew nothing about either mountaineering or aviation, but after reading of Mallory and Irvine he conceived a plan to crash-land a plane on the Rongbuk Glacier, then climb alone to the summit. He obtained financial backing, learned how to fly, bought a used plane, trained for endurance, and made a remarkable illegal solo flight over the objections of almost every nation involved—all the way to India, where his aircraft was impounded.

Disguised as a deaf and dumb monk, Wilson reached Rongbuk Monastery and was accepted by the head lama as a kindred spirit. With no climbing experience, he floundered up the glacier to the old Camp III, then spent four days attempting to reach the North Col, only 1,500 feet above. He camped for several nights in the middle of the steep face, then retreated and died at its base, probably the victim of sheer exhaustion.

Yet another British expedition in 1935 was notable for several reasons. First, Eric Shipton and Charles Warren found Wilson's body near Camp III, a short way from his tent.

Noel Odell.

88

Second, Shipton planned a considerable departure from the massive, polar-style journeys of the past. He used fewer climbers, less equipment, and would leave fewer fixed camps on the slopes. "I was anxious for the opportunity to demonstrate that, for one-tenth of the former cost and a fraction of the bother and disruption of the local countryside, a party could be placed on the North Col, adequately equipped to make a strong summit bid." Unfortunately, bad weather kept them from their objective. Third, he introduced a significant figure to the history of Everest.

At the last minute he had hired two extra Sherpas in Darjeeling. One of them was a strapping nineteen-year-old named Tenzing Bhotia, later to become known as Tenzing Norgay, partner of Edmund Hillary on the first successful climb of Everest in 1953. *Bhotia* meant Tibetan, for Tenzing was not technically a Sherpa. He was one of a handful of men who had lived on both the Tibetan and Nepalese sides of Everest. Nepal and India later fought over his nationality to claim his success on Everest, but actually he had been born in Tibet east of Everest near Makalu. His mother's brother was the head lama of Rongbuk, and his sister later lived there too. When he was a child, his family moved to Thami on the Nepal side of the border. Many such "Khamba" immigrants became part of Sherpa society, but life was hard for these unlanded families. As a young teenager Tenzing had moved to Darjeeling in India to find work in the city.

Tenzing enjoyed working for Shipton's expedition and was to return three more times to Rongbuk before turning his attentions to Everest climbs from Nepal after the doors of Tibet were closed by the Chinese in 1950.

After failing to reach the summit in 1935, Shipton, Tilman, and the other six members of the party made twenty-six ascents of peaks over 20,000 feet on the Tibetan side of Everest, but added little to the knowledge of Everest itself. They counted on returning the next year for an all-out attempt.

The 1936 expedition was a far cry from Shipton's lightweight dreams. He was one of twelve climbers on an expedition led by Hugh Ruttledge, who had also led the 1933 effort. Bad weather held the party back until the majority of the expedition—thirty-eight men including Sherpas—were camped on the North Col. The monsoon was coming especially early, and a dreadful scenario came to their minds. What if heavy snows cut off their retreat down the col? To descend in avalanche conditions was to invite the worst disaster in Himalayan history. They retreated to Camp I,

watched the monsoon arrive in full force, and never regained the col.

In 1938 it was H. W. Tilman's turn to try a lightweight expedition. He had gone to Nanda Devi with an Anglo-American expedition instead of to Everest in 1936, where he reached the 25,645-foot summit with just such a light team. Nanda Devi was to remain the highest peak climbed in the world until the ascent of Annapurna after World War II. For his 1938 Everest attempt, he selected seven tried-and-true men; six had been to Everest, three to Nanda Devi. Among this illustrious cast were Odell, Shipton, and Frank Smythe (who had reached 28,000 feet in 1933). Another early monsoon dashed their hopes. Vain hope pushed Shipton and Smythe through waist-deep powder to 27,250 feet, where Mallory and Irvine had clambored over bare rock.

The conquest of Everest was pursued as part of British destiny in the Asian subcontinent. With not a little poetic justice British exclusivity in Tibet was terminated by the fickle winds of politics rather than those of Everest itself. Proposed expeditions for 1940, 1941, and 1942 were canceled because of the war. A 1947 trip proposed by Shipton from his remote post in Kashgar coincided with the year the British raj, under duress, gave back control of India, beginning a war between India and Pakistan that killed millions. Also in 1947 a Tibetan seer appeared in a trance before the Dalai Lama with swollen red face, rolling eyes, and protruding tongue. He foretold dire threats from foreigners, and upon his advice the Dalai Lama banned all travel permits until 1950, precisely the year the Chinese invaded Tibet.

With the new Chinese rule Russia inherited the same friendly-power status that Britain had cultivated under the previous two Dalai Lamas. In late 1952 rumors surfaced of a Russian tragedy high on Everest. Six summit climbers supposedly disappeared above 27,000 feet, but neither the Russians nor the Chinese admitted to even the existence of the expedition.

The Russians did admit to a successful reconnaissance of Everest in 1959 with the Chinese. Because of a growing rift between the two nations, the planned 1960 Sino-Soviet expedition became wholly Chinese. Russians were carefully eliminated from all descriptions of Chinese mountaineering history. The Chinese claimed Everest reconnaissances in 1958 and 1959 plus the 1960 expedition as entirely their own.

On March 19, 1960, the main contingent of a 214-member expedition reached base camp below the Rongbuk Glacier.

None of the members had more than a few years' experience, the average age being an unusually young twenty-four. On May 3 the leader of the expedition, Shih Chan Chun, headed for the summit with Wang Feng Tung. They spent long hours trying to climb the Second Step at 28,200, then bivouacked right there with their oxygen turned off. On May 24 four climbers made another bid. In the lead was Gongbu, a Tibetan. Behind him were Chu Yin-hua, a woodsman from Yunnan; Wang Fu-chou, a cadre who belonged to the Central Communist Party; and Liu Lian-man, another Han Chinese.

The party moved more slowly than the most pallid British Everester. Lack of technical ability accounted for the three days it took them to reach the North Col from Camp III, which Mallory had climbed on sight in half a day. The traverse from high camp at 27,900 feet to the Second Step just 200 feet higher took over two hours. They avoided the step itself by a chimney that ended in a 15-foot cliff at the top. Here Liu Lian-man placed a piton and took four falls. Wearing crampons, his feet wouldn't stay on the holds. Gongbu tried twice and failed. Chu took over, succeeded in placing a higher piton, but couldn't make the last 10 feet either. The total years of mountain experience of this trio could be counted on one hand.

What Chu did next was unprecedented in high-altitude climbing. He stripped off his boots to just inner socks so he could "get closer to the rock" and stand on Liu's shoulders without hurting him. Gripping the rock with toes that quickly went numb, he reached the top of the step and belayed the other men with his rope. It was 5:00 P.M. His feet never regained feeling.

Not far above the step, Liu could go no further. He stayed behind while the others moved on. The terrain was not difficult now, but the men were almost as spent as Liu. Just sixty feet below the summit the last of their oxygen ran out. Chu related those final moments:

At this moment we remembered the decision made at the Party meeting . . . nothing would make us turn back! But our legs refused to carry us any further, so we had to go on all fours. Gongbu took the lead . . . we saw the star-studded sky above us on the top peak of Chomolungma. To the south of the crest was gleaming white snow, and to the north was nothing but dull grey rocks.

A bust of Chairman Mao wrapped in the national flag was left on top along with a note laboriously written in Chinese characters by starlight: "Wang Fu-chou and two others conquered Chomolungma at 4:20 A.M., May 25, 1960."

The last 800 feet above the Second Step had taken eleven hours. For these utterly spent men the descent to camp took even longer. Storms made the descent an epic to match the climb itself.

The barefoot climber, Chu Yin-hua, lost all joints of all ten toes to frostbite. The other summiteers lost parts of fingers and suffered frostbitten ears and noses. In Peking they were national heroes, but the Western world remained in doubt. Chinese propaganda was notoriously untrustworthy. No summit photographs and few facts were supplied.

The highest published photograph was taken on the descent by Chu Yin-hua, blown up from a frame of movie footage. R. L. G. Irving, who had been Mallory's schoolmaster and original climbing mentor, calculated the height at which this photo was made and told the world that the Chinese were lying because the photo had been made *below* the Second Step instead of above, 650 feet lower than claimed.

Lawrence Wager, who had climbed to the highest known point on the Tibetan side of Everest in 1933, analyzed the Chinese photo against his own and Hillary's from the successful ascent through Nepal in 1953. He proved beyond a doubt that the photo was indeed made where the Chinese claimed: above the Second Step. A Swiss expert, G. O. Dhyrenfurth, was certain the photo was an aerial.

Whether the photo had been taken from the air or thousands of feet lower on the mountain really proved nothing. It could have been captioned for propaganda by Peking bureaucrats without the climbers' knowledge. The armchair critics did not realize that the time of arrival on the summit was not a true 4:20 A.M., because Mao had put all China on Peking time. Thus the three men had climbed upward in the darkness only until an effective 1:20 A.M. just a month from the longest day of the year.

Nevertheless, Western skepticism reigned supreme. We asked for proof that just wasn't there. The Chinese reached the summit in darkness, fighting to stay alive. Their last concern was whether people halfway around the world would doubt what they were doing. Throughout the world the foundation of mountaineering is based on trust. It is a sport without referees, a way of life without written laws.

In spite of this mountaineering tradition, the Chinese

Ruins of the "Shining Crystal Monastery," Shekar-Dzong.

Stupa and mani stones, Rongbuk Monastery.

Everest expedition was judged by courtroom standards. No one talked to witnesses or advised the Chinese of their rights. Discrepancies in accounts translated and rewritten for the media became evidence against their deeds in world opinion. That they later didn't reply to the hundreds of American and European mountaineers who wrote to invite themselves to the mountains of Tibet is hardly surprising.

The Chinese mounted another massive expedition to Everest in 1975. This time they placed nine climbers on the summit. Again the Western world refused to believe them— until a British expedition climbing Everest from Nepal came upon a Chinese survey tripod on the summit.

The Tibetan, the woodsman, and the bureaucrat who made the first ascent of Everest from Tibet in 1960 carried a bust of Chairman Mao to the top for the same reasons that American expeditions promote capitalist sponsors. They were mountaineers above all else.

Propaganda is not a Chinese invention. We in the West continue to vilify a fictional Nazi death cult in mountaineering in which men like Heinrich Harrer climbed the Eiger "for the glory of their Fuehrer." Similarly, we wrote off Chinese mountaineering by saying their "claim has lacked so far any credible evidence," and that their account was "full of glaring discrepancies and has since been discredited in the Western Hemisphere."

Many of the same journalists and historians who judged the Chinese climb for us are equally sure there is no chance Mallory or Irvine climbed Everest in 1924.

Moonlight on Chomolungma
from Rongbuk Monastery.

94

Chapter 8: In the Tracks of Mallory

"TELL THEM THAT WE HAVE ONLY THREE DAYS. We would like to explore as much of Chomolungma as we can. How far toward the North Col can we go?"

After the interpreter relayed the question, Wang Fu-chou and Chu Yin-hua looked at one another without a spoken word. They had climbed Everest together in 1960. It had taken them most of a month to reach the North Col—acclimatizing, exploring, and moving an expedition of 214 over twenty miles of the Rongbuk Glacier's moraines and ice pinnacles.

Now we were at 17,200 feet in the massive base camp of the 1981 *Expédition Militaire Française*. General Pierre Astorg, head of all alpine troops for France, was leader of this million-dollar effort. Chinese trucks brought the expedition all the way to base camp over the world's highest road system. The two Chinese who pondered my question were the liaison officers. Wang Fu-chou was also the secretary-general of the Chinese Mountaineering Association, and Chu Yin-hua (my liaison officer on Mustagh Ata in 1980) was about to be appointed CMA director for Tibet.

Wang's answer came slowly with a hint of a cunning smile, "You may climb as high as you wish on Chomolungma so long as you return in three days."

My partner was Harold Knutson, whose side trips during years of geological field work in Nepal included the South Col of Everest, the upper realms of Dhaulagiri, and the top of Ganesh Himal. At forty—just five days older than I—he was one of the top masters marathon runners in the United States as well as a veteran skier. He had left his geology hammer behind.

We returned to our camp outside Rongbuk Monastery, six miles below the base camp. Our itinerary was padded with five unstructured days to scramble up lower peaks, visit the Rongbuk Glacier, hike around for views, or just relax. The other twelve people in our trekking group would be under the guidance of my assistant leader, Jo Sanders, while we were on the mountain.

On May 12 at dawn Harold and I left the monastery. Everest filled the southern sky even though it was twenty-two miles away as the crow flies. And crows do fly here; Everest-size giant crows, called *goraks*, have raided camps at over 27,000 feet on the mountain. If a camp is ever placed on the summit, goraks may drop in for dinner.

Bar-headed geese have been seen many times flying in V formation at extreme altitudes, yet something in human nature wants to deny that the realm of Everest is attainable

pale in comparison to the West's patent obliviousness to Tibetan nomenclature: the name we use is no less political than a Soviet gem such as "Nineteenth Party Congress Peak." We honor Sir George Everest, who happened to be surveyor-general in India when the mountain's height, not the mountain itself, was discovered.

Tibetans were never interested in calculating Chomolungma's height, nor in climbing it. That they have done so with the Chinese is only an indication of their forced redirection of goals. We are all—Tibetan, Chinese, British, American—prisoners of our culture and time. We may briefly escape toward narrowly defined goals, but even those are defined by the matrix in which we have lived, hidden wombs that have shaped our beings.

There was nothing logical in my own and Harold's drive to climb fast and far on Everest. There was nothing logical in Mallory and Irvine's drive to keep going into the clouds. A case could be made that the Chinese method of moving massive waves of people up the mountain in a continual ebb and flow until someone reaches the summit for the purpose of collective glory is far more logical.

To climb for the glory of Mao seems ridiculous to us, but we did not emerge from serfdom through a revolution that denied much of our individuality for national goals. We did not live out the subtle weakening of that revolution. We were not part of Mao's attempts to overcome its declining momentum by remotivating new generations of youth. Climbing Chomolungma was just such an artificial revolutionary experience, one far less damaging than the Great Leap Forward or the Cultural Revolution.

Because the meaning of mountaineering in China was far beyond individual achievement, very few facts about the 1975 Chinese expedition reached the Western world. Untold hundreds of men and women traveled the Rongbuk Glacier on this largest of all Everest efforts. Thirty-three men and seven women were positioned for the final assault in Camp VI at 26,900 feet with oxygen and plenty of food and equipment. Of the nine who reached the summit, only one was Han Chinese. All the others were Tibetan, including a thirty-seven-year-old woman and mother of three children.

Tibetan disinterest in mountaineering is evident. Not one Tibetan introduced to the sport by the British or the Chinese ever pursued it independently. The true mountaineer is motivated by his or her inner spirit. Tibetans simply live in a spiritual world vastly different from ours. Their Hindu-

to any living thing besides man. When the Great Trigonometric Survey of India investigated native names for Everest in the nineteenth century one was "Mi-ti Gu-ti Cha-pu Long-nga," which scholars translated "You cannot see the summit from near it, but you can see the summit from nine directions, and a bird which flies as high as the summit goes blind."

The most common Tibetan name for Everest is Chomolungma, meaning something close to "Mother Goddess of the Earth." The Chinese use the same name, Qomolungma, spelled in their new Pinyin style in which "Q" is pronounced "Ch." Recent criticisms of their full official name, "Qomolungma Feng" (in which Feng simply means "peak" in order to separate the name of a range from an individual summit),

Buddhist roots in ancient India are chasms apart from our own Greco-Roman heritage. The Greeks sought to make the universe comfortable with architecture, philosophy, and science; the Indian chased "a phantasmagoria of universe fleeing away from him in spirals beyond the horizon of the mind."

Explorers and climbers beyond all else seek personal, tangible events to define their existence; Tibetans have the wild forces of nature and life answered by their gods. They don't ask the internal questions that give the Western mountaineer a more personal definition of life: Can I succeed on this mountain? Can I make the right choices to live through danger? If I do this once, can I do it again? And again?

Somewhere down the line the logical Western mind may fall into a sloppy, mystical trap. After enough successes the "again?" comes without the original question or purpose. The climber enters a state of imagined immortality as the quest switches from a discovery of what life allows in the face of risk into a roulette game by a compulsive gambler who ignores the odds. The gambler-climber may reach such a totally positive state that the possibility of the negative—accident or death—is no longer seriously considered.

Harold and I had a small degree of this confidence from other fast ventures to above 20,000 feet. We saw no mountaineering dangers that were life-threatening, so we were complacent about our safety as we set off for the heights, perhaps in the same way that Mallory and Irvine had been when they set off from so much higher in 1924.

Mountaineers rarely die surmounting great difficulties. They fall on easy terrain or pass away in the night.

Two hours after leaving Rongbuk we passed the French base camp and were invited to a leisurely breakfast in their house-size cook tent. They told us not to bother with a tent or sleeping pads, since we could use theirs at Camps I, II, and III. At 11:00 A.M. we walked off in T-shirts and running shoes with thirty-five-pound loads of food, clothing, boots, and climbing gear over as good a trail as many in the High Sierra.

All around the camp were the remains of blue sheep, snow cocks, and chukar partridges shot by Tibetans working for the expedition. The old taboos of not killing any animal in the Rongbuk Valley were gone. Some wildlife had survived here only because there were no longer any permanent residents. The blue sheep, creatures of habit, still occasionally came down to the monastery walls early in the morning.

We were starting off on the best day in several months. Unusually continuous storms had kept the French from making a summit bid. As we drew closer, the single mountain in front of us began to dwarf the panorama of finely sculpted peaks to the west. Even Nuptse, number twenty-one among the world's peaks, dropped its sawtooth crest below the shoulder of Chomolungma's long West Ridge. Pumori's perfect pyramid, high anywhere else in Tibet, looked like a minor pinnacle.

At 1:00 P.M. we passed the tents of Camp I, feeling fresh and fit. We had been told Camp II was a full day's travel further for a heavily laden porter.

As we left the steep hillsides and moraines for the rock-strewn ice itself, our sense of wildness was weakened by something less than a quarter inch in diameter: an insulated wire. Twenty miles of it ran in and out of rock and snow, following us and leading us everywhere we went. If we lost track of it for fifty feet, it always reappeared, for it had been placed by people (the Chinese in 1975) who were headed where we were headed. We wondered why they hadn't chosen wireless communications.

The wire made nothing easier for us. If anything the distraction made it more difficult to be at one with our surroundings and to lose consciousness of ourselves, an ideal state that comes after some time on the trail. We had left sea level just eight days earlier, and our pace began to slow drastically as we headed for Camp II at 20,000 feet, our third stage of the day.

Both of us tried to shrug off a growing lassitude. Harold, never complaining, always strong, always steady, finally said, "I can't go on. We're going to have to bivouac." We gave it one more half-hour push; then another. I was far ahead when Camp II suddenly came into view. Dropping my pack, I went back to carry Harold's, and within the hour we were brewing tea in a comfortable wall tent, ready to crash for ten hours of much-needed sleep.

The next morning both of us felt surprisingly fresh. The same natural pathway that the British had found in 1922 led through a maze of ice pinnacles. Soon the rock under our feet gave way to snow. Only now, in 10° F. temperatures at nearly 21,000 feet, did we switch from running shoes to double mountaineering boots.

By late morning we reached Camp III, occupied by half a dozen Frenchmen who had come down from a high camp at 26,900 to rest and recover after a bout with bad weather.

Base camp at 17,200 feet under Chomolungma.

The North Col loomed above the camp, guarded by a 1,000-foot headwall that in this head-on view looked more vertical, but closer and less high than in photographs. We gladly accepted an invitation for lunch and tea before continuing up.

As soon as we set foot on the steep snow, it was apparent that no members of the French team had traveled the route recently. Fixed ropes were often three feet under the surface. Because of the avalanche hazard, I vowed to turn around if I came to a point where I could no longer stay clipped to the ropes. Digging and step-plugging were laborious, but more than compensated for by the time we were saving on technical climbing. Big crevasses were bridged with aluminum ladders. Other ladders were screwed into glistening ice to surmount short headwalls.

I wondered how Mallory, without any of this modern paraphernalia, had climbed this so easily in 1921 when the route was unknown. Then I remembered that we were not on the route where he had been avalanched and the seven Sherpas had perished. The French had wisely chosen a steeper but safer line to the left. Today, however, the avalanche danger seemed extreme.

I continued on, breaking trail through windblown powder, well above Harold. As I struggled toward a ladder, I heard a low "whump" and the ladder moved uphill. It seemed that way because the snow slope was not moving relative to me; it was going down with me. The optical illusion, like that of another car moving when it is your own that is sliding back, lasted a split second. Before I had time to be really scared, I stopped facefirst in the snow about five feet below where I had been. The rope was tight on my waist, and the avalanche was filling a huge crevasse not far below. Harold was out of its path.

I kept on leading. Several hundred feet higher the snow again slipped away, and again the rope held. At six in the evening I wallowed like a fish out of water over the final cornice with Harold not far behind. The weather had deteriorated. The northeast ridge disappeared into the mist, as it had done on that afternoon for Noel Odell more than half a century before. Toward Nepal I could see only cloud. Looking into Tibet, I watched the ceiling lower to eye level with me on 23,000-foot Khartaphu.

I felt tired but quite normal. Strength seemed to surge back as I thought of my original plan to try Changtse, the North Peak of Chomolungma, an easy 1,700 feet above and

oh so close now. If only we hadn't stopped so long for lunch, or started earlier! But this was my head talking, not my body. My euphoria was evidence of how little oxygen was getting to my brain. I knew this, and I felt a strange sense of control as if I could switch from intuitive complacency to logical urgency (and a sense of how weak I really was).

Harold, too, was ready to go down. We had very positive feelings over having such an intimate connection with the north side of Everest in so short a time, having reached a height exceeded by only one other American party, Woodrow Wilson Sayre's illegal "Four Against Everest" expedition in 1962.

As we neared the base of the wall, less than a mile from Camp III, I had to rest several times a minute just to be able to walk downhill. Our energies were reversed from the previous day. Harold felt stronger, and it was his turn to offer to carry my pack into camp.

The author below the North Col; summit at upper left.

The French would not allow us to eat our freeze-dried cuisine. They insisted on sharing their own declining rations. As we talked long into the darkness, one man asked in broken English if we knew about the American who was trying to solve the mystery of Mallory and Irvine. He showed us a long letter from Tom Holzel of Massachusetts, asking them to look for Mallory's body on a terrace at 8,200 meters and if they found a camera, to go through some elaborate technical precautions to save the film. Eastman Kodak had given him expectations that printable images might still exist after fifty-seven years in the Chomolungma "freezer." If the film were rewarmed before processing, the latent image would in all probability disappear.

The reopening of mountaineering in Tibet in 1980 kindled new interest in Mallory and Irvine's fate. Back in 1971 I had read Holzel's theoretical scenario published in *Mountain* magazine, which showed how Mallory and Irvine might have made the summit. I had also read the extremely logical rebuke in a later issue from Sir Percy Wyn Harris, whose credibility was solidly backed by history. More accurately, Sir Percy *was* history. In 1933 he had reached the highest known point of all British North Colers, 28,125 feet, and had found Mallory or Irvine's ice ax.

I had come to share Sir Percy's opinion that "a detailed examination of the article must lead to the conclusion that Mr. Holzel has never done any serious mountaineering or had any practical experience of the problems of high-altitude climbing." I wrote off Holzel as another zealot who pursues a cause forever regardless of its worthiness. As events began to unfold, I reversed that hasty conclusion.

If, as it now appears, the Chinese had withheld information that might jeopardize their claim to the first ascent of Everest from Tibet, could Sir Percy be totally objective—with his own supremacy among prewar Everesters at stake? In any case, Holzel's controversy faded into obscurity for eight long years. It seemed to be one of those sensational missing-person mysteries that might remain unsolved forever.

Holzel didn't give up. In 1979 he wrote a letter to a Japanese team that had just been given the first foreign permit for the north side of Everest since 1938. He asked them to search a snow terrace at 26,900 feet for bodies or other evidence. The Japanese expedition was for 1980, when eight Chinese and Tibetan peaks were first being opened, but they obtained special permission to reconnoiter the lower mountain in 1979 with six Chinese climbers who knew the area.

Five months later Holzel received a reply from the Japanese Alpine Club. A tragedy had occurred. As six climbers neared the North Col, three were swept to their deaths in an avalanche. Among them was Wang Hong Bao, who had repeatedly climbed to over 26,000 feet on the 1975 Chinese expedition. The day before his death Wang told Ryoten Hasegawa, who survived the avalanche, that he had seen "two deads" on his 1975 climb. The first, near Camp III, was undoubtedly Maurice Wilson (already found by Shipton in 1935). The other was at 26,575 feet. "When he had touched the clothes of the dead at 8,100 meters," Hasegawa reported, "the clothes had been broken to pieces and blown off by the wind."

Hasegawa asked Wang if the body could be Russian. Wang said Russians never climbed that high. Although he spoke no English, he repeated the words "English, English."

Typical stone home of the
Tibetan Plateau, Shekar.

Hasegawa further reported that Wang had etched two crucial words in the snow in characters common to Chinese and Japanese: "Englishman, 8,100." Hasegawa's certainty was quoted in the *London Times*: "There can be no mistake."

Holzel applied to the CMA for a permit to go to Chomolungma to search for Mallory and Irvine. They responded:

About the information that a Chinese climber had found the bodies of Mallory and Irvine at the altitude of 8,100 meters high on Qomolungma, this is an entire rumor. Our association tried to clarify the news reported by the Japanese newspaper *Yomiuri* on many occasions and in different ways. So we hold it is not necessary for your team to go to Qomolungma to make a research.

Our French friends had questioned both Chu Yin-hua and two Tibetans who had reached the summit in 1975. All three said the body must have been that of Wu Tsung-yueh who fell from 27,900 feet in 1975.

Holzel responded, "What does that do to Wang's testimony? He could not possibly have confused a just-dead, modernly clothed Oriental corpse with that of a desiccated body of a Westerner dressed in disintegrating, old-fashioned clothing." And if he did lie about it, how would he "obtain such expert knowledge of where an 'English' body might be found?"

Mallory & Irvine leaving the North Col on their last climb, 6 June 1924

A 1981 book on Chinese mountains was published by the CMA with Japanese and English translations under the same cover. One essay was titled, "Things Left Behind on Mt. Qomolungma." Zeng Shusheng gave minute details on the discovery in 1960 of a body near Camp III (again almost certainly Wilson). He had been on the 1975 expedition, and he said, "We saw no more remains of the foreign climber." The only other item mentioned was an oxygen cylinder found at 25,560 feet that was brought back to Peking.

Holzel learned that a British climber (who does not want his name used in the controversy) had been present when a Chinese climber was questioned about the body Wang found. He answered assertively that "there was no substantiation of any other body found on Mt. Everest," then lowered his voice so the group couldn't hear to tell the Britisher that there might be a camera on the body, and that "the CMA is not eager to have a picture prove that the Chinese did not make the first ascent from the north."

When Shih Chan Chun, director of the CMA, visited the United States in 1981, he was repeatedly interviewed about Mallory and Irvine. He, too, was history. He had led both the 1960 and 1975 expeditions, reaching 28,100 feet at the foot of the famous Second Step. He steadfastly claimed that no body had been found on the upper mountain, not even that of Wu Tsung-yueh mentioned by Chu and the two Tibetans. He did, however, have some additions to "Things Left Behind on Mt. Qomolungma." The *Los Angeles Times* ran a long story, "Was Hillary 29 Years Too Late?" with some surprising revelations:

Shi . . . told *The Times* that since 1960 he has had physical evidence, never before made public, that George Leigh-Mallory was within an hour's hike of scaling the 29,028-foot summit before he and a companion disappeared in 1924. Shi said a 1960 expedition he led up Everest's difficult North Face found a short wooden pole and a length of rope belonging to Leigh-Mallory 8,500 meters (27,900 feet) up the Himalayan mountain. Two oxygen bottles were found at slightly lower levels, Shi said.

Tom Holzel, an American alpinist who has studied the 1924 Leigh-Mallory expedition extensively, said Shi's statements put Leigh-Mallory several hundred feet higher than has previously been known. More importantly, Holzel said, they place Leigh-Mallory past the last major obstacle to conquering Everest, a sheer rock wall known as the Second Step. . . .

Shi did not explain why he had delayed for more than 20 years in disclosing his findings. . . . Holding out his hands to indicate a distance of about three feet, Shi indicated the length of "a pole, wooden, and a rope also, from Mallory and Irvine." Asked if this evidence convinces him that Leigh-Mallory and Irvine ascended to at least 8,500 meters, he said that was the case. Did either of them make it to the summit? "It is a mystery and I couldn't judge," Shi replied.

The Mallory and Irvine mystery had always revolved around whether they reached the top of the Second Step. Both sides presented laborious calculations. Noel Odell, the one eyewitness, is alive, clear of mind at ninety, and still not sure which step he saw through a hole in the clouds.

The Second Step controversy is too complex and emotional to rehash here. The important thing to keep in mind is that even if one or the other were proven, it would not determine (based on present evidence) whether Mallory and Irvine reached the summit. There would merely be a new flurry of guesswork. It is all too easy to build logical sequences of evidence around sparse outlines. In cases like this, people who are certain are usually wrong.

Nothing will ever deny the genuine uncertainty and curiosity of men like Hillary, who in his moment of ultimate gratification on top of Everest, mind dimmed by lack of oxygen, made a conscious effort to look about for traces of Mallory and Irvine. Or Odell, who holds in his old mind nuances of that moment that can never be fully described; impressions based on the intuition of a man who knew his mountains, impressions that led him to conclude that Mallory may have reached the top and perished on the descent. Or Younghusband, who knew both men and mountain, and maintained until his dying day that one of them "must have very nearly, perhaps actually, reached the top."

Some of the *Los Angeles Times*'s pyramid of logic tumbled after Leo LeBon of Mountain Travel conducted a more in-depth interview with Shih. LeBon discovered that Shih's nomenclature for the steps was the opposite of that in Western literature. What he called the Second Step was the second one *below* the summit, not the second one encountered in climbing up. Shih confirmed this on a photograph, which explains why his stated 8,500-meter discovery of the stick and rope is below, not above, the accepted height of the Second Step.

To see the issue in its broadest dimensions, we must avoid getting caught up in the "step controversy." Let us take the lowest accepted altitude for Mallory and Irvine: 27,900 feet. Let us try to prove beyond a doubt, as Sir Percy Wyn Harris

attempted to do, that they couldn't have made the summit after Odell sighted them at 12:50 P.M. Sir Percy stated, "Any reasonable person would agree that an estimate suggesting a rate of climb higher than 300 feet per hour . . . had not been worked out objectively."

Most early Everesters did indeed climb slower than 300 feet per hour, but there were exceptions, and those exceptions are now becoming the rule among men in good physical condition using oxygen, as Mallory was. Among the early exceptions was George Finch, rejected once because he was anemic and flabby, who climbed to 26,500 feet at a rate of 900 feet per hour in 1922. Odell, spurred by the urgency of Mallory's disappearance, climbed at 800 feet per hour *without* oxygen for over three hours to 25,300 feet.

Ordinary people, not professional climbers, have matched these rates on recent expeditions from Nepal. Climbing with oxygen in 1981, Peter Hackett, a medical doctor who was not a highly experienced climber, soloed the last 2,750 feet to the summit of Everest at 340 feet per hour. Chris Kopczynski of Spokane, Washington, averaged over 600 feet per hour for 4.5 hours when he made the summit with a Sherpa. For Mallory to have climbed the maximum remaining 1,128 feet by six in the evening would have required a rate of climb of just 218 feet per hour.

Mallory almost certainly would have run out of oxygen before reaching the top. He almost certainly would have been benighted either on his ascent or on the return. But are these conditions as impossible as the old Everesters claim? Certainly not. With a goal like the first ascent of Everest in mind, superhuman performances are not just remote possibilities, but predictable occurrences. Anyone who watched Bruce Jenner run an effortless victory lap in the 1976 Olympics after the fastest 1,500 meters of his life, while his fellow competitors were sprawled on the grass, cannot deny the power of psychic energy. Such a thing did indeed happen to Chu Yin-hua in 1960 on Mallory's exact route. He ran out of oxygen (above 28,200 according to the CMA), and climbed long into the night. Are we to say that Mallory could not have done the same? Panduo, the Tibetan mother of three, climbed the route in 1975 with eight companions, using oxygen only sporadically, and not at all for over an hour near the summit.

The mystery of Mallory and Irvine could go forever unsolved, or the answer may be known by the time these words are in print. The search for evidence is the grandest

ABOVE *Rongbuk Monastery in 1981.*

RIGHT *Rongbuk Monastery in 1921.*

of mountaineering ironies. We hope they left things on their climb. We—today's ecology-oriented mountaineers—are eager to locate "things left behind" by Mallory and Irvine while the core of our own ethic is to climb leaving no trace at all. Some of the same climbers who would relish knowledge of Mallory and Irvine advocate doing away with guidebooks so that everyone can have a "first ascent" experience.

Mallory and Irvine have done well by this new ethic. Several generations of climbers have not been able to determine where they went. And the search continues.

Everesters of all nationalities have a rather poor record as environmentalists. As early as 1922, George Finch and Charles Bruce "laughed aloud at the thought that there goes another five pounds off our backs" every time a bottle "bumped its way over the precipice and the good steel clanged like a church bell at each impact." Although these bottles are now considered historical finds, the difference between litter and artifacts is simply age. The South Col on the other side of Everest has been called the world's highest junkyard.

The greatest sacrilege perpetrated by Everesters was at a considerably lower elevation: 16,500 feet at Rongbuk Monastery. After our climb of the North Col, Harold and I returned in a long third day. Here were relics of expeditions that made the Chinese twenty-mile wire seem innocuous. The monastery itself has been destroyed. The Red Guard of the People's Liberation Army fanned the Tibetans into a frenzy of collective destruction. The Chinese would not give us a date, but a Tibetan yak driver who spoke Nepali indicated to another trekker that the monastery was intact until 1974. Tibetan and Chinese alike admitted that both races had joined together to turn the highest and one of the most sacred places of Lamaistic Buddhism into a shambles. As I walked through the ruins I spoke my thoughts into a tape recorder:

This is a depressing place. Spots of snow form distant dots in gullies, surrounded by barren rock slopes. There are occasional black dots—junipers, the highest timberline scrub—in between boulders. Otherwise this is as desolate a place as man could imagine. Next to our camp here is the Rongbuk Monastery without a single ceiling; just broken walls stretching a hundred yards up a hillside devoid of life, where hundreds of lamas and pilgrims once worshiped.

To my left is Chomolungma, the Goddess Mother, this huge mountain rising above desolation unlike any I have seen. I cannot recall being in such a rain shadow, in such a barren area so high. Questions come to mind. How did people live here? It would be interesting to try to reconstruct the life of a lama. Where did his food come from? His heat? His butter for the lamps? The paint for the walls? Who carried them up? Why? And how? I'm awed.

All the ease and all the quietness of spirit that I felt is suddenly erased in the presence of this desecrated monastery and this great mountain, a mountain that I might attempt to climb. It would give me a supreme test. Do I want that test? I can still wonder, but this monastery is beyond any test, beyond any help. Gone.

LEFT *Gold-leafed Buddha on the ruined walls of Rongbuk Monastery.*

RIGHT *Peeling face on a crumbling wall, Rongbuk.*

Seracs on the East Rongbuk Glacier.

Among these walls, where the wind blasts fading paintings and carved stone, expeditions have performed a sacrilege that turns my stomach. What I have seen here is irretrievably horrible and grotesque. I had to sit down and regain my composure after I looked into the first of dozens of rooms filled with trash. Tears came to my eyes, and I rarely cry. Cans. Thousands of cans. None of them very rusted. All from expeditions since 1975. Chinese labels. Japanese labels. German labels. Boxes, paper, decaying food, metal, and just plain junk. And Rongbuk is accessible by truck! The Chinese could have simply carried it all out!

The essence of this place is contained in a wall painting that I just photographed. The elements have obliterated all but a pair of mournful eyes staring from a featureless face.

The rape of Rongbuk was the culmination of a tour of destruction that had begun for us as soon as we left the restored showcase of Lhasa. Shekar, the "Shining Crystal Monastery," seen by Mallory on the 1921 expedition was in far worse condition. Not even a wall was intact. As we walked through the rubble a thousand feet above the town, I felt something unusual about this "artifact" of destruction, something I would never have found in America: the silence. No signs, fences, trails, people, horns, police, rangers, and all those things that make our historical sights not quite as real as TV documentaries about them.

In Gyantse, where Younghusband had sieged the Tibetans in 1904, we saw pilgrims circumambulating Tibet's greatest *chorten* in timeless fashion. It had been built by Rapten Kunsang-phapa in the early fifteenth century, the Sistine Chapel of Lamaism. This Kumbum (place of a hundred thousand images) was the ultimate *chorten*: a structure of worship that can vary from a pile of rocks on a mountain pass to this giant wedding cake of stone formed from circular tiers of interlocking chapels.

In 1948 the famed Tibetologist Giuseppe Tucci visited Gyantse and brought back photographs of the Kumbum surrounded by a monastic city. He described the Kumbum as a "superb psychocosmogram, wherein the very breathing of the universe is portrayed." Its architecture had come a long way from "beginnings in the Babylonian ziggurat to find a haven on the Roof of the World." The dazzling progression of frescoes and Buddha images were arranged to form a circuit so that pilgrims (like those we now watched) were put into an orbit with the core of the structure, magically but not literally identified with the earth's axis, on their right.

We watched the pilgrims walk round and round in circles, gaining holiness from what was on their right, oblivious to the devastation to their left.

The remainder of the monastic city is gone. The ancient wall that had once contained it now sits very much alone on a barren hillside. The place has the feel of an abandoned quarry. Buildings have been crushed into rubble here, but, as in Lhasa, an inner force prevented the combined Red Guard and Tibetan insurgents from touching the holiest place of all.

The difference with Rongbuk was that we became more than passive observers of cultural destruction. Our kind of people—trekkers and climbers from the West—had trashed the floors of the monastery. Here we were suddenly part of it all, partners with the Tibetans and Chinese. When Pan Yu (our interpreter) translated a request from Chang Jiang Yuan (our liaison officer) to preserve Rongbuk's artifacts, the clash of ethics and philosophies would have burst the walls and the ceilings, were they not already in ruins. Sitting on a stone floor that had so recently emerged from centuries of darkness, Tom Cole, Jo Sanders, and I talked about our feelings.

Jo said indignantly, "The Chinese Mountaineering Association must become aware of this. The garbage is just abhorrent. All along we've had indications of their lack of concern."

Tom was indignant about something else. "Our interpreter, Pan, was very sheepish when he reminded us of the rules about not taking cultural artifacts. It is insane to imagine that they would go and destroy a temple, then call the rubble 'cultural artifacts'."

I replied, "But if they don't take credit for the destruction, and they've gone through enough time, I can see how they might consider what's left as cultural artifacts."

"The Chinese are good at that," Tom concurred. "They switched the Gang of Four for this, and the Cultural Revolution for that, and it's easy for them to blame those who came before. It all washes to a certain extent, I guess."

I brought up the fact that our liaison officer told us we could each take one of the hundreds of identical clay Buddhas that were lying on the ground near a damaged kiln, so long as we hid them from the customs agents. "If we don't take one," I concluded, "the first Japanese trekking group up here is going to scoop them up."

Tom looked me straight in the eye and said, "If you saw a person dead in the streets and he had gold jewelry on, would you take off the jewelry on the basis that the next guy is going to come along and take it?"

I returned the stare and answered, "It would depend on how the situation evolved. In my own civilization and home, no. But I can imagine a desperate situation where I would do just that."

Tom's eyes dropped and so did his voice. "I could too," he almost whispered. "This place makes me so sad I don't want to think about it."

Jo had the last word, "It's an individual decision that each one of us has to address ourselves. There are people who will take them home and put them on the shelf with all their other collectible items, and it won't mean anything to them, and there are others to whom it will mean the world. When you handed that little tiny Buddha to me and I held it in my hands, I couldn't believe the feeling, the respect, the sadness I felt. Tremendously sad. That sadness will stay with me for the rest of my life."

To have left Tibet immediately after Rongbuk would have been an emotional disaster. We had the good fortune to make a three-day side trip to Tingri, a trading center where Sherpas from Nepal used to bring rice, grain, raw iron, and livestock to trade for Tibetan salt, wool, and other commodities. Trade virtually ceased after the 1959 rebellion in Tibet, not because it became illegal (although the border was closed for short periods), but because the Sherpas found the Chinese authorities in Tingri unpredictable and often unfair in their dealings.

During the Cultural Revolution, a hill near Tingri was hollowed out to provide hidden quarters for soldiers and vehicles. We were not allowed to stay in the city because of "security reasons." This was a blessing because the Chinese were always trying to make us stay in dingy quarters for a hundred dollars a night per person, while we wanted to be out camping on the land.

What we found on the plains of Tingri was the Tibetan camp of our dreams. We set up tents by a stream that snaked through a green meadow. The meadow wove its way around low hills until it ran into the Himalayan crest, thirty miles distant through invisibly clear air. A tremendous gap led into Nepal. This pass, the Nangpa La, appeared to cut so deeply between the massifs of Cho Oyu and Gaurisankar that even I, who had seen the glaciers and rubble from the Nepal side, imagined that a carpet of grassland parted the snows.

Yaks and sheep wandered peacefully. Here for the first time I understood why Tibetans believe that their homeland, barren and cold though it may be, is the most wonderful place on earth.

One evening I opened my duffel, took out running shoes and shorts, and ran to the top of a nearby hill. The sun was setting on the skyline of Cho Oyu, where Herbert Tichy's party of three had made the highest-ever first ascent by a small expedition, climbing a short way into Tibet from Nepal in 1954. On the plains below, Harrer and Aufschnaiter had passed in 1945 and Mallory had lived in a base camp in 1921.

My experience in Tingri was hardly that of the early explorers. Here, where they had barely survived in various disguises, moving with yaks and donkeys, wearing Tibetan clothing, I stood draped with thousands of dollars of Nikon cameras. Behind me was a Chinese truck with everything my group needed, everything necessary to make a portable environment where we could sleep in the same bags and tents, eat the same food, wear the same clothes, and talk with the same friends as if we were camping in the California Sierra.

The scene even looked like the Sierra to me. The mountains were just twice as high. Everest was just two Mt. Whitneys; twice 14,496 feet is 28,992, only ten feet shy of the top of the world. Or was it? As I ran back to camp, I recalled the quandary of the British surveyors when six different calculations averaged out to 29,000 feet exactly. They thought no one would believe them, so they considered alternative heights: 28,999 would be rounded off, as would 29,001; they chose 29,002 as the official height. In a lower snow year, or with a different correction factor for refraction in the air, Everest might just be the perfect double. The past took on a heightened immediacy, as if I had lived it myself.

The plains were empty now, empty of explorers, empty of nomadic families, empty of wild ass and gazelle. All this had vanished in one long generation. Captain Noel, who had passed through here in 1913 and sparked the British toward Everest, was alive and well in his nineties in England. Another captain before him, C. H. D. Ryder, had ridden across these plains in 1904 when he left Younghusband's Lhasa mission to explore. Ryder, who later became a successor to Sir George Everest as Surveyor General of the Great Trigonometric Survey of India, was the first of his countrymen to see the mountain as I saw it now—supremacy assured as the sun left the top of each neighboring peak.

*Devastation from the Cultural
Revolution surrounds the
Kumbum of Gyantse.* 109

*High grasslands on the edge of
the Tibetan Plateau.*

PART FIVE: MINYA KONKA

Minya Konka from the air.

Chapter 9: The Long Road to Minya Konka

LUNCHTIME IN SHANGHAI. Nine members of an American expedition were dining together, savoring luxury in the diplomatic community before departing for the wilds of China. Their goal was to find and measure a mysterious peak reported to be higher than Everest.

Lunch went uneaten. Terris Moore, a twenty-three-year-old Harvard graduate student, had just latched the doors to the balcony when they blew open with a tremendous noise. Out in the Yellow River a powder barge was exploding. As he scrambled to the roof for a better view, a battleship began shelling the city. Planes flew over, dropping bombs.

The date was January 28, 1932. Japan was at war with China.

Although the expedition's leader was an old China hand with foreign service experience, the majority of the group were men in their early twenties from eastern colleges, men used to a planned, purposeful, progressive existence, men unprepared for such events.

Within hours most of the expedition members became volunteer U.S. Marines patrolling with helmets, rifles, and bayonets. British troops arrived to break the siege of Shanghai on the fifth day, but the expedition never regained its unity. The official permit was denied because of the war, and the members became split between two objectives, both

rumored to rival Everest, Anye Machin, and Minya Konka. The leaders were determined to explore Anye Machin regardless of permission, but their doctors, who had plans for a medical program among the natives, refused to go on without official sanction of their work for professional reasons.

Four of the youngest members—Moore, Young, Emmons, and Burdsall—formed an entirely new expedition bound for Minya Konka. Their ace-in-the-hole was Jack Young, born in Hawaii and educated at New York University, but also a member of an influential Chinese family in mainland China. He had been an interpreter and full member of a 1929 expedition near Minya Konka with Kermit and Theodore Roosevelt, Jr., in search of the giant panda.

On Young's recommendation they enrolled at the North China Union Language School to learn conversational Mandarin. America was in the midst of the Great Depression, and the foursome had little reason to hurry back to chaos and unemployment. A letter one of them received said it all:

We're all having the worst "hard times" in human memory. . . . Better off for you to stay in China for a while, especially if you have something worthwhile you can do there.

The tiny expedition's new objective took form from Young's experience in Szechwan and Moore's fascination with Minya Konka. Moore had first become aware of the peak in the Explorer's Club library in New York two years earlier. One of America's top mountaineers, Allen Carpé, showed him a crude map of the uncharted border regions of eastern Tibet and Szechwan in a new book by the Roosevelt brothers, *Trailing the Giant Panda*. Near the town of Tatsienlu was a peak labeled, "MT. KOONKA, 30,000'?" The text was vague:

Early one morning we got our first glimpse of mysterious Mount Koonka, rising high in white majesty . . . and regretted the lack of time that made it impossible for us to make a reconnaissance. . . . The altitude of this mighty peak is unknown, but there are those who claim that it rises more than thirty thousand feet and is the highest in the world. A geologist from Chengtu made a special expedition to establish Koonka's height, but after he had taken his observations he refused for some entirely unaccountable reason to divulge them. Perhaps some slip had occurred in his calculations and he was unwilling to dwell upon the error.

Carpé then dug up a recent *National Geographic* with Joseph Rock's account of yet another Chinese range with a suspected giant that ended with the statement: "I came to the conclusion that the Amne Machin towers more than 28,000 feet." Carpé and Moore talked to Albert Bumstead, chief cartographer of the National Geographic Society and learned the inside story. Rock had cabled the society: "MINYA KONKA HIGHEST PEAK ON GLOBE 30,250 FEET ROCK." Bumstead told them that he had advised Dr. Grosvenor not to publish any such figure until Rock could return and convince them from his observational data. When Rock did return to Washington, they decided that with sighting compass and aneroid as his only instruments for determining altitudes, 28,000 feet was the maximum they were willing to publish.

When Rock wrote a second China article in October 1930 with his measurement of Minya Konka's height as 25,600 feet, Moore and Carpé made a logical deduction: "If Dr. Rock found the Amne Machin to be 4,000 feet higher than Minya Konka, then, crude though his methods may have been, apparently he used the same method on both. Since Amne Machin must therefore be the higher, let's head for it." Thus, they joined the prospective 1932 expedition to explore and possibly climb Anye Machin.

Another mark against Minya Konka was the inconsistency of data. The Roosevelts claimed 30,000 feet, Dr. Rock said 25,600, and the latest available map from the British war office made by explorers who had been within twenty-five miles of the mountain showed no contour lines over 16,500 feet in the entire region.

Carpé invited Moore to test expedition climbing techniques with him in Alaska. There the two men made impressive first ascents of Mts. Bona and Fairweather. Both peaks rose over 10,000 feet above their bases in true Himalayan proportions. On both they utilized a peculiarly Alaskan style of mountaineering. Instead of the Himalayan and Arctic method of fixing and stocking a series of camps before the final assault, the Alaskan method involved moving a single camp toward the summit by multiple carries if necessary. Because native porters were not available, equipment was kept to a bare minimum, and the party just kept moving up with their camp on their backs.

Could this method be used on higher peaks in Asia? Carpé and Moore believed so. Despite some highly publicized big expeditions, an analysis of successful Himalayan climbs before 1930 showed that not one summit had been reached by one of these massive sieges with high-altitude porters. Peaks up to 24,000 feet had been climbed by small parties moving lightly, quickly, and with little fanfare.

Carpé was not in China to help organize the Minya Konka climb. He had dropped out a year earlier to pursue cosmic ray research on Mt. McKinley. In May 1932, as the Minya Konka foursome were concluding negotiations for an expedition permit, they read a front-page story in the English-language Shanghai newspaper: Allen Carpé, noted scientist and America's leading mountaineer, had perished on Mt. McKinley in a crevasse fall.

Carpé had been present at an early Explorer's Club meeting of the expedition when airplanes were ruled out for exploration of the Anye Machin massif because of the difficulty of high-altitude take-offs and lack of landing sites. He and others in the group were anything but ignorant of the exploration potential of aircraft. They were, in fact, in the forefront of such exploration. Ironically, Carpé's fatal journey to Mt. McKinley began as a passenger on the first airplane ever to successfully land on and take off from a glacier. In later years Moore was to devote more of his life to bush flying than to mountaineering, and to help design the first retractable wheel-skis to allow snow landings after hard-surface take-offs.

In 1932 these men did not think that flying into Tibet was reasonable. An even stronger rationale for surface travel was their belief that with existing instruments "no accurate altitude determinations of high mountains could be made in flight," strong words borne out just a decade later when World War II pilots made international headlines with distorted eyewitness accounts of flying next to mountains rivaling Everest in the Minya Konka and Anye Machin ranges.

The four members of the Minya Konka team were all in their early twenties except for one elder statesman, 36-year-old Dick Burdsall. Only Terry Moore had previous high-altitude experience. Art Emmons, a Harvard undergraduate, had climbed in the Alps and Alaska. Jack Young, who had been with the Roosevelts, had never climbed, and Burdsall had limited experience. Leadership was determined by what Moore called "an informal partnership of four, the managing partner for a particular purpose being chosen by action of the other three as the occasion arose."

Thus, four young men, now familiar with the ways of China and its language, pursued a dream. Their amazingly liberal permit gave them freedoms no foreign mountaineering expedition has had since: to travel at will across China onto the Tibetan Plateau while surveying, taking photographs, climbing mountains, and conversing with the native people without official liaisons or interpreters. In a long article for the *Alpine Journal* of London, Moore later summarized the journey to this point with appropriate British understatement:

By a combination of circumstances, not all of which were of a strictly mountaineering nature, we found ourselves a small party of friends in Shanghai, in June 1932, with the time and means for a modest excursion to these ranges in West China.

Burdsall and Emmons left Shanghai in June to survey the mountain region while Moore and Young remained back to gather mountaineering equipment, much of which had been lost in transport to the Orient.

Over a month later Moore and Young started their own six-week journey to meet the others in base camp. A fifteen-hundred-mile boat trip up the Yangtze River, followed by weeks of overland travel through villages and cloud forests where giant pandas lived, brought them face to face with one of the most spectacularly situated mountains on earth. Unlike Everest, Minya Konka is not in a group of summits starting from a high base. It is a blade of granite and ice set on the edge of the Tibetan Plateau, forming one of the greatest land escarpments on earth. Where Everest domi-

En route to Minya Konka Burdsall and Emmons crest a pass above a sea of clouds.
© *National Geographic Society*

nates the scene from Rongbuk with a 12,500-foot rise above that point in seventeen miles, Minya Konka rises 21,500 feet above a point just twenty-two miles from its summit.

The mountain defines the juncture of the Tibetan Plateau and China not only geologically, but also politically and ethnically. When Sir Joseph Hooker studied the Himalaya in 1848 (bringing back important evidence for his friend Charles Darwin's unpublished theory of evolution), he remarked how human cultures were stratified by altitude changes in the same way as life zones in plants and animals. Minya Konka, however, is part of such an enormous geographical boundary that human borders (always overprecise compared to natural ones), were drawn on either side of it. The political border of Tibet lay considerably west of the peak, but the cultural boundary was to the east. Thus, the mountain was situated, as if by its own design, in an area with Chinese administration, Tibetan culture, and Tibetan people. At its base are areas of moist Southeast Asian forest separated by fingers of the "great desert of grass" of Tibet.

As Burdsall and Emmons neared the mountain, they left behind the rounded, grassy hills of the Yulong Valley, topped a 15,000-foot pass, then dropped into the Buchu Valley, where heavy rhododendron forest formed a canopy for berries, birds, and countless varieties of wildflowers. When geologist Arnold Heim worked in the region the previous

The Konka Gompa, 1930.

of sunlit snow streaming from its summit in the early dawn. It seemed so remote that it was almost ethereal in its aloof austerity. . . . Climb it? There appeared not the remotest chance!

In the two years since their first plans of visiting Minya Konka, some of the mystery of its height had disappeared. Altitudes reported by modern explorers began to cluster around the first measurement made in 1879 by the expedition of a Hungarian count, Bela Szechenyi, who computed 24,934 feet from a distance of thirty-five miles. Exactly fifty years passed before another foreign visitor measured the peak from near its base, the same period when a flurry of reports came in from travelers who had seen at a distance a great peak rivaling Everest in height. Joseph Rock reached the Konka Gompa in 1929 and measured the peak at 25,600 feet for the *National Geographic*. A year later Edward Imhof and Arnold Heim made a geological study and surveyed the peak at 25,262 feet. Burdsall and Emmons roughly surveyed it at 24,000 feet. After further measurements and corrections for atmospheric refraction, their final figure of exactly 24,900 feet was only 34 feet (0.14 percent) from the amazingly accurate 1879 survey.

Burdsall and Emmons bided time until the others arrived. They surveyed peaks and valleys, climbed to 18,000 feet to check out a possible route, and were thrilled to find a herd of forty-two blue sheep on the mountain. Time passed quickly. All too soon the larch trees were turning gold. Winter was in the air on September 19 when Moore and Young finally arrived with a flea-bitten horse. They looked like a scruffy pair of local bandits.

Their journey had been far more adventurous than their companions'. One morning they had awakened in the Tibetan hill country to find their horse missing. Local people told them that a passing band of soldiers commandeered the animal, a frequent practice taken for granted in the region. The horse was a necessity for transporting the expedition, so Moore and Young organized a posse and trailed the soldiers over a pass. They found their horse with its mane clipped to change its appearance, but the soldiers failed to heed their request to stop.

Moore and Young took the law into their own hands by firing a couple of rounds past the soldiers' ears, halting them in their tracks. Young questioned them in Chinese while Moore covered with a pistol. They got their horse back only after disarming the soldier leading it of a long knife and putting him under house arrest.

year, he described a similar valley below the peak as "the most remote and romantic valley of the world."

In the heart of the Buchu Valley, they found their trail marked by piles of stones and birch bark embossed with Tibetan characters. This holy path led to the Konka Gompa, a cluster of buildings with shingled roofs spectacularly perched on a hillside. They were greeted cordially by several old lamas, shown to a large room, and told to make themselves at home. Other buildings housed religious objects, student lamas, and a large kitchen where a group of women cooked over a square hearth. They were quite surprised to see women in a Buddhist monastery until they learned that the gompa was of the Nyingma-pa sect in which lamas are not required to be celibate.

The gompa community also included a small herd of cows and a lone rooster, who woke them to their first close view of the mountain as it emerged from days of cloud cover. Emmons wrote his impressions:

There stood the resplendent Konka in the clear morning air, the very embodiment of majesty and awe, with a golden plume

They also used their firearms to obtain a collection of zoological specimens that Young had undertaken for the *Academia Sinica*, the Chinese Academy of Sciences. Just four days after the expedition regrouped in the Buchu Valley, Young shot a fine ram from a different herd than the forty-two seen earlier. By the end of the expedition, he had collected five blue sheep, one Asiatic brown bear, one Himalayan black bear, two wild boars, three gorals, one musk deer, and a golden monkey. During a side trip on the way out he procured a giant panda for the American Museum of Natural History and two live brown bear cubs for the Bronx Zoo. He found evidence, but no sightings, of the rare *takin*, a robust goat-antelope with a head like a miniature musk ox. The year before, Imhof and Heim had seen a whole herd of *takin* next to the Hailoko Glacier on the south side of the mountain.

The odds of climbing the mountain seemed slim indeed. The steep slopes were too difficult; the more gentle ones were scoured by frequent avalanches that often woke them in the night. Their only hope seemed to be the narrow, corniced Northwest Ridge. Emmons assessed their chances:

The season was so far advanced that if our climb succeeded at this late date, it would be almost unprecedented in the annals of Himalayan mountaineering, and severe storms could be expected at any time from now on. The route appeared difficult in the extreme. Our total climbing personnel consisted of only four men, two of whom had little previous mountain experience, a woefully small number to tackle an unknown 25,000-foot giant. . . . Our food and fuel supplies, while perhaps adequate, left little or no margin in case of emergency. We had little or no faith in the local men as porters.

Six porters were found to work for the customary wage of a half rupee (three cents) per day as far as the snowline at 17,700 feet. Above there, the four men would be on their own. The base camp tent, purchased used in Peking, was a relic from one of Sven Hedin's expeditions. Food for the assault consisted of dried fruits, soups, milk supplemented with local yak butter, cheese, bread, noodles, and *tsampa* (ground barley).

On October 2, 1932, the small band of climbers and porters finally left the lamasery for the mountain, almost a year after they had set sail with the original expedition from New York. Five days later Moore and Emmons reached the crest of the Northwest Ridge at 19,800 feet. The route above looked reasonable all the way to the base of the summit

pyramid at 23,000 feet. As they hastily descended to camp, Moore dropped from sight without warning. Emmons braced himself as the rope came tight. Moore ended up dangling ten feet below the surface in a large crevasse.

For one of the party's less experienced members, the crevasse could well have become a final resting place. Moore knew what to do. With a belay from Emmons he spread-eagled himself, sunk his crampons into the opposing walls of ice, and climbed out under his own power.

Crevasses were not the most serious hazard. Each sunrise was invariably greeted with "a crashing volley of avalanches that continued throughout the day with spectacular volume, sending thousands of tons of blue-green ice far across the valley four or five thousand feet below." The climbing route

Moore and Emmons on the Northwest Ridge of Minya Konka. © National Geographic Society

Terry Moore holding the "wrong" Republic of China flag on the summit of Minya Konka.

was out of the path of these ice monsters, but open to a more subtle menace: loose snow avalanches that could be started at any time by the sun's heat or the weight of climbers on an unstable slope.

On October 12 Moore and Emmons were at 20,700 feet trying to traverse a feature called "The Hump." Two feet of fresh snow lay on very steep slopes. "Without the slightest warning, there came a low hissing sound. We stood gazing in fascinated horror as the entire snowfield to the depth of two feet slid away from immediately *below* our tracks. We had cut the slope as neatly as with a knife."

Moore and Emmons continued to push the route, sleeping in the same bag to conserve weight, finally reaching 23,000 feet on October 16. Exhausted from a week's work above 20,000 feet, Moore wrote in his diary of "a tremendous yearning to spend two or three days dozing in the sun on the green grass about the base camp" (14,400 feet).

Young, with no previous mountain experience, had pushed himself equally hard to reach 20,000 feet. He accompanied Moore and Emmons back to the green grass, while only Burdsall remained at the snowline camp.

After two days of rest and eight more of climbing, the team was in position for a summit bid. Young had stayed back to continue his zoological work, while the other three gradually moved loads to 22,000 feet.

On the night of October 27 Emmons had difficulty eating a frozen biscuit. He got out his pocket knife and forced the blade clean through the biscuit into the palm of his hand, severing the nerves to his two little fingers with a deep gash. With great disappointment Emmons bowed out of the summit team. He had been far more fit than Burdsall, who had trouble sleeping and acclimatizing.

After a windy, fitful night, Moore and Burdsall got up at 3:40 A.M. for the summit bid. By five they were walking by flashlight under star-filled blackness. As the purple of impending dawn marked the horizon far away in Tibet, Jupiter remained above the summit in an absolutely clear sky.

Their careful study of the route enabled them to avoid most of the icy obstacles. They climbed roped together wearing crampons, cutting only an occasional step. One area of ice seracs coated with hoarfrost slowed them down, but otherwise the crooked ridge proved easier than expected. At 2:40 P.M. they reached an oval platform about twenty feet across, the highest of three grouped closely together. Nothing but sky was above them. The visible horizon was so far

below that Moore felt he was actually seeing the curvature of the earth. Peaks that had dominated the sky from 20,000 feet "now dwindled to a series of mere white patches against the brown plain." They lingered on the summit long enough to take more than thirty photographs, including complete panoramas and shots of Moore holding first a Chinese Nationalist flag, then an American one.

Twenty-five years after the climb, Terry Moore was invited to attend the centenary of The Alpine Club in London. Minya Konka remained the highest summit ever reached by Americans, and because of this Moore had been selected for introduction to Queen Elizabeth. He was dressed in white tie and tails, awaiting her arrival when an Alpine Club member asked, "Dr. Moore, what are you saying to the Chinese?"

Moore answered that he had heard of their June 1957 ascent of Minya Konka, but had not yet seen their account. The man persisted, "Then you haven't yet read what they've written about you in Chinese propaganda magazines? The Chinese claim the first ascent of Minya Konka. They discount your climb because they found no evidence of it on top."

Two years passed before the Foreign Languages Press of Peking published an illustrated fifty-four-page book, *The Conquest of Minya Konka*, by Shih Chan Chun (leader of the Mustagh Ata and Everest expeditions of 1959, 1960, and 1975). The account described how six Chinese climbers reached the summit, and three of them died in a fall on the descent. Another climber died in an avalanche set off by a party of thirteen ascending together through steep, waist-deep snow low on the peak.

The 1932 climb was repudiated:

[The American expedition] claimed that Moore and Burdsall reached the summit where they planted the American flag amidst a violent snowstorm and that the flag was left there as evidence of America's success in distant conquest. . . . It is regrettable that we were unable to discover any traces left by the Americans on top. . . . It remained for our youthful mountaineering party— the All-China Trade Union Mountaineering Party, in June 1957, to triumphantly conquer this world-famous peak, and eradicate the blank spot on the map of the motherland.

In truth Moore and Burdsall had reached the top, had done so in perfect weather, had no motive of American conquest, had not left an American flag planted, and had flown and photographed the flag of the Republic of China first in recognition of the government that had permitted the journey.

Moore contacted Jack Young and Art Emmons. In the intervening years Young had become a brigadier general in the U.S. Army with a chestful of medals including three Bronze Stars, two Silver Stars, and two Legion of Merits awarded after he retired as a major general in the Republic of China Army. Emmons had switched from engineering to become a diplomat in the foreign service. These men knew their politics, and they told Moore, "You're not reading the words of Shih Chan Chun. . . .You're reading what the Foreign Languages Press in Peking, in the year 1959, wants the readers of its book in English to believe. You and Dick committed the crime in 1932 of putting up the wrong flag: the one that's now in exile on Taiwan!"

The 1932 climbers analyzed the Chinese photos and found none that could be identified as above 20,500 feet. The labeled summit photo showed no horizon, just snow and sky. The group generously accepted the Chinese claim, despite the lack of photographic proof and strange references to rock cairns, "because we suppose that all their high-altitude pictures were lost with the bodies of the three members of the summit party."

The result of the propaganda was the opposite of the Chinese intentions. Mountaineers all over the Western world began to doubt *their* ascent. The *Alpine Journal* of England printed an editorial note with Shih Chan Chun's article on his climb:

Indeed the tables have now been turned, for although Terris Moore is . . . accepting the ascent by the Chinese party, doubts are introduced over the burying of a container under a stone cairn, since the Americans found no rocks within a thousand feet of the summit."

Soon thereafter Chinese accounts changed the reference to building a stone cairn on top of the peak. In the 1959 Chinese book, Shih Chan Chun is quoted, "I inserted into a tin can a record of our ascent and buried it in the snow." A 1981 Chinese Mountaineering Association book that gives con-

The south face of Minya Konka during a 1932 reconnaissance.

siderable detail on the summit day states, "according to international practice we put into the *box* [emphasis added] a piece of paper recording our climb," and makes no mention of the deaths of the three summit climbers later that same day.

Moore, ironically, had become a mountaineering historian in his own right. His 1967 book, *Mount McKinley: The Pioneer Climbs*, delved thoroughly and objectively into the controversy over Frederick Cook's bogus claims to have climbed the mountain and reached the North Pole. Moore knew that history would find the truth on his side. He had no need to castigate the Chinese for their written words, especially until he could talk personally to the mountaineers themselves. His time would come.

*Aerial of southeast Tibet—
snowy peaks in all directions, a
vision off the scale of my experience.*

Chapter 10: Through Hidden Corridors

ON THE MORNING of May 4, 1981, I was lost in a dream world, a mountaineer's heaven at 27,000 feet near the border of southern Tibet. I could see hundreds of miles of snowy peaks in all directions, a vision off the scale of my experience. I understood how a World War II pilot coming on this scene unexpectedly could have announced the discovery of the highest mountains in the world. Sightings from the air of both Minya Konka and Anye Machin had prompted such reports.

In a month I would be bound for Anye Machin, the still-unclimbed peak that had lured Americans in 1932 and made headlines as being higher than Everest in 1944. A pilot flying "The Hump" from Burma to China had reported then that he was blown off course in a storm only to come out of the clouds at 30,000 feet—below the top of a mountain. Now, in 1981, I, too, was in an airplane above a landscape that did not agree with my map, the latest U.S. government's Operational Navigation Chart (ONC), revised March 1978.

I saw distant peaks that indeed looked Everest-size. They rose on the horizon behind an ocean of lesser whitecaps, too far away to compare to an altimeter reading. I love to follow map symbols everywhere I travel in much the same way that a musician follows a score, but I began to have an uneasy feeling, as if I had lost my place or turned to the wrong sheet. Slowly it dawned on me that the map lacked the necessary symbols to orchestrate my journey.

Most of the map was toned in green, which the key indicated as "flat or relatively level terrain regardless of altitude." These sections of about three thousand square miles had only a few contour lines and a handful of marked elevations, usually below 20,000 feet. Other areas of the map had even less information. They were toned gray with such labels as: "RELIEF DATA INCOMPLETE; MAXIMUM ELEVATIONS ARE BELIEVED NOT TO EXCEED 23,500 FEET." These no-man's-lands had been given deceivingly unique shapes, like states of the union, that gave them the official look of real places. I much preferred the old tradition of leaving such hinterlands blank except for a fierce emblem denoting something to the effect that "There be dragons here!" My smug belief that I intimately knew the great ranges of the earth vanished as I compared my memory of the view from summits over 20,000 feet in the Karakoram Range of Pakistan, the Nepal Himalaya, and the lower but geographically wilder Alaska Range with what was now in front of me: more miles of more jagged peaks, with a greater feeling of height, than anything I knew existed on the planet. I saw no "flat or relatively level

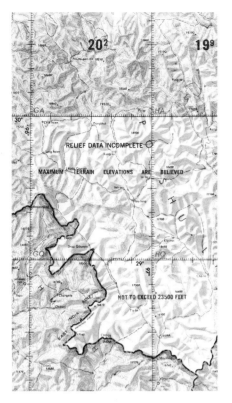

Section of ONC map, revised 1978.

terrain," just wildly sculpted ice and rock with unlimited variation. Granite peaks with monolithic facades alternated with banded metamorphic crests reminiscent of the Canadian Rockies. Still other mountains had plunging, asymmetrical folds that set them free from the normal limits of form.

The map in my lap was designed for military pilots. MEFs (maximum elevation figures) overlaid each quadrangle of latitude and longitude in large purple letters. In one quadrangle, for example, 23^5 meant 23,500 feet, but within that area was no marked summit over 21,700 feet. Another quadrangle, half gray, was keyed 24^8 with no marked summit over 21,310 feet.

Only by following these purple abbreviations could I gain a hint of the scope of these Tibetan ranges. Ten linked squares, a breadth of over six hundred miles, were consecutively labeled: 20^2, 22^1, 25^1, 23^2, 21^0, 20^9, 23^2, 23^5, 25^8, 24^0. Here were thirty thousand square miles of high peaks, enough to keep all the world's mountaineers busy well into the next century.

The addition of one known entity suddenly shifted the world outside my window into focus. I recognized a peak from an old photograph: Namche Barwa, the world's highest unclimbed summit. Its shape and location inside the "Great Bend" of the Tsangpo River were unmistakable. Since I knew that the Great Trigonometric Survey of India had measured it with considerable accuracy in 1912, I was very glad not to be in a U-2 on a mission to observe hidden installations in Tibet, trying to fly with 300 feet of clearance over known obstacles by my ONC H-10 map. As I passed over a quadrangle marked "25¹" and a peak labeled "24,440," I would have chanced splattering myself onto the upper ramparts of 25,445-foot Namche Barwa as it came out of the clouds.

In fact, I was in a Russian turbo-prop Ilyushin 18, a standard Chinese airliner. For an hour we had been flying over high peaks. Before Namche Barwa, the last landmark I recognized had been four hundred miles back: Minya Konka poking through a layer of cloud.

I have never set foot on Minya Konka, nor viewed it from the ground. To include a modern perspective of a mountain so significant in the annals of American mountaineering and exploration, it is necessary—for this chapter only—to depart from the simple alternation of historic explorations and first-person revisits that I have used in this book so far. In this chapter I will explore the Minya Konka region through ex-

periences of people I know personally who have been there, and through their connections with each other.

People who frequently travel to wild places are more closely linked than the public generally supposes. I first became aware of this as a teenager, when I was astounded to read that three of my heroes knew each other long before their individual works made them famous. What coincidence! But it wasn't. After my first Himalayan expedition and many "chance" meetings, I intuitively understood how the nature writer Loren Eiseley, the photographer Edward Weston, and the poet Robinson Jeffers became friends. Such meetings are almost predictable. Climbers and other wilderness explorers travel the world through hidden corridors, which converge at the most unexpected times and places. Even here, beneath the plane in these unfathomable wild mountains, such connections exist on a considerable scale.

As I flew past Minya Konka, I thought of Kim Schmitz, my favorite partner on four Himalayan expeditions and countless other climbs, who just seven months before had climbed on Minya Konka with the first group of foreigners permitted since 1932—actually two simultaneous American expeditions to the same peak. Kim attempted the original Northwest Ridge route. Descending in deep snow from just 18,000 feet early in the climb, his three companions inadvertently triggered a slab avalanche. Kim was above the slide, but roped to them. As they slipped away, he dug in his ice ax. For a moment the entire party stopped. Snow kept sliding around them. As Kim held the weight of all three men, his ax slowly pulled out, projecting him as if from a slingshot into the white cascade. He bobbed under the surface, came up again, fell over a sixty-foot cliff, felt his back hit a rock, and stopped.

Kim ended up fifteen hundred feet below the fracture line, bent double in excruciating pain with a broken back. Near him was Jonathan Wright, a twenty-eight-year-old photographer on assignment for ABC-TV and *National Geographic*. Jonathan's eyes were open and clear, but he was speechless and motionless. His neck was broken. He died quietly within minutes.

Below them were Rick Ridgeway and Yvon Chouinard, battered but relatively unhurt. Other expedition members rushed to the rescue, and the survivors were evacuated to base camp. There Kim's chest was tightly wrapped in an Ensolite sleeping pad. He walked and rode for the better part of a week to civilization, rather than wait longer to be carried out. After enduring that ordeal, he felt no need to be put into a body cast, and two months later he was skiing at Squaw Valley.

Now he was the leader of the expedition to Anye Machin that I was to meet in a few weeks in the city of Lanchow in central China.

Three American expeditions had come to China during the opening year of 1980. I had been on the first one to Mustagh Ata. Both the other two had gone to Minya Konka. Kim's expedition was the brainchild of Leo LeBon, president of Mountain Travel, an American adventure travel agency. LeBon had first conceived the expedition as a commercial, guided climb, but costs quoted by the CMA proved so extreme and unprecedented that he reconsidered. The cream of American mountaineers were invited, the project sold to television, and the few remaining spots on the team sold to qualified (and wealthy) clients. A commercial trek was arranged to the base of Minya Konka with the climb as the center-ring attraction.

LeBon was experienced at such ventures. He had put together the highest successful guided climb done by Americans, a 1977 expedition to Nun Kun in India (at one-fourth the cost of China). Kim and I had been the leaders.

The other 1980 Minya Konka expedition had also assembled some of America's best climbers for an attempt on the unclimbed south face. They, too, failed more than 5,000 feet below the summit due to difficulty, weather, and avalanche danger. Among those participating in the initial organization of this American Alpine Club expedition was Terry Moore, who was as surprised as anyone that after forty-nine years of progress, two experienced American teams simultaneously failed on the peak he had climbed on the very first attempt so long before.

Since then, I had had the good fortune to sit next to Terry Moore at a banquet in Washington, D.C. He told me of the time—in the early fifties, while he was president of the University of Alaska—that a group of faculty wives complained about a student living in a tent right on campus. Moore didn't share their indignation, so he spied on the student before accosting him. When he watched a raven drop from the sky and land on the student's hand, Moore knew that this was no ordinary undergraduate. Young George Schaller had a special understanding of animal behavior far beyond any curriculum. From that day on Schaller became a frequent guest at the presidential residence.

Minya Konka. © *National Geographic Society*

In an earlier chapter I mentioned how Schaller took off to climb an Alaskan mountain with Heinrich Harrer, who was a visiting lecturer at the university. Schaller and Harrer made the first ascent of Mt. Drum, one of the major peaks of the Wrangell Range. The influence of Harrer, fresh from his seven years in Tibet, and Moore, the last American to climb a peak in China, whetted Schaller's appetite for the high places of Asia. Between 1969 and 1975, in conducting various wildlife surveys, he logged more time in the Himalayan outback than any Western mountaineer.

He was, of course, already respected as one of America's best field zoologists. His behavioral studies of African lions, mountain gorillas, and Bengal tigers were unprecedented successes. He had won a National Book Award, and *National Geographic* had published his first-ever photographs of a snow leopard in the wilds. After 1978 he became something of a cult hero, not from his own publications, but from one short journey in the Himalaya with Peter Matthiessen, who returned home to write the bestseller *The Snow Leopard*.

Today, however, the same hidden corridors that linked Schaller with Moore and Harrer placed me directly above Schaller, a hundred-odd miles northeast of Minya Konka, where he was engaged in a study of giant pandas in cooperation with the World Wildlife Fund and the government of China. Once again he was in the forefront of research on the behavior of an animal unstudied in the wild, and he himself became the first Westerner in over fifty years to see a wild panda.

Because I had previously written about Schaller's work, *Audubon* magazine invited me to do a story on the panda project. Just before I left for Tibet I received a letter from Schaller from the Wolong Panda Reserve:

There are several good reasons why you cannot do a story on the panda project for *Audubon*. (a) The Chinese would probably not give you permission . . . (b) Working on behalf of WWF, I cannot invite you. . . . They have tried to get someone in on their behalf without success. (c) If someone does a piece on me in the field, it will be myself doing it the first time around. . . . Work goes slowly. Pandas tend to stick to such thick bamboo and are so scarce that one seldom sees one, much less has an opportunity to photograph. So it's a study of looking at droppings, feeding sites, etc. Right now we're trying to trap one and radio-collar it. Terry Moore climbed here in 1932. I have seen his mountain—Minya Konka—several times. Lovely peak.

Minya Konka was, in Schaller's terms, Terry Moore's mountain. Something about that concept was vaguely disturbing. I let it filter through my mind and concluded that Schaller was right. Minya Konka deserved to be Terry Moore's mountain. What other major climb by Americans had not been repeated by Westerners for half a century? But I was not thinking like Schaller. I was trying to overinterpret his simple statement of the obvious. He saw an undeniable connection between man and mountain, and that was that. Lovely peak.

In Schaller's simplicity of thought was a deeper meaning that helped me to understand why some people travel the hidden corridors and others never find them. I saw that Schaller had no fear of saying "his mountain," a human overlay on nature that most biologists avoid with a phobia. By not holding human emotion totally separate from his science, he enriched his perceptions. For example, I remembered how he had explained that gorillas do not deserve their fierce reputations, even though they really do beat their chests occasionally, by making a human comparison: "Man behaves

remarkably like a gorilla in conflicting situations. A marital squabble, for example . . . may end with shouting, thrown objects, slamming doors, furniture pounded and kicked—all ways of reducing tension."

It is hardly coincidental that Loren Eiseley, in whose work and choice of friends I first became aware of such human interconnectedness, had the same staggering capacity to integrate intuition and analysis. I saw a similarity between Terry Moore's mountain and George Schaller's animals. Moore's mountain was very big and previously unclimbed. Schaller's subjects were big, virtually unstudied in the wild, and on the whole anthropomorphic. He hadn't written any books on bats or mice.

Studying the panda, however, was rarely as glamorous as it seemed. Its habitat of thick forest and mountainside resembled Vermont overlaying the Grand Canyon. Crumbling cliffs draped with thick timber and bamboo rose out of deep river valleys separating highlands of 8,000 to 15,000 feet.

In the heart of this unique area the Tibetans call the "Land of Great Corrugations," two hundred miles west of Minya Konka, is a narrow strip of land just fifty miles wide through which three of the world's major rivers flow on their way toward oceans two thousand miles apart. The Yangtze swings east across China to the Pacific. The Mekong flows southeast through Vietnam. The Salween runs due south through Burma to the Indian Ocean.

Another two hundred miles beyond this strip is another great river, the Tsangpo of Tibet, which crosses the main Himalaya to become the Brahmaputra and eventually joins the Ganges near the sea.

The trail through this region crosses thirteen major rivers at right angles. A person never sees more than two at once. Today, however, I had flown in a single hour over waters that nourish a billion people in Tibet, China, India, Burma, Laos, Cambodia, Vietnam, Thailand, and Bangladesh. Without these Tibetan waters, hundreds of millions of people would perish.

As water is the lifeblood of human societies, bamboo is for the giant panda. The panda lives in bamboo, eats bamboo, thinks bamboo, and consumes up to forty pounds a day, receiving from it much of its liquid needs as well. In the past, healthy bamboo forests meant healthy pandas. Their range extended throughout southern China and Tibet.

Unique in many ways, the giant panda is the only member of the order Carnivora that normally has a vegetarian

Hoopoe, Upupa epops, *flashy resident of the Tibetan steppes.*

The petals of this poppy,
Mcconopsis integrifolia, *are*
collected by lamas to make
yellow dye.

126

diet. An extension of the wristbone gives the animal something close to a thumb with which to make an opposable grip. Zoologists still disagree over what family the panda belongs to. Some place it in the raccoon family, others give it a category all its own. Most agree that it is not, as it appears, a close relative of the bear.

In the late seventies the Chinese government became aware that their national animal was endangered. Villagers found bodies of pandas that had starved to death. Fewer than a thousand remained in the wilds. The Western world also became concerned. Schaller headed up an American contingent for a joint research project with the Chinese. With his love of high Asia and studies of large, elusive mammals, he was the ideal candidate to decode the habits and needs of everybody's beloved teddy bear.

Bamboo, like water, ebbs and flows in cycles. Instead of coming with annual monsoons, it marches to a far slower beat. Depending on the species, life cycles run from a decade to over a century. What separates bamboo cycles from the life and death of all other plants is that each species flowers and dies by an internal clock. No matter where on the globe a bamboo plant grows, it will commit mass suicide in synchronization with all others of its species, flowering first, to ensure new growth a few years later.

These die-offs used to have little effect on pandas. Forests of different species grew contiguously, and pandas just moved to new homes.

After Chinese Liberation in 1949, the lifestyle of the hill peoples of Szechwan and Tibet underwent considerable change. In 1958 the Great Leap Forward (a Marxist campaign of modernization) brought agricultural communes into what had once been continuous forests of spruce, hemlock, rhododendron, oak, and bamboo. Millions of acres of fields were cleared. The pandas' range had been gradually shrinking for over a million years, and their population became concentrated into a small region of umbrella bamboo with a life cycle of about a century. When this species began its cyclical die-off in the mid-1970s, pandas were cut off by human encroachments on their habitat and had no place to go. They began to starve.

I tried to arrange a brief visit to the Wolong Panda Reserve while in Chengdu en route to Tibet. I had already planned to leave the group with Harold Knutson on the way back in order to join Kim Schmitz for the Anye Machin expedition. I asked if with two extra days in our itinerary,

we could hire a jeep, drive through the panda reserve, and camp beneath Siguniang, an unclimbed peak just opened to foreigners.

The Szechwan arm of the Chinese Mountaineering Association said yes. There was one slight hitch: the cost. Charter travel, the most expensive part of treks and expeditions to China, was usually hidden within an already exorbitant overall fee. To drive eight hours in a jeep, sleep in our own bags near a commune, eat four meals on the road, and return the next night would cost eighteen hundred dollars. Prices were fixed. I agreed only because I was willing to be extorted for such a once-in-a-lifetime visit. But how it clashed with the three cents per day per porter that Joseph Rock, Terris Moore, and the Roosevelt brothers paid fifty years before.

The outcome was beyond my worst imagination. The CMA arranged for my group to fly back to Chengdu on a day when no flights were scheduled, although they assured me reservations had been booked months in advance. A second day was lost because of weather. With no Chinese accountability for travel within the country, my group of fifteen was billed eight thousand dollars for two extra days in Lhasa, the most expensive place in Asia. The Panda Reserve trip was cancelled.

Soon after I returned home, *Geo* magazine came out with a cover story on Schaller's panda research. I thumbed through a series of double-page photographs taken by a *Geo* photographer. I felt a lump in my stomach as I looked at what I had hoped to do for *Audubon*. "For the first time ever," the article began, "a Western journalist has been permitted to photograph these remarkable creatures in their natural setting." A large print of a panda in the wild was offered as a subscription bonus.

Something didn't equate. I knew Schaller too well to think that I had gotten a bum steer. I wondered why none of his photographs were used. Despite his protests about "just taking snaps," he regularly returns with better animal pictures than the pros who share some of his travels (but not his understanding of wildlife). My own Tibetan material was to be published by *National Geographic*. While I worked at their headquarters in Washington, D.C., I was surprised to see a copy of their forthcoming cover story on the panda with text and photos by Schaller. He had succeeded in radio-collaring several pandas to study their behavior, and his pictures, as usual, were fabulous.

At the same time an article in the *Washington Post* disclosed that *Geo*'s wild panda shots were frauds. Schaller was quoted as being very surprised to see images of his captive pandas captioned as taken in the wild.

Death on Minya Konka and the struggle for life among the pandas were the glamor stories from the mountains of Szechwan this opening year. Trekking went virtually unnoticed except for a chatty *New Yorker* piece on what a Manhattan surgeon was putting into his medical kit for a guided walk around Mt. Siguniang.

In my travels and lectures I encountered many of the people who had walked to the base of Minya Konka with Mountain Travel in 1980. They had a far more positive feeling about their experience than others I knew who had gone to different ranges in China and Tibet. Despite agricultural encroachment at lower elevations, the landscape was nearly as primeval as the American expedition had found it in 1932.

Whereas trekkers in the Pamirs, Tian Shan, and Everest regions saw virtually no wildlife in 1980, a considerable number of wild creatures still roamed the flanks of Minya Konka. Black bear, blue sheep, and sambar deer were seen. Leo LeBon met a friendly, toothless Tibetan in the village of Tshumi who had been a young monk at the Konka Gompa in 1932 and remembered Terry Moore. The gompa, however, had been destroyed in the late sixties during the Cultural Revolution. Only a few painted walls remained.

In the bar of the main tourist hotel in Chengdu, the capital of Szechwan, I met a small group of Japanese mountaineers. Eight of their party had not returned from an ill-fated attempt on Minya Konka in April 1981. One climber had been just three hundred feet from the top when he fell, unroped. His seven companions radioed base camp and were instructed to rope up and descend. One man slipped and all were pulled down to their deaths.

A few months later, in December 1981, the hidden corridors of Szechwan converged on one of the largest Chinese communities outside Asia. At a dinner in San Francisco's Chinatown, I sat at a table with Leo LeBon, Terry Moore, and Shih Chan Chun, who was on his first visit to America. The man whose name was signed to official Chinese accounts disclaiming the first ascent of Minya Konka was now face to face with one of the summiteers. Shih did not speak English, but he looked Moore in the eye and said through his interpreter, "We want you to know that you got to the top."

*"The Land of Great Corruga-
tions" of eastern Tibet.*

129

*Lone Golok rider, Anye Machin
Range.*

PART SIX: ANYE MACHIN

*Sunrise on the summit of
Anye Machin.*

Chapter 11: The Legend of Anye Machin

IN THE LAND OF GREAT CORRUGATIONS surrounding Minya Konka the weather is so continuously awful that the name of the neighboring province, Yunnan, means "south of the clouds." Nudged against the monsoon forests of Burma and Laos, Yunnan was off the track of most Central Asian travelers. In 1922, however, two explorers met there by chance. The burning desire of Joseph Rock's life for most of the next decade was sparked in a conversation in Yunnan with General George Pereira.

Rock had been in China for a year doing botanical exploration for the U.S. Department of Agriculture when he met the British general, who recounted his grand loop of exploration from Peking through Lhasa, India, and Burma, undertaken for its own sake rather than for any military objective. Rock was especially impressed by Pereira's description of the Anye Machin Range, eight hundred miles to the north. While traversing the grasslands of Kokonor high on the Tibetan Plateau, the general had seen a great snow peak he was certain would prove higher than Everest. He said that the reason the region was unexplored was that it was inhabited by Goloks, the fiercest of all Tibetan tribes, who were led by a militant queen.

Right then Rock decided to visit Anye Machin. He hoped to unravel three mysteries: the height of the mountain, the legend of the Golok queen, and the area's little-known natural history. Captain P. K. Kozloff's Russian expedition, which skirted the edge of the region in 1900, had reported a splendid variety of flowering plants and a "fabulous quantity of wild mammals to be found everywhere."

By 1924 Rock's reputation as an explorer of western China was solidly established. He published an article on the Nakhi tribe in *National Geographic* and enlisted support from both the National Geographic Society and Harvard's Arnold Arboretum for a journey into the land of the Goloks.

It seemed incongruous that such a large group of lawless people could actually control so much Chinese territory, but the history of the Goloks and their land made the reasons very clear. The Anye Machin Range is on the eastern edge of the Tibetan Plateau. The mountains were in Amdo Province of Tibet until 1724, when the Chinese became nominal overlords of Tibet. In exchange for continued autonomy in the central and western regions, much of eastern Tibet was ceded to China as Chinghai Province. The Goloks, however, were ethnically but not politically Tibetan. Having never given allegiance to Lhasa or any other government, they weren't about to become subjects of China. The Anye Machin area remained a no-man's land; no Golok gave allegiance to China and no Chinese dared to go there.

Goloks in a snowstorm.

Rock's first attempts to reach the range were thwarted by civil wars between the plains Moslems and the Tibetan hill tribes—spearheaded by the Goloks. He reported seeing Tibetans hung by their thumbs, disemboweled alive and filled with hot stones. Their revenge was just as brutal. Rock came across a mosque utterly destroyed by the Tibetans: "The Moslems had been driven into it, the gates locked, and the building set on fire . . . the dead lay six feet deep."

When Rock reached Labrang, a sprawling Buddhist monastery on an upper tributary of the Yellow River, he found Tibetan heads "strung about the walls of the Moslem garrison like a garland of flowers." Decorating posts in front of the barracks were the heads of young Tibetan girls. Moslem riders galloped through town with heads bobbing from their saddles, while Tibetan nomads "charged against the Moslems at full speed on horseback, impaling them on their thirty-foot lances like men spearing frogs."

Rock lost a year and a half's time, which he spent in other explorations, before it was safe to travel across the plateau toward his uncharted dream mountains. His life was rarely as spartan as those who read his exploits in *National Geographic* imagined. When Edgar Snow, an American writer later famous for his portrayal of the Communist revolution in China, traveled with Rock in Yunnan, his description of life on the trail included details that Rock never mentioned:

During the march, his [Rock's] tribal retainers divided into a vanguard and a rear guard. The advance party, led by a cook, an assistant cook, and a butler, would spot a sheltered place with a good view, unfold the table and chairs on a leopard skin rug, and lay out clean linen cloth, silver and napkins. By the time we arrived our meal would be almost ready. At night it was several courses ending with tea and liqueurs.

Rock used grant money from Harvard and the National Geographic Society to fund his fetish for clandestine luxuries. During his childhood in Austria, he had been prepared to enter the priesthood by a stern father who worked as a servant. His biographer, S. B. Sutton, links his upbringing to his strong adult repressions about academia, religion, and being waited upon.

His fantasies of exploring China began even before he began to teach himself Chinese at the age of thirteen. For him, life moved in sudden spurts rather than by the slow progress of academia. As a teenager he was a shy truant; at twenty-one a penniless American immigrant. This was

ABOVE *Labrang Monastery as Joseph Rock saw it.* © *National Geographic Society*

LEFT *Moslem army in snowstorm in the foothills of Anye Machin.*

hardly the breeding one expected in a man who would blossom in later life, in the words of his biographer, into "one of the most flamboyant and exasperating individuals ever to have crossed Harvard Yard."

Crossing Harvard Yard in no way implied that Rock spent his formative years in those halls of ivy, or in any others. Like so many explorers of remote parts of the world, he was a maverick who followed his personal lust for adventure

135

Rock then devoted a decade to botany, became the unchallenged authority on the flora of Hawaii, and published five books plus dozens of monographs, two of which became classics in their field. In 1921 he left for the mainland after a row with the school administration. The U.S. Department of Agriculture hired this now-distinguished botanist, and, because of his language skills, shipped him to China, where he stayed for most of the next twenty-seven years. Once again he bypassed academia by never publishing a single paper on Chinese flora, although he was funded for botanical studies by distinguished institutions.

Rock claimed an academic background that included a degree from the University of Vienna and a position as professor of Chinese at the College of Hawaii. Neither is in the records of the respective institutions. This complex man of wildly fluctuating moods explored more of western China in his time than any other American, was borne into cities in a sedan chair, and often mistaken for a foreign prince. His life took on an unconscious rhythm, unequivocally described by Sutton:

He could endure about two years of the Chinese wilderness at one stretch. Then he would develop some pretext—such as organizing an expedition, purchasing new equipment, or consulting a volume in a Parisian library—for returning to the West. He would gorge himself on operas, fancy hotels, rich foods, and social gatherings, at which he was usually the star attraction, but he never really felt comfortable or quite sure of himself where no one believed that he was a "foreign prince." And so, after a few months, he would begin to complain about the "excesses of civilization" and hasten back to what he liked to call the simple life.

When Rock returned to Labrang in early May 1926, he found the monastery back in the hands of the Tibetans. Over five thousand lamas lived in the sprawling cloister. The kitchen for four thousand used kettles six feet across. The main chanting hall also held four thousand in a single room supported by 140 columns forty feet high. The complex had hundreds of buildings, thirty of which contained chanting halls or served as homes for the "living Buddhas," who were perpetuated by discovering a new incarnation in the form of a child after the old incarnation died. The practical reasons for perpetuating these celibate high lamas through discovered reincarnations were clear, but Rock found political expediency as well. In Radja Gompa, just eighty miles from Anye Machin, a Tibetan water-carrier explained to him how

and thirst for knowledge rather than the plans of any institution. The path that brought him to Harvard was as unusual as it was crooked.

By the age of twenty-three Rock had taught himself nine or ten languages, including Chinese. He never graduated from college, but soon bluffed his way into teaching natural history and Latin in Hawaii. His biography contains an undocumented story that Rock walked into the national headquarters of the U.S. Forest Service in Washington, D.C., "informed the startled officer in charge that the division needed a herbarium," then "identified himself as a botanist and proposed that he be the man to collect it for the division. Arrogance, charm, and the fact that no one checked his credentials carried the day for him."

Yaks below Anye Machin.

Living Buddha in 1934.

was instantly shattered whenever Golok tribesmen were around. Rock found them arrogant, rude, and unpredictable. "Such hostile and unfriendly people I have never met anywhere else in the world," Rock wrote in one of his monographs. "They are at home in these bleak mountain fastnesses, and seeing a caravan of a foreigner incites the wild curiosity and the pleasant anticipation of robbing him to find out what treasures he carries and to come into their possession."

Earlier explorers rarely had a chance to describe the Goloks firsthand. Some never returned. Word filtered back after the disappearance of Dutreuil de Rhins in 1891 that he had been laced alive into a yak skin and tossed into the Yellow River. Dr. Migot, a Buddhist scholar, was set afoot naked onto the Tibetan Plateau. Other more legendary explorers—Huc, Rockhill, Przewalski—never penetrated the region but wrote secondhand of reports of Golok savagery.

Rock found Golok history to be almost entirely unwritten. In the seventh century the Tibetan Empire expanded westward to the present Soviet border, eastward into Szechwan (where the imperial capital of China was seized), and northward beyond Kokonor, China's largest lake. King Tusong deployed his fiercest warriors to fight in the northern mountains against angry Moslems and Chinese. These soldiers found the rugged mountains beyond Kokonor a fine place to live. When the empire began to shrink, an isolated enclave of warriors remained to live by their wits, independent of both China and Tibet. These were the first Goloks.

Modern Goloks speak a dialect little changed from the seventh century, unintelligible to other Tibetans. Isolation preserved other elements of their old ways as well. The men Rock came face to face with were essentially seventh-century warriors, but with their spears replaced by rifles. They had no desire to join the modern world.

Human obstacles rather than geographical ones hid the secret of Anye Machin from Joseph Rock. His description of Golok character ends with a manifesto of how he must proceed:

The struggle for existence has left its mark on their wild, coarse faces, which are never broadened by a smile. Their life is spent on horseback, always ready for battle. . . . They are a marauding fraternity, going often six hundred strong on robbing expeditions, making the caravan roads west of Amnye Machen unsafe. . . . A foreigner can only travel here if he is adequately armed with

the living Buddha business always worked out for the benefit of the rich:

The local Buddha was very rich; so was his steward; and when "reincarnations" occurred, it seemed to him that this "miracle" always happened just as it might have been desired by the chief Buddha. For example, when the daughter of a powerful chief died, she was soon afterward reincarnated in the person of a small boy, a nephew of the Buddha's steward—a business and political arrangement agreeable to all concerned! When one of the minor Buddhas of Radja died he, too, was happily, conveniently, and quickly reincarnated, this time in the person of the steward's brother!

I smiled and asked the water-carrier how it happened that none of his children was the reincarnation of some departed Buddha. With a twinkle in his eye, he remarked that it was because the sum of all his worldly goods was two goats.

Beyond Radja Gompa, Rock found that the "whole region between the Yellow River and Amnyi Machen is one great zoological garden. Wherever I looked I saw wild animals grazing contentedly." The peacefulness of this scene

Shrine on a hilltop, Anye Machin Range.

139

modern weapons and in a large group, but the larger the party the more cumbersome his caravan. When traveling in this area one must be mobile, have no slow yak, but only fast horses, plenty of ammunition, and superior rifles.

During Rock's three years of travels, he was never able to approach Anye Machin closer than fifty miles. He did make extensive cultural and scientific notes, which he published years later as a monograph. The legend of the Golok queen was not at all what it had first seemed. She was a Golok woman who had been captured and brought to Labrang. There she had an intimate relationship with a Moslem general who called her his Golok queen. In reality, her people wanted her head. She later turned coat again and regained the favor of her people by arranging the ransom of a Golok chief's mother, who had also been captured. The chief had abandoned her to save his own skin, but he bought her back for five hundred yaks.

Rock also learned that Anye Machin was a holy mountain that up to ten thousand Goloks a year circumambulated in a pilgrimage that took seven days of hard walking. He correctly stated, "It is the northwestern dome of the range which is the highest prominence, with Chenrezig, the southeastern

Golok headman.

one, the second highest." Chinese surveyors many decades later concluded the opposite, leading to a false claim that the highest summit had been climbed. Rock was not as accurate in his assessment of the mountain's height. With no theodolite for precise measuring of trigonometric angles, he combined compass sightings, altitudes calculated from the boiling point of water, and his usual zeal to come up with an astounding figure.

Thus the National Geographic Society's most prominent explorer of China mailed in an article reporting the discovery of a 30,000-foot mountain. The magazine's chief editor, Gilbert Grosvenor, consulted with its chief cartographer, Albert Bumstead, who advised not publishing any such figure until Rock returned with hard data in hand. Rock had previously drawn detailed maps of unknown regions by his own measurements, but Bumstead did not trust them, and he had gently suggested to Rock that the accuracy of his work could be greatly improved by learning a few basics of cartography. Rock, offended, said he didn't know much about math and didn't have the time to learn.

Grosvenor decided to be conservative about Rock's claims. Still not aware of his true background, Grosvenor assumed that the good professor had a Ph.D. and called him "Dr. Rock" in person and in print. The February 1930 *National Geographic* published Rock's article, "Seeking the Mountains of Mystery: An Expedition on the China–Tibet Frontier to the Unexplored Amnyi Machen Range, One of Whose Peaks Rivals Everest." Needing an altitude for the peak, the editors chose a figure lower than Everest that would not invite embarrassing questions about the article's paucity of hard data. Their rewrite made Rock's convoluted prose flow like liquid gold, furthering his credibility as a botanist-explorer-linguist:

"To-day the map has no secrets." Idle minds repeat that parrot phrase. But who knows all Tibet, or its far-away frontiers on western China? . . . the headwaters of the 2000-mile-long Yellow River and the towering, unexplored range of Amnyi Machin. Twenty-eight thousand feet, or almost as high as Everest, its tallest peak lifts its snow-white head, majestic as the Matterhorn. Here, in remote, almost inaccessible valleys, I found countless wild animals still unafraid of man, peaceful as in Eden. . . . I shouted for joy as I beheld the majestic peaks of one of the grandest mountain ranges of all Asia.

Over the next two decades three more groups of explorers investigated the Anye Machin region by land and by air. All

Worn prayer wheels in the Kumbum near Sining, Chinghai.

Lamas of the Kumbum near
Sining, Chinghai.

three involved Americans. The last of these men, Leonard Clark, visited the region on the eve of the Communist Liberation. He stepped into Joseph Rock's shoes with an equally strong desire to find his own identity in the mountain and its secrets. In order to do this, he had to ignore conflicting data from other recent explorers.

In 1943 Captain Brooke Dolan and Lieutenant Colonel Ilya Tolstoy had traveled on the edge of the Anye Machin Range on a U.S. intelligence mission for the Office of Strategic Services, forerunner of the CIA. They reported no unusually high mountain in the area, nor had Dolan seen one a decade earlier when he collected Tibetan fauna for the Philadelphia Academy of Natural Sciences near the east side of the Anye Machin Range in 1934. What he did confirm, however, were Rock's reports of profuse wildlife there. He brought back 2,615 bird specimens and 310 mammal specimens, including all the large creatures of the Tibetan steppes except the snow leopard and the forest leopard.

The other American enterprise came about in late 1947 when *Life* asked Bradford Washburn to fly over China to find the highest mountain in the world. Washburn, a world-renowned expert on mountains and mapping, told them that no peak exists higher than Everest. He refused to go on a highly promoted "search for the highest mountain," but did agree to pursue a more academic determination of what was there. For planning and advice he enlisted Terry Moore and Jack Young, Minya Konka veterans familiar with China's inner ranges. Flight plans came to a halt when neither *Life* nor any other source would fund such a limited objective.

Life turned to Milton Reynolds, wealthy promoter of the fastest flight around the world to date. He was eager for both the flight and the column inches it would draw him. He beat his drums beforehand, drawing headlines about himself and the 30,000-foot mountain.

Washburn went to China to assist in the planning. He found a superb Chinese pilot, Moon Chin, to fly with Reynolds, but Bill Odom, his personal pilot, objected. "Odom was totally obdurate," Washburn later said. "He wouldn't sit on the flight deck with any 'damned Chinee'." Washburn was not entirely happy with Odom's nonchalant flying style, especially when he ran off the runway and mired Reynolds' converted B-24 deep in the mud, threatening the entire project. The Chinese, in turn, were even less happy when Odom filed a flight plan for Calcutta, then took off for Anye Machin with Reynolds and his crew chief, Tex

Lamas near Anye Machin with a pet Tibetan gazelle, 1949.

Sallee, without permission. Not a single peak showed above a cloud layer near 30,000 feet. Reynolds and Odom returned home to more headlines about their search for the 30,000-foot mountain.

With Washburn's urging *Life* photographer Jack Birns later flew the entire region with Moon Chin. Phenomenal photographs were made on a clear day. Several summits appeared to be slightly over 20,000 feet, but no more than that. *Life* editors decided not to print a nonstory that would only gratify Reynolds' desire for free ink. The photos from Moon Chin's flight have remained unpublished to this day.

Like Milton Reynolds, Leonard Clark knew how to promote himself; like Brooke Dolan, he had been an OSS officer in China during World War II. Clark had spent two years in northern China handling intelligence and guerrilla activities. His fascination for Anye Machin grew out of 1944 news stories of the flight crew that reported seeing a mountain 30,000 feet high in China. Bold, fearless, and politically astute, Clark devised a plan for penetrating the Golok stronghold.

From his intelligence days Clark knew of the secret wars in northwestern China and Tibet. "These flights and battles were never to my knowledge—but for Dr. Rock's report—reported in detail to the outside world. . . . The Chinese government did not hesitate to brand as a liar any traveler who dared suggest such troubles existed in their own Tibetan backyard."

Tibetan guards of Leonard Clark's expedition.

Goloks and other Tibetan tribes for cooperation with their traditional enemy, the Moslems, for the greater good of routing the Communists, who were threatening to take over all of China and Tibet.

As a diplomatic courtesy, Clark called on the Panchen Lama in Kumbum Monastery not far from Sining. This second most powerful figure of Tibet, surrounded by flowers, rubies, diamonds, and sapphires in his heavenly throne room, was twelve years old. During his audience with Clark, the young ruler ordered his aides out of the room and made a hushed request. Could Clark ask the powerful General Ma "to place him—the Panchen Lama—at the head of a Moslem army so that he could invade Lhasa. Once beyond the Turquoise Bridge there, he would install himself at the Potala. . . ." Such were the dreams of a youth who was already ruler of all that he had ever seen.

The Kumbum Monastery was one of the holiest places of Tibet, even though it was now outside the formal borders. The temple of Serdong, "The Golden Tree," surrounds a tree that grew on the spot where the founder of the reformed, "Yellow Hat" Ge-lug-pa sect, Tsong-ka-pa, was born in 1358. Since the monastery itself was founded in 1516, several Dalai Lamas had been "discovered" in the surrounding area. Among these was Tenzing Gyatso, a thirteen-year-old boy born in Tengster just thirty-five miles from Kumbum. He was now the Fourteenth Dalai Lama, master of all Tibet.

Clark himself was a man with a lust for power. Rather than a personal urge to rule, he pursued constant associations with powerful people, powerful forces, powerful land masses. The OSS, the Goloks, Anye Machin, and General Ma made him feel right at home.

In the great grasslands of the Kokonor region, Clark saw not beauty, nor freedom, nor open space, but a source of power. "The basic foundation . . . of this inherent Mongol power for war is grass, strong grass converted into excellent animal flesh—among the finest in the world. I was taking grass samples and seeds, hoping to transfer its power to the pastures of America and Europe now desperately engaged in building a way of life bedded solidly in 'security,' and doing it mainly—from our mid-Asian angle of view—ostrich fashion."

Clark set out for Fort Ta Ho Pa in the dead of winter, guarded around the clock by soldiers with machine guns. He encountered temperatures down to –36° F. as his party lived off gazelle meat on the road. Besides herds of gazelle, they

Clark understood the power wielded by General Ma Pufang, warlord of over a million Moslem soldiers rebelling against the Communists. In February 1949 he bluffed his way into the interior of China, then arranged a daring meeting with the general from which he expected one of two results: either he would be taken into the courtyard and shot, or he would be commissioned, funded, equipped, and supported to penetrate the Anye Machin Range. General Ma chose the latter course, although reports from the time show no indication he ever considered direct support of Chiang Kai-shek's Nationalist Army.

At Fort Ta Ho Pa beneath the Anye Machin Range, Clark planned to begin phase two of his operations. "Unique in Tibetan history," he later recounted, "is this arrangement where a traveler has acted as emissary (however unofficial) to a government in order to carry out his own work of discovery." He would try to negotiate some sort of treaty with the

Golok women in full dress,
Ta Ho Pa.

LEFT *Golok woman, Ta Ho Pa.*

RIGHT *Cape of 108 braids interwoven with coral, turquoise, and silver.*

146

came across large bands of wild asses and blue sheep, as well as a very large mountain sheep, the Tibetan argali, or *nyan*, a close relative of the Marco Polo sheep of the Pamirs. Musk deer were solitary but plentiful, as were the large brown bears that sometimes walked through camp at night.

Once inside the walled compound of Fort Ta Ho Pa, Clark began to work out his plans with some of the Moslem officers while others were en route from the lowlands. During his first night at the fort, guards opened up the gates at one in the morning for a lone rider. In came a somber warning from the Goloks that Clark described in detail:

A horse with a man on its back was standing there. A single survivor [of the arriving officers' party] had been tortured, his eyes gouged out, his tongue, ears and nose cut off; his belly was filled with stones (mani stones consigning him to heaven) and his body mounted on a horse, tied in upright position and now driven back to Fort Ta Ho Pa as a grim warning that Tibetans must be consulted on such serious matters as the movements of Moslems and foreign strangers.

Clark's cavalry continued with 240 animals and numerous machine guns. Even with this noisy army, he encountered vast herds of wildlife. Day after day he passed hundreds of gazelles and wild asses. "It seemed every few minutes we would spot a bear or a hunting wolf, herds of musk deer, kyangs, gazelles, bighorn sheep, or foxes. This must be one of the last unspoiled big-game paradises remaining in Asia."

Clark arrived at the northwestern end of the main peaks of the Anye Machin range, unaware that he was not in line of sight with the highest summit, which was hidden behind a front range fifteen miles to the southeast.

May 6, 1949, was Leonard Francis Clark's day for numbers. Leaving camp at 6:30 A.M. in 28.4° temperature, measuring a ridge at 12,792 feet, seeing four herds totaling 700 to 750 wild asses, he proceeded to the far end of the valley "only two miles" from the "actual base of the peak." There he made two one-thousand-meter base lines, took sightings through an English-made theodolite that he had borrowed from the Chinghai Highway Bureau, measured the boiling point of water to determine the elevation of his instruments, and used trigonometry to calculate the following conclusion: Anye Machin Peak, 29,661 feet above sea level; Mt. Everest, 29,144 feet above sea level; so Anye Machin Peak is *517 feet higher* than Everest.

In October 1949 *Life* magazine ran a sensational account of Clark's discovery of the world's highest mountain. Al-

though the majority of readers accepted this new high point on the planet, most mountain experts did not. Some went so far as to say that there was something fishy about Clark's entire account. Those who had been there themselves, such as Joseph Rock, recognized that Clark had been where he had said, even if his math was poor. The kindest criticism came from the U.S. Geological Survey, which concluded that because his theodolite lacked a seconds' measurement for angles, he could have determined the mountain's height only within 2,500 feet.

Clark's book on his journey, *The Marching Wind*, relates a curse that has brought misfortune to "every explorer, flyer, and adventurer . . . after even briefly sighting this so-called god mountain." Possibly Clark thought that a curse like that of King Tut's Tomb would keep others from proving his errors of measurement. He told how General Pereira, the originator of the legend of Anye Machin's height, died in the field before returning to Peking after his meeting with Joseph Rock. He also related how "The Hump" pilots who reported the mountain's great height during the war were all "subsequently either lost in Tibet after reporting the mountain by radio, or were invariably lost later during battle or in crashes."

Clark's necrology was highly selective. Besides ignoring the recent visits of the pilot Moon Chin and the Brooke Dolan expedition, he left out the early measurement published by a French explorer, F. Grenard, who lived long after he reported the mountain at 6,500 meters (21,325 feet) in the 1894 book, *Mission Scientifique dans la Haute Asie*. He even left out Joseph Rock himself, who was not only alive and well in his sixties, but still writing about Anye Machin. In a 1952 monograph on Anye Machin, Rock stated: "After long experience among the snow mountains of West China and Eastern Tibet, I have come to the conclusion that the Am-nye Ma-chhen is not much higher than 21,000 feet."

Leonard Clark was better at mysticism than mathematics. His prediction of a curse came true—for him personally, that is. A few years after seeing Anye Machin, he disappeared among savage tribes in South America without a trace.

In October 1949—coincidentally the same month that *Life* published Clark's article—Mao Tse-tung founded the People's Republic of China. How to deal with the Goloks was not high on his priorities, but by the midfifties the Goloks were in an all-out war against Communist land reforms and taxation (explained in Chapter 6). Following their heri-

Leonard Clark with a sextant in the Anye Machin Range.

tage of banditry, they made such frequent raids on the highway to Lhasa that Mao could not count on it as a supply line for his troops. As the situation in central Tibet became more tense, Mao saw two courses of action: subdue the Goloks or plan an alternate military route into Tibet. He tried both.

Attempting the first in February 1956, Mao's troops suffered a major defeat. The outside world, however, heard virtually nothing about it. The People's Liberation Army, called in to stop the Golok raids on the road to Lhasa, seriously underestimated their adversaries. Goloks captured two hundred Chinese soldiers, cut off their noses flush with their faces, and drove the mutilated men into the frozen desert as a warning. When Mao counterattacked, over seven thousand of his best troops were ambushed and routed.

One of the few reports to reach America was a short article in the July 29, 1956, *Boston Globe* from an Asian correspondent:

The wild Golok tribesmen in the remote northeast were the first to rebel. But better armies than the Chinese occupation forces have tried to subdue the Goloks and have been mauled in the attempt. The Goloks fought, the Chinese lost, and nobody took much notice.

Chinese attempts to build a railroad to Lhasa through the Kokonor grasslands were continually thwarted. In April 1961 the *New York Times* reported more violent guerrilla warfare in Golok country. The Chinese air force was called in: "Bombers went into action in the north-east, where the Chinese had to abandon construction of the Lhasa-Lanchow railway because of rebel activity." The railroad was still uncompleted in 1981.

The Chinese realized that they could not count on the road from Lanchow through Golok country as a backup to the only other road to Lhasa, the thousand-mile mountain twister from Chengdu, recently completed in 1954. With a minimum of organization, Tibet could block all ground access to Lhasa. Mao began to put effort into the second course of action—an alternate route into Tibet.

Several divisions of Mao's troops were deployed in Sinkiang Province because of peasant rebellions there. Those soldiers could assist in Tibet, though, only if a road could be built from Sinkiang to Lhasa. The Chinese made a daring move. The barren plains of Aksai Chin were an area under Indian control (classically part of Tibet until the British brought it under Indian domination in the nineteenth century), but no Indian troops were stationed in the uninhabited region, so the Chinese simply built an emergency road there, which the Indians took years to discover.

This sequence of events explains some of the mysteries of the 1962 war between India and China. Anti-Communist phobia in the West first led political analysts toward the false conclusion that China was preparing to invade India. After a month of Chinese victories, much of India was wide open to conquest. Suddenly the invasion stopped and the Chinese "inexplicably" withdrew to hold only the highlands with their road.

Lack of knowledge of the Golok situation prevented otherwise astute journalists from understanding China's limited goal in the "war." The road was simply a necessary safety valve, and the territory, like all others "invaded by Red China" (Korea, Vietnam, Laos, Cambodia), was part of the land area that originally belonged to Imperial China before encroachments of the past two centuries, part of what the People's Republic considered its rightful heritage.

In the Golok heartland Mao resorted to major air raids to partially break the resistance. Unlike other Tibetan minorities within China, the Goloks ended up keeping their rifles, Buddhist practices, and nomadic lifestyle.

So little information has come to the outside world from Chinghai Province in the last thirty years that one American China-watcher stationed in Hong Kong called it "the black hole of China." In 1965 the Foreign Languages Press of Peking released a new book, *Mountaineering in China*. One short chapter was titled, "Unveiling the Mystery of Amne Machin." It told of a climbing expedition from the Peking Geological Institute that had surveyed Anye Machin to 23,491 feet in 1960, then miraculously climbed the peak in two days: "The mountaineering group left Base Camp at 5,119 meters [16,795 feet] on June 1 to further unveil the 'mystery' of this mountain. They reached the top at 13:20 hours, Peking time, the following day."

A later CMA publication gave more details. Base camp was actually at just 13,380 feet, a far more realistic altitude.

Beginning on May 20, several reconnaissances were made and two higher camps were established at 14,760 feet and 16,400 feet. The final base camp was set on May 29, and the summit was reached on June 2.

Among the eight members of the summit party was Wang Hong Bao, the same man who today is at the center of the Mallory and Irvine controversy for disclosing to the Japanese, on the day before he died, his 1975 discovery of the body of an Englishman at 26,575 feet on Everest.

The mystery of Anye Machin was far from over. Among other things, the Chinese had climbed the wrong mountain and had again misjudged its height by thousands of feet.

Ice lake beneath Anye Machin.

Chapter 12: Dreamland's End

THE ANYE MACHIN RANGE has a lush beauty, a blend of green grass and ice, quite unlike the steppes of central Tibet. I have sardonically called these arid steppes "freeze-dried Nevada," but this place is like the Brooks Range of Alaska in the summer. Wildflowers carpet grassy hills that roll mile after mile toward broad horizons, broken only by a wall of peaks to the east. The ground is real tundra here, moist grassland marked with frost polygons and other features of the high Arctic. The plant life is familiar, part of the circumpolar zone of cold-weather vegetation given to us by the Ice Ages.

Seeing flowers of the Holarctic—cinquefoil, gentians, buttercups, monkshood—gives me something of the feel of the High Sierra or the Rockies. The personal experience, however, bears no resemblance whatsoever. This morning was absolutely unique in my life, blazed into my memory as if it is happening now.

I am running uphill with a Golok rider close at my heels. Half a mile above me is a hilltop shrine, a cluster of rock piles, poles, and cloth flags. A low sound that seems born of the earth itself grows ever louder as I draw near. At first I do not realize that it is coming from behind me. It speeds up when I speed up, slows down when I slow down. The Golok rider is chanting in rhythm with my footsteps.

My lungs feel ready to burst with each stride. I can only run here at 15,500 feet because I am acclimatized from climbing to the North Col of Everest last month and to the top of Anye Machin last week.

Now my goal is just to reach the hilltop, lie down, and rest. I feel the euphoria of oxygen debt as I push hard up the final grade. The Golok doesn't stop at the top as I expect; he moves ahead of me, dismounts from his horse, and leads it briskly along a well-worn path. I follow him on three complete circles of the shrine with its two-hundred-foot wall of intricately carved mani stones.

Just when I think things are going well, the Golok turns serious. I stand very still as he draws a long knife and holds it to my face. He cuts a lock of my hair; then one of his own; finally one from his horse. He ties them to a rope on one of the poles as an offering to the gods.

Neither of us speaks the other's language. We are alone in the shadow of a mountain. Explorers from the West created the legend of its height, but here in the East there is an equally lofty belief about Anye Machin.

Each circumambulation of the shrine sends a prayer to the deities of the earth, sky, moon, and stars, represented by heaps of mani stones a little apart from the main wall. The

Golok patron saint, Machin Bomra, owner of the earth, lord of the mountains, has the highest stone heap of all: Anye Machin itself. Chong Hun is a yak driver for my trekking party; we are on day five of a circumambulation of this greatest shrine of all.

Before the Communist Liberation, up to ten thousand Goloks a year circumambulated the holy peak by the same 120-mile trail. Never in my wildest dreams did I imagine myself in this situation—running alone with a Golok horseman.

A year ago the CMA granted permission for me to lead the first group of Westerners on the Anye Machin pilgrimage. Because they reported abundant wildlife, as had every early explorer, I invited some of America's best field zoologists, geographers, geologists, botanists, ornithologists, and ecologists to join me. Nearly all of them had Asian experience and expertise.

We began as a party of fifteen. After a couple of days on the trail, nine quit the pilgrimage because of the inhospitable nature of the Goloks and the failure of the CMA to provide adequate food, support, and information about the route. Our headstrong liaison officer's dealings with the Goloks proved about as effective as I imagined Nikita Khrushchev

might have been alone dealing with a tribe in New Guinea. The liaison officer stayed back with the other nine, while I set off with the remaining five trekkers, one interpreter, two Goloks, three horses, and a yak train of supplies to complete the pilgrimage.

In my party were Harold Knutson, the geologist who had been with me in Tibet; Rodney Jackson, winner of a Rolex Award for a study of snow leopards; John Harte, an expert in freshwater ecology from the University of California; plus Bob and Wendelanne Henn, a couple out for an adventure.

I am alone now with Chong Hun, one of our yak drivers, because I stayed back from the group to find a minirecorder that fell out of my pack. After searching in vain for an hour, I gave up and started to walk as fast as I could. Around the first bend I found Chong Hun waiting with his horse. He motioned for me to give him my backpack with thirty pounds of cameras so I could walk faster while he rode. Gradually, I was able to break into a run next to the trotting horse. When we caught up with the others, Chong Hun kept on going. Not about to let my cameras out of sight, I ran after him. We continued side by side until we were once again alone on the grasslands under Anye Machin.

The Goloks have not answered personal or historical questions through our Chinese interpreter. Chong Hun has been particularly insolent, but I have begun to understand his need to display his independence. The Liberation of 1949 stripped most of the people of Tibet of their arms, their religious practices, their nomadic traditions, and much of their dignity. The Goloks, however, kept their traditions far more intact.

Being here gives me a feeling of journeying back in time before 1949. In all my travels through eight provinces of China I have never seen anything like this unconstrained tribe. Wild-looking men ride through the hills with carbines and modern AK-47 rifles. They live year-round in black tents made of yak hair, own their own horses, and graze hundreds of yaks and sheep per family. Fierce Tibetan mastiffs guard every home. The communes beneath Anye Machin have no Chinese members.

Now as Chong Hun and I circle the shrine for the last time, he stops to pray. I recognize a series of Tibetan characters on a flag, point and say, "*Om mani padme hum,*" a universal prayer that transcends the separate dialects of the Goloks and the Lhasa Tibetans. Chong Hun's face lights up. When

High meadow on the Anye Machin pilgrimage.

White-lipped deer, Cervus albirostris, *at Snow Mountain Commune.*

154

I mention the holy places I have been to in Tibet—Drepung, Jokhang, Tashilhunpo, Gyantse, Rongbuk—he proudly gestures that he has visited those places also. I doubt that any Han Chinese has ever shared such interest and respect for his religion, and it is clear that he is deeply moved.

I sit alone with Chong Hun for half an hour before the arrival of the others. They photograph the unusual scene of a Golok reclining in the grass with a hand on a foreigner's shoulder instead of his neck. When cameras begin to click, even though I encourage it, I feel something of the sense of intrusion that a native must experience when foreign guests arrive.

Chong Hun is a born ham. Whenever I turn his way, he gives the traditional Tibetan greeting: sticking his tongue out part way with his mouth slightly open. It is the first time that a Golok has shown us any openness and warmth.

I realize that now is an ideal time to ask questions through Gung Jian Chun, our twenty-four-year-old Chinese interpreter. Chong Hun answers in earnest, the first of his haughty tribe to talk of his past. Even his commune director, Chang La, refused my invitation to talk over tea.

Chong Hun first tells me of his personal six horses, fourteen yaks, and twenty sheep; then of the one hundred yaks and three hundred sheep he grazes for the commune; then of his four sons and three daughters. He has lived his whole life in black tents, and he has been to Datsu, this hilltop shrine, seven times before. "When I was eight years old," he relates, "I came here with my family on a pilgrimage around the mountain as you are doing now. Everyone, even the incarnate lama, was required to walk the whole distance. We saw wolves, bears, musk deer, great herds of gazelles, blue sheep, and *nyan*."

Rod Jackson, our zoologist, interjects that *nyan* is the Tibetan name for the argali, mountain sheep with horns up to a foot in diameter. *Nyan* is also a horned Tibetan god of the earth. To Jackson, one *nyan* is as mythical as the other. He craves a sighting of a wild *nyan* more than that of any other creature, even that of the snow leopard, which is his specialty. "Where can we see *nyan* at this time of year?" he asks.

"They are gone," Chong Hun replies wistfully. "I saw my last *nyan* when I was eighteen; now I am forty-three. None of my comrades has seen any sign of them in many, many years."

Disappointment passes across Jackson's face like the shad-

Golok with a lynx.

ow of a cloud, the real cloud, that is crossing the Anye Machin of our dreams. He realizes once and for all that there is no secret Shangri-la of rare animals here, as the CMA promised. "That explains why I haven't even found an old *nyan* skull," he ponders aloud. Nor has he found many bones of other animals said to be present in the CMA description. His recorded incidence of wildlife signs—tracks, droppings, bones—is just one every seven kilometers, a factor far worse than most of the "decimated" parts of the Himalaya in India and Nepal. "And why," he addresses Chong Hun, "do you think the animals have left?"

"Guns. The people have guns now and free bullets from the communes. Horses too. Everyone has a horse to ride and *nyan* have no place to hide. There are more people, more yaks, more goats, more guns, more bullets, and no more *nyan*."

Just two days earlier we had crossed paths with another American trekking group. To our great surprise we learned that they had seen two snow leopards. One casually rose

*The Goloks of Snow Mountain
Commune, among the last of the
"people of the black tents."*

from a tawny boulder, the same color as its coat, in broad daylight. The other was brought into camp, freshly killed by one of their armed Golok guides. Jackson interviewed the trekkers and concluded that both animals were small sub-adults that were trying to establish a range here. "I have seen no sign of tracks, scratchings, or droppings of adults here. They've probably been shot out, as any newcomers will be."

Nothing is as expected here. I can hardly blame early explorers for overestimating Anye Machin's height. After watching white ice merge with white cloud day after day, there are times I can't tell whether the peaks are 15,000 or 50,000 feet above a sea that has no meaning here.

Although most of the grassland is deplorably overgrazed, I can't ignore the benefit: a veritable golf green of closely cropped grass to walk on makes this some of the most pleasurable high-altitude trekking in the world.

The Goloks are not eager to encourage trekking. Through Chong Hun I learn one reason why. They have no financial incentive to work for us. The money we pay in one lump sum to the CMA for their services will be halved with the national administration, halved with the province, halved with the county and then divided four hundred ways with the members of their brigade at the end of the year. Now I understand why these legendary horsemen consistently lose their horses every morning: to discourage us so that they can return home to their land, their animals, and their families, and also to flaunt their independence at the Chinese.

To really understand the story of my trek and climb here, we need to move around in time to other incidents, events that fill in the picture of the modern Golok people, their land, and how one of the greatest concentrations of high-altitude wildlife in the world came to be decimated in just thirty years.

In Dawu, capital of the Golok Tibetan Autonomous Prefecture, I interviewed a cheerful Golok policeman, Gung-dung Jian Tso. Fear of the Chinese was etched into his features as he talked to our interpreter. His tension eased as he told the romantic legend of how the kingdom of Tibet changed in the seventh century after a king married a Chinese princess, Wen Cheng, who brought the holiest of images with her through Golok lands on the way to meet her husband-to-be in Lhasa. I tried to change the subject. "Tell me about the modern change of kingdoms in Chinghai. How did your people become part of the Chinese Liberation?"

My interpreter refused to translate the question. I insisted.

The policemen's face withdrew into the stiff mask I had seen on thousands of faces in China's major cities. "There are no legends about modern times," he said with his eyes glued to the hotel ceiling, totally afraid to discuss what those same eyes must have witnessed.

Peng Rui Yung, general secretary of Machin County in which Anye Machin was situated, answered questions clearly and directly. A tiny Chinese bureaucrat with ivory skin and thick, dirty glasses, he looked me in the eye as he rattled off answers with confidence. He was so proud of his knowledge of demographics and production figures that I saw a perfect opportunity for inquiry into environmental degradation. I suspected that the lack of wildlife was at least as much due to habitat destruction as to hunting pressure.

I asked him to tell me about the progress of the livestock industry. "Before there was a commune at Anye Machin, there were only one hundred or two hundred people living near the mountain with just seven thousand animals. Now," he related with obvious pride, "the same region—the seven hundred square kilometers of Snow Mountain Commune—has eight hundred people and over seventy thousand yaks and sheep. Many people own their own animals as well."

This tenfold increase in livestock and people virtually destroyed the prime wildlife habitat on the valley bottoms. As Mr. Peng extolled the virtues of his country's pasture-lands, I asked him about the average per-capita income. "We are very well off. Our people make thirty to forty yuan (eighteen to twenty-four dollars) each month, but through personal sales many make one hundred yuan a month."

"What do they sell?"

"Mostly products from their private animals and musk. The commune sells one hundred thousand yuan of musk in a year."

"Are the musk deer raised on a farm?"

"No. They are wild animals."

"I was told that all wild animals around Anye Machin—deer, mountain sheep, snow leopards—were legally protected."

"That is correct, but the commune leader can give special permission for a person to collect musk. Each deer can bring as much as four hundred yuan of musk, you know."

"What happens if a musk deer is killed illegally?"

"There is a fine, a big fine of two hundred yuan!"

"How often is an illegal hunter fined?"

"I do not know."

In typical Tibetan fashion, a Golok woman gives a warm greeting with her tongue.

"When was the last time you remember a hunter being fined?"

"I do not know."

"Do you have any records of hunters being fined?"

"No."

It was soon clear to me that not one person in recent years had been fined for poaching. There was even a fifteen-yuan bounty on snow leopards, which were supposedly protected throughout China by international agreement. Wolves brought a ten-yuan bounty. Significantly, these bounties were paid directly to the individual instead of going into the commune slush fund to be divided.

Killing predators brought easy pocket change; killing wild sheep or deer for food was encouraged by the simple economics of not killing a valuable personal animal and by the lack of enforcement of game laws.

Mr. Peng's information underscored what I had long suspected: the Chinese government gives lip service to environmental concerns to procure favorable world opinion and foreign capital; at the local level there is essentially no action. The public image of the PRC looks good. Some sixty-odd nature preserves now exist in important locations throughout China. The management of these preserves, however, is not general public knowledge. When the Chinese Environmental Protection Office sent a "leading group of the state council" to America in 1981 to find out how we handle such problems, I went to dinner with one of the principals, Ms. Cao Xuan Xuan. In order to learn the most from the American example, she had prepared a sincere and revealing description of the state of her agency:

First priorities are pollution problems from industries and municipalities. The restoration of degraded landscapes and the protection of wildlife are also important. . . . Neither the central organization nor the local ones have clearly defined functions and responsibilities. None of them have perfect working regulations. . . . The work of environmental management is still in a state of lack of coordination.

I summarized that evening in my notes: "The law of environmental protection appears to provide for organization and structures, but not base-level enforcement. There are objectives, not results."

This environmental contradiction was especially obvious in Machin County, which, by Mr. Peng's statistics, must be one of the world's safest places to raise sheep and goats. The

Tibetan blue sheep shot by Clark's 1949 expedition.

annual predation loss was just 0.14 percent (a figure that correlates almost perfectly with Chong Hun's loss of just one lamb to wolves in two years, a 0.11 percent loss). This is nearly insignificant among animals that have a natural mortality rate of up to 8 percent per year even in areas such as New Zealand, where predators are totally absent. Although his facts indicated a near-eradication of large carnivores, Mr. Peng told me that Golok herdsmen carry AK-47s with full banana clips of bullets (supplied free by their commune) "in case the wolves attack the sheep."

A more likely explanation for Golok armaments came from Tarthang Tulku, one of the few Goloks living in America, who spoke openly of his early life and his people. When I spoke with him in Berkeley in 1981, he had just published the largest work on Tibetan Buddhism ever written in a modern language, a 120-volume edition tagged at fifteen thousand dollars per set, when I interviewed him in the Nyingma Institute in Berkeley, California, where he was the head lama.

"I was born fifteen days' ride east of Anye Machin in the village of Darthung. My people have always been horsemen, and they measure distance by days on horseback. They are rebels, like your old American cowboys, and their horses

159

represent the same freedom that a motorcycle does to a modern rebel.

"My people have a code of absolute honesty within each clan, and no Golok will steal from another's home. Horses are a different matter. One clan will always try to take horses from another. The Golok sense of loyalty is absolute to things they understand. They are not what you might call intellectual. When they don't understand they go crazy. They will never back down from battle or support of their people. This is why they always win against the odds. And if there is even so much as a hint that a man has shirked his place in battle or support of a comrade, all the women of his clan including his wife and daughters will spit in his face when he returns. It is a fate worse than death, so it is easy for him to face death.

"My people will never lay down their weapons or their religion. Luckily for us we practiced our faith more in small shrines and in the home than in great monasteries and temples as in Lhasa. The Chinese never broke our spirit."

The Chinese very nearly succeeded in breaking the spirit of both my trek around Anye Machin and my climb. Planning began in Peking in July 1980 when the red carpet was out in celebration of the ascent of Mustagh Ata, the first American climb in the People's Republic of China. Jo Sanders eagerly negotiated permission for the first American trek through Tibet to the north side of Mt. Everest in 1981. Then came a sales pitch from the CMA. Were we interested in climbing or trekking in the Anye Machin Range, which would be opened in 1981 for the first time ever?

A virtual news blackout had been in effect in all of Chinghai Province since Liberation. The only written information available was a single-page description of the region that the CMA had prepared in English. It said the mountain was 23,491 feet and had been climbed once, by a Chinese party in 1960. The surrounding area contained "a wealth of rare birds and animals . . . thick virgin forests where deer, leopards, and bear thrive, while the grasslands and gravel slopes near the snowline are alive with hordes of gazelles, wild asses, and rare musk deer." The rainy season was reported as June to September. As further confirmation of this wildlife paradise, we were given a slide show on the area with fine close-ups of rare white-lipped deer in thick willows.

With a handshake to be followed by a signed protocol, we arranged to bring fifteen people on a three-week trek. The sale was no small potato. In-China costs paid to the CMA would exceed forty thousand dollars. The route would circle the Anye Machin massif at 13,000 to 16,000 feet by way of the old Golok pilgrimage with three extra days in the itinerary for an optional ascent of an easy 18,000-foot peak.

The CMA assured us that no Westerners had been on the pilgrimage and further guaranteed that we would be the first to attempt to do so. This was very important to Jo for the marketing of the trip and to me for selling a story. *National Geographic* subsequently assigned me an article.

Our trip was to begin in early June, a time the CMA recommended as after the snow melt and before the monsoon rains. They added the surprising bit of information that the peak had been "recently resurveyed" at 20,610 feet instead of 23,491, and that it had not been climbed. The summit reached in 1960 was actually 85 feet lower. I was offered a permit for the highest peak, but I declined in favor of exploring the area's natural wealth by way of the pilgrimage trek.

Two months before departure, Kim Schmitz, my partner on four Himalayan expeditions, told me that he had signed on with Mountain Travel to lead the first ascent of Anye Machin. I began juggling some complex, but highly intriguing time schedules. If I didn't return to Peking between my Tibetan Everest trek and the Anye Machin trek, I would have two weeks of free time precisely when Kim's expedition was coming from America to the mountain. Could I leave my trek in Chengdu, travel by train into central China, meet the climbers, truck and trek to base camp, climb the peak in six days or less, and join my trekkers for the pilgrimage?

It was worth the gamble. I signed on the climb as assistant leader. Harold Knutson, who would be with me in Tibet, also joined. Jo Sanders, co-leader of my Anye Machin trek, would bring that group to the mountains from Peking. Logistics were completed for three back-to-back adventures: Everest, Anye Machin climb, Anye Machin pilgrimage trek.

Then these well-laid plans began to come apart. I was very surprised to learn that Mountain Travel had been granted a permit to bring in trekkers to do the Anye Machin pilgrimage at the same time as our climb. The CMA had broken their solemn promise that no other group would be permitted on the pilgrimage before us. A later bombshell was that the CMA had sold the Japanese and the West Germans permits to climb the peak ahead of us.

LEFT *Interior of a black Golok tent.*

RIGHT *Golok child and fox pelt, Anye Machin.*

Nyan *is Tibetan for both this wild sheep,* Ovis ammon hodgsoni, *and the name of the horned god of the earth. Now one is as mythical as the other.*

Harold and I left our Everest group on May 27, 1981, in Chengdu, Szechwan Province. For the first time we had been granted a permit to travel without a liaison officer or interpreter, as far as Lanchow. I recorded the unique day in my diary:

Left for Lanchow on the "Hard Sleeping Train" this morning. Just H. and I with hundreds of Chinese who do not speak English. Hundreds of miles go by in this most populous province without a spadeful of natural world left unturned. China seems to be a voracious machine bent on consuming itself, slowly and pastorally, yet assuredly. It is pleasant, clicking along in an electric train, watching the countryside and relaxing as the others in our berth for six devour my copy of *National Geographic*.

On May 29 I almost lost Harold in Lanchow:

Up at six for a seven-mile run through town. Girls titter at hairy Harold without a shirt. We run quite fast, and I come back with mild cramps and diarrhea. Harold's symptoms are worse. He's vomiting. Bad food?

[15 minutes later] No! He's shivering with a high fever, a brief recurrence of malaria from geological fieldwork days in Africa. Every year or so he gets symptoms that last a day, but he still runs 2:36 marathons at age forty, so he's not in too bad health, I guess.

Harold lets our Sports Federation hosts take him to the hospital for an examination. Big mistake. They take a stool sample and diagnose "bacterial dysentery." An English-speaking doctor tells me, "Mister Kananudasona isa vely sick." His main doctor is a woman with the bedside manner of a dean of girls. She insists he stay in the hospital for three days because of his "infectious disease." We must leave tomorrow at dawn for Anye Machin. His symptoms are gone now, he can drink and eat very well, but because he had vomiting and diarrhea for an hour in the morning, she's pumping him full of intravenous fluids. The Chinese refuse my request to place him in the care of the American doctor who is coming with our climbing expedition on the plane tonight.

Now they want to take a stool sample from me because I have been traveling with Harold! I refuse with considerable difficulty. How can I get Harold out of here? I question the medical procedures. The IV fluids are premature. Dysentery may be present, but does not account for the two-hour episode that resembles his earlier malarial attacks, and that's why they brought him here. I plan for our doctor to meet with the hospital staff at five, after his plane lands here. But the plane does not land. We find out it came down for some mechanical difficulty in Taiyuan, just three hundred miles from Peking. Poor Harold is a prisoner in a Chinese hospital! The Sports Federation people are nowhere to be found when I take a taxi to look for them.

The plane comes in at midnight. I rush Dr. Lon Hoover and John Thune [leader of the MT trekking group] to the hospital. Hours pass. The Chinese hang on tenaciously in great fear of repercussions if Harold turns for the worse after they release him. After a stage play to save them face, during which Harold appeared in the office in his underwear holding his IV bottle in one hand, looking like a tanned Olympian about to set a discus record, the Chinese let him go into our care. But at 4:00 A.M. they call John Thune's room and plead for Kananudasona to stay back.

In the morning the CMA has no travel permit for us to proceed to Sining [in Chinghai] with the expedition, even though they approved our plan in writing months ago. Long negotiations follow. The Chinese direct our movements by what Kim calls "the hurry-up-and-wait" system. Finally we're off. Harold too.

In the mountains it rained and snowed for our first eight days. By chance we met a Chinese glaciological team in the field. They didn't consider the weather at all unusual, because weather records show a fierce rainy season from May to July. Our trek and climb were scheduled squarely in the middle of the bad weather. The team had a topographical map that showed Anye Machin to be 20,610 feet, just as the CMA had told us, but the date of this "latest" survey was 1971. Thus the Chinese had known for ten years that the peak was 3,000 feet lower, and that their 1960 expedition climbed a summit several miles from the highest point.

The Japanese were leaving just when we arrived. The Chinese told us they had reached the summit in storm after a month-long siege. The West Germans were on the mountain, fixing camps on a different route than ours. We sat in base camp plagued by bad weather until there were only three days left before I was to meet my trekking party. All we had managed to do was to carry a supply dump up to 15,500 feet. When the storm finally broke, Kim, Harold, and I made a fast, alpine-style bid on the unattempted northeast ridge.

On the first day we climbed from 14,000 feet to a camp high on a subsidiary ridge at 19,000 feet. The next morning we followed a corniced knife edge that led onto the main ridge of the peak. Ice cliffs that looked ominous from below proved passable on either side. As we used our ice axes and the front points of our crampons to negotiate steep spots, we were thankful that the storm had covered the blue ice just under the surface. No technical gear such as ice screws or

Knutson and Schmitz traverse the northeast ridge of Anye Machin in high winds.

fixed rope were needed. We could move roped together, reasonably quickly, up the steepening ridge that put us into the summit plateau shortly after noon.

The ordeal was far from over. In front of us a mile-wide basin of thigh-deep powder with a wind crust separated us from the summit. Walking here at over 20,000 feet with our full complement of climbing gear was far more strenuous than front-pointing up the ridge had been. We took turns breaking trail for an hour and a half, until we emerged onto the summit, as large and level as a football field.

The sun was shining, and it was obvious that we were on the highest point in sight. Our elation was surprisingly subdued as we posed for photographs, ate salami and crackers, and gazed below us in all directions toward the land where Harold and I would be trekking in just a couple of days. Kim was not going with us. As leader of the expedition, he planned to descend, pick up the four remaining Mountain Travel clients, and make a second summit climb.

We were surprised to find nothing on the summit, no evidence of a previous ascent and no marks on the south ridge coming up from the Japanese base camp. We looked for telltale lines from compaction of the snow that often re-

main in exposed places for weeks after a party passes, but saw nothing. Even so, we weren't sure whether we had made the first, the second, or the third ascent of the mountain.

After we descended, we learned that we weren't third when the West Germans reported reaching the top one day after we did. They found our tracks, names, snow pickets, and marker wands on top. Our CMA liaison officer, Yu Liangpu, was as unsure about things as we were. He told us that the Japanese had climbed the lower summit reached by the Chinese in 1960, then later informed us that they climbed the highest peak.

Immediately after the climb I had more pressing concerns than the pedantics of who reached the summit first. The afternoon after I stood on the top, I met my trekking group on schedule. Nobody was smiling.

In Peking they had learned of a small error in calculations. The pilgrimage was 120 miles instead of 70. Logistics were still set for the shorter distance. The only way to complete the circular route was to give up the optional three-day climb —for which some had specially trained and bought new equipment—and walk considerably farther each day.

They were also prohibited from camping during the three-day drive into the mountains on dirt roads. This cost $2,690 extra for $30-per-night, dirt-floor rooms. Chartering a truck and a bus for the 460 miles each way made Hertz seem like a bargain: $8,802. The fee for parking one truck in a yak pasture for ten days while we were on the trail was $940.

The trekkers found CMA trail food meager and barely edible. Breakfast was sugar cookies crumbled into powdered skim milk. Bread was unsealed and coated with green mold, and butter was already rancid. For transport in monsoon rains on the backs of yaks, the CMA had supplied cardboard boxes tied shut with string.

Since maps of the region were classified as secret, we were given a hand-drawn chart with a dotted line to follow across white paper, where in reality we would find countless peaks, rivers, and valleys.

I did discover where the fine photos of rare white-lipped deer that I had been shown in Peking were made. I took similar close-ups in the thick foliage of the Snow Mountain Commune Deer Farm, created in 1967 to harvest antlers for aphrodisiacs and herbal medicines after wild deer became scarce. The results of our extensive searches for wild mammals were very sparse. We saw five wild blue sheep atop a

Golok family of Snow Moun-
tain Commune.   165

The dilemma of the Goloks is symbolized by this boy with a Chinese military cap. Either they lose their cultural heritage piece by piece or, hopelessly out-numbered, resist all who bear the red star.

rocky promontory, and three MacNeill's deer, a rare relative of the elk, on a distant hillside. Two musk deer were flushed out of the brush, but they could hardly be called "abundant," as they were by almost every earlier explorer.

We were lucky to be able to investigate bird life far more thoroughly. With us was Ben King, an ornithologist for the American Museum of Natural History. Festooned with binoculars, spotting scope, and notebook, dressed in khaki everything, King was the quintessential birder. Besides his credentials as author of a bird guide to Southeast Asia, Fulbright Fellow, and record holder for Asian bird sightings (1,640 out of the 2,200 known species), he had the honor of having two bird parasites, a fly and a louse, named after him. Of the 78 species King identified in the mountains, 59 had not been previously reported from there, since King was the first ornithologist ever to visit and return.

On the day I met King, having just descended from high camp on Anye Machin, I made a side trip to a nest I had seen on the ascent at 15,500 feet. A falcon dived on me, whistling its talons past my hair as I climbed a crumbling cliff to its eyrie. In the nest I found four almost fully grown fledglings on the verge of being able to fly. I thought they were peregrine falcons, but King later identified them as a cousin, the Barbary falcon, known to range from North Africa to Mongolia. My sighting was five hundred miles from the nearest recorded one.

Within a stone's throw was an even bigger nest of willow sticks. This was the home of a lammergeier, the Tibetan counterpart of a condor. Later we came upon one of these great vultures that had eaten too much to fly. I took photographs from arm's length, then watched King pick up the bird from behind and set it on a high place. Spreading its nine-foot wings, it took to the air like an overloaded 747 using all its runway. The sound of wingtips touching the earth echoed in my ears.

For sheer unusual data, John Harte pulled the brass ring. He wanted to see how much acid rain reached mountains so distant from the world's great industrial centers. In the high mountains he found no acidity, due to the native limestone and airborne alkali dust from the dry lakes of the Kokonor region. But in the little hamlet of Dawu, he collected fresh rainwater with a pH of 2.25, as acid as strong vinegar. Here, from the only town within hundreds of miles with one main street and a few thousand souls, was taken "one of the most acidic precipitation samples ever recorded in the world."

The reason? Uncontrolled coal burning for heat and cooking in a high, cold place without a viable wood supply.

The last days of our trek around the mountain were increasingly enjoyable. Our Golok yak drivers became much more friendly after my time with Chong Hun at the shrine. Before, they always tried to keep us moving past any habitation while the inhabitants scowled at us and their dogs barked. Now they introduced us to these "people of the black tents," the last remnants of the great nomadic culture of Tibet. We shared food, tea, and simple things like looking at each other's rings, hair, and eyes. At my suggestion, we left our cameras in our packs until we were fully accepted as friends. Then and only then would these proud people gather their best finery and pose for us.

Toward the end of our journey a storm broke in the evening with a double rainbow. Everyone—American and Golok alike—stood outside in wonder. Time stood still. The past and the present came together, and the future seemed unimportant. We were no longer fighting a schedule, each other, or the elements. We were at one with our existence.

To reach this state, which I so often have found in the mountains, took me longer than ever before. This time we

ABOVE *Harold Knutson crossing a glacial river.*

BELOW *Ben King and friend.*

The last days of the pilgrimage.

with blizzards, avalanches, high winds, and invading armies, but they were only now accepting trekkers and climbers.

At the end of the pilgrimage, I understood two of the three legendary superlatives of Anye Machin. I saw how the fierce Golok warriors of old had integrated themselves—by intimidation and courage—into a bare suggestion of communal life with a maximum of autonomy. I also saw why the wildlife Shangri-la was long gone. But after climbing Anye Machin, I had no idea how a pilot could ever think it was higher than Everest.

Months after I returned home to California, my eighty-year-old mother handed me a letter sent her by Dick Leonard, a student of my late father, a long-time family friend, and a pioneer of Yosemite climbing in the thirties. During World War II he had maneuvered himself into an intelligence assignment in Asia because of his love of the Himalaya.

Leonard had prodigiously studied books on the Himalaya, and as he flew next to the range in October 1944, he proudly called aloud the names of the great peaks as they passed by his DC-3 window. An air force captain across the aisle said, "Major, you seem to know a lot about the Himalaya. Have you heard of the peak higher than Everest?"

"Oh yes," Leonard replied. "Anye Machin is one of the greatest geographical discoveries of the century!"

"Well, it's all a fake," the captain revealed. "We made it up. Those British correspondents kept pestering us for exciting stories to cable home, so we told them about a DC-3 that got blown off course in a terrific storm and discovered a mountain over 30,000 feet. We said they figured they were two hundred miles off course, but they recovered and landed in Chungking. Of course, a fully loaded DC-3 can't fly anywhere near as high as we said, and it couldn't carry enough fuel to get back from that far off course even if the pilot knew the way. It was a great practical joke—serious reports of it were published all over the world."

needed an extra struggle to move us finally beyond worry and complaint. Just days before we had argued over whether to attempt the pilgrimage, and I had written down all the "what if" worries that were paralyzing members of my party from being able to accept what nature would deal us. What if: (1) someone gets sick? (2) someone gets too tired? (3) the Goloks rebel? (4) food is insufficient? (5) bears raid camp? (6) the weather is bad? (7) the distance is yet again longer than the Chinese say?

But here we were standing in the rain with the rebels, tired, almost out of food, walking more miles per day than necessary, and loving it. I suspected that the Goloks were going through a similar awakening. They had accepted life

A Golok surveys his wounded homeland, a far cry from descriptions issued from Peking as late as 1981 of a place where the "slopes near snowline are alive with hordes of gazelles, wild asses, and musk deer."

169

RIGHT *Snow leopard,* Panthera uncia, *image of all that is wild, mysterious, and vanishing in the mountains of Asia.*

OPPOSITE *Chong Hun leads his horse on a small circumambulation of Datsu, a hilltop shrine beneath the main subject of our circular pilgrimage, Anye Machin.* © *National Geographic Society*

A Chronology of Mountain Exploration

John Martinek

This chronology covers the major exploration and climbing expeditions up to the current opening of each region to tourism, and does not necessarily include all of those who have traveled these remote parts of Asia.

THE REFERENCE NUMBERS AT THE END OF PARAGRAPHS REFER TO ENTRIES IN THE BIBLIOGRAPHY.

EXPLORATION OF THE MUSTAGH ATA REGION

C. A.D. 150   Ptolemy, the Greek geographer and astronomer, wrote of Tashkurgan, a city at 13,000 feet within twenty miles of Mustagh Ata, as being the western edge of China. Ptolemy quoted another geographer, named Marinus, who in turn took his information from a Macedonian trader, Maes, who had sent agents to China along a route that skirted the northern Pamirs. Some historians doubt that Ptolemy's Tashkurgan is the same city as the modern one. *References: 20, 89*

519   Sung Yun and Hui-sheng, Chinese Buddhist pilgrims, traveled across the southern reach of the Pamirs on an imperial mission to Afghanistan, then ruled by the Huns. *Reference: 89*

642   Hsuan Tsang, another Chinese Buddhist pilgrim, traveled through the Pamirs to India. His journal, "Memoirs of the Western Countries," became the most valuable source of information on the state of Buddhism in the seventh century in India and Central Asia, along with the first detailed accounts of the culture, wildlife, and appearance of the Tagdhumbash Pamir. *References: 6, 44, 89*

747   Kao Hsien-chih, Chinese general, led ten thousand soldiers from Kashgar across the Pamirs to the Oxus. There they defeated the combined forces of the Arabs and the Tibetans, thus reducing the Tibetan empire, which had reached its greatest westward expansion. As a result, the Chinese controlled the Tarim Basin for the first time. *Reference: 89*

747   Dharmachandra, an Indian monk, died in the Tarim Basin after turning back from crossing the Pamirs en route home from China because of the "disturbed condition of the region," that is, the Sino-Tibetan conflicts. *Reference: 88*

752   Wu-kung, yet another Chinese Buddhist pilgrim, passed through the Pamirs on his way to and from India. *Reference: 88*

1272-1273   Maffeo, Marco, and Niccolo Polo traveled for three and a half years from their home in Venice to the court of Kublai Khan near present Peking. Marco, just seventeen at the start of the trip, kept a detailed journal. He traveled with his father and his uncle across the Pamirs under Mustagh Ata via the Silk Road. Marco described for the first time the great wild sheep which now bear his name (although a subspecies with slightly smaller horns was described by von Rubruck, a French Franciscan missionary, north of the Pamirs in 1252). The Polos stayed in the

Khan's court for twenty years. Marco's journal became a book, *The Travels of Marco Polo*, with the help of a romance writer, Rustichello of Pisa. *References: 20, 64, 88*

1603 Benedict de Goes, a Spanish Jesuit, traveled on a mission to the Moghul Emperor Akbar's court in India. He then joined a trading caravan to China with his friend Isaac the Armenian. They traveled through Afghanistan and across the Sarikol Plains of the Pamirs, where Isaac almost died falling into a river, and many of their men actually froze to death. De Goes never returned; he died in China in 1607. *References: 54, 88*

c. 1827 Alexander Gardiner, self-acclaimed American soldier-of-fortune and historical enigma, traveled through the East with the style of an Old West gunfighter. His reports of crossing all the six great mountain systems of Asia before maps acknowledged their existence have many errors, and whether he crossed the Pamirs is uncertain. His reports of life in Yarkand (south of Kashgar) are highly credible. Why Gardiner drew criticism from British historians is partially explained by John Keay: "Gardiner was just a desperado, a hired gun on the run. His moral standards . . . were those of Boot Hill, not Sandhurst. If, instead of a Tartar turban, the old colonel had worn a ten-gallon hat . . . his whole career would have been more readily understood." *References: 47, 63*

1837–1840 Lieutenant John Wood, a British naval officer, made a winter journey on behalf of the East India Company to open relations with the Afghani hill tribes. Receiving coveted permission to go to the Pamirs, he left his group to search for the source of the Oxus River. In February 1840, accompanied by several Kirghiz, he reached Lake Sarikol with a frostbitten and exhausted party, and disproved the belief that this lake fed two major rivers (it is a source only of the Oxus). He rediscovered the great wild sheep described by Marco Polo. *References: 47, 105*

1886–1887 Ney Elias, an independent explorer forced into the employ of the British government to continue his travels, investigated Russian movements in the Pamirs. The Wakhan corridor, a remarkable result of his recommendations, created a buffer of neutral Afghan territory between the British and Russian empires. He was so independent from the hierarchy of British India that his findings were downplayed as much as possible during his lifetime. Later he was begrudgingly accepted as the outstanding British explorer of his time. One of his discoveries, a peak he named Mt. Dufferin, later became known as Mustagh Ata. *References: 47, 58*

1889–1891 Francis Younghusband, a British lieutenant, was sent to investigate raids on caravans near the Pamirs and to assess Russian intentions in the region. On the Chinese side he met Russian Captain Grombchevsky traveling with a German naturalist, Herr Conrad. At Tashkurgan near Mustagh Ata he crossed paths with a British Major Cumberland and a Lieutenant Bower, who were with a Frenchman, M. Dauvergne. As Kenneth Mason later wrote: "It is a curious commentary on the political state of affairs at this time that in this no-man's-land a Russian, a Frenchman, a German, and no less than three Britishers should meet as friendly, if rival, explorers without an official passport of any kind." Younghusband encountered a group of Russian soldiers led by Colonel Yanoff, who proclaimed the Pamirs to be Russian territory. The two men treated each other as gentlemen, dining together and drinking vodka and brandy while discussing their explorations. Three days later Yanoff received notice from his government to escort Younghusband off Russian soil. Younghusband asked what would happen if he refused; Yanoff said he would use force. Younghusband had no soldiers; Yanoff had thirty. These were the stakes of the Great Game in 1891. They dined again and agreed that Younghusband should leave under his own power after signing a statement of protest. *References: 54, 111*

1894 Sven Hedin, a Swedish explorer, made four attempts to climb Mustagh Ata while en route to Tibet. In April he backed down because of an inflammation of his eyes. In early August he tried to climb the peak astride a yak, accompanied by several Kirghiz (not the least important of whom led his animal by nose-ring up the mountain). Hedin claims to have reached 20,600 feet on his beast, but at the same time mentions rock under the snow in the animal's tracks (the elevation was probably not more than 18,500 feet). A third attempt that month ended after yaks and men fell into crevasses. The fourth attempt ended low on the mountain in high winds and blowing snow with Kirghiz, Swede, and yak alike suffering altitude sickness. *References: 32, 35*

1894 George Nathaniel Curzon, later to be viceroy of India at a young age, traveled extensively through the Pamirs in search of the source of the Oxus while a member of Parliament. He discovered the glacier that is recognized today as the true source of the Oxus. Curzon's intimate knowledge of the region was an important factor in the later politics of the Great Game. *References: 14, 46*

1900   Sir Aurel Stein, British archaeologist and explorer, made numerous visits to the Pamirs to investigate the routes and descriptions of classical travelers in this area. In July 1900 Stein attempted Mustagh Ata, spending five days and reaching about 20,000 feet. He brought an experienced climber named Punyali, who became exhausted at 19,000 feet and dropped out. Stein, feeling more fit, climbed another thousand feet before turning back. *References: 56, 87*

1925   Theodore and Kermit Roosevelt, sons of the U.S. president, visited the Pamirs in search of Marco Polo sheep. Traveling by way of Yarkand and Kashgar, they headed for Subashi, below Mustagh Ata. In the valleys nearby they climbed to over 17,000 feet in blizzards to shoot two adult males. Near a smaller village of "four or five yourts" they shot the remaining specimens to complete a family exhibit for the American Museum of Natural History. *Reference: 76*

1935   Peter Fleming, a British travel writer, went overland from Peking to Srinigar with a Swiss woman, Kini Maillart. They crossed the eastern end of the Pamirs via the 15,000-foot Chichilik Pass. Fleming's account adds a new dimension to high-altitude physiology: "The Turkis stabbed the wretched ponies midway between the eye and nostril with long iron skewers which they carried for the purpose; this let a good deal of blood, and though it looked a barbarous and cruel practice, it undoubtedly made the animals' breathing easier at high altitudes." *Reference: 27*

1940-1948   Eric Shipton, Himalayan explorer and mountaineer, became British consul of Kashgar in 1940. He traveled through the Pamirs beneath Mustagh Ata en route to his position. H. W. Tilman, his longtime mountain companion, joined him in 1947 for attempts on Mustagh Ata and Chacragil, a 22,000-foot neighboring peak, failing on both peaks. On Mustagh Ata the climb went well until a summit push from a high camp of just 20,000 feet failed in deep snow and extreme cold somewhere around 24,000 feet. Shipton suffered frostbite on all the toes of one foot. *References: 82, 83, 94, 96*

1956   A joint Sino-Soviet expedition made the first ascent of Mustagh Ata, 24,757 feet. The Soviets played a leading role. They supplied a majority of the climbers and equipment. The entire expedition trained and acclimatized for a month in the Soviet Pamirs before moving to Mustagh Ata. After establishing four camps up to 22,300 feet, they evacuated the mountain, rested, celebrated political pleasantries with the local Kirghiz, and held a joint meeting of the Soviet and Chinese Communist parties to order thirty-one climbers to the summit. All thirty-one made the top; nineteen Soviets and twelve Chinese, including Shih Chan Chun (later Everest leader and director of the CMA). Accompanying scientists performed meteorological and glaciological studies. *Reference: 108*

1959   A Chinese expedition made the second ascent of Mustagh Ata, placing twenty-five men and eight women on the summit, including several Tibetans. After extensive acclimatization the actual ascent was made in five days from base camp with no casualties. A women's altitude record was set. The Chinese later dropped the 1956 climb with the Russians from their literature, holding out this ascent and that of Minya Konka as the genesis of their Everest successes. *Reference: 59*

EXPLORATION OF THE TIAN SHAN

c. 629   Hsuan Tsang, a Chinese Buddhist pilgrim, traveled from ancient Chang-an (Sian) past Bogda Ola to Kucha in the foothills of the Tian Shan near Mt. Tomur (Peak Pobeda). He stayed for sixty days at the Ascharya Monastery, where he proved himself so worthy that the ruler of the region supplied him with transport animals for the journey home. His elephant drowned en route. *References: 6, 43*

1856-1857   P. P. Semjonov, a Russian geographer, penetrated far into the Tian Shan Range and described the peak of Khan Tengri. Later explorations included another Russian, Ignatjev. *Reference: 62*

1879-1883   Nicholas M. Przewalski crossed the eastern extremity of the Tian Shan over the Kamil Pass en route to Tibet on his third and fourth journeys. *References: 53, 65*

1903   Dr. Gottfried Merzbacher, an Austrian explorer, mapped the Bogda Range and set the height of the highest peak as 21,350 feet (true elevation: 17,864 feet). *Reference: 2*

1914   Sir Aurel Stein, British archaeologist and Sinologist, traversed the northern edge of the Bogda Range and the Karlik-tagh, then took a direct route "across a rugged portion of the T'ien-shan Range rising to numerous snowy peaks by a pass close on 12,000 feet." *Reference: 87*

1929   M. Pogrebezky led three Ukrainian expeditions to Khan Tengri, which he climbed with two other men via the west ridge in 1931. During the same year a Russian, Suchodolsky, tried the same peak from the north and failed at 20,000 feet. *Reference: 62*

1932   Sven Hedin, the great Swedish explorer, surveyed the height of Bogda at exactly 18,000 feet, much closer than previous exaggerations. *Reference: 35*

1936–1937   Two Russian expeditions climbed Khan Tengri, one with a Swiss member, Lorenz Saladin, who died from extreme frostbite. *Reference: 62*

1938   The Letavet Russian expedition climbed Khan Tengri, then three members climbed Mt. Tomur (Peak Pobeda), still unaware of its height, which was calculated in 1946 as 24,392. They were not credited with the ascent until after 1977, when photos of a Chinese ascent perfectly matched their description. *Reference: 62*

1941   Wilfred Skrede, a nineteen-year-old Norwegian, decided to join the Canadian army by traveling overland from Oslo across Europe and Central Asia with four other youths. They traversed under the northern edge of the Tian Shan all the way to the Bogda Range, cut south to Turfan, then skirted the southern foothills back to Kashgar, from where they reached India the hard way. *Reference: 85*

1948   Eric Shipton and H. William Tilman, British mountaineers, made two unsuccessful attempts to climb Bogda Ola while Shipton was British consul of Kashgar. They reached a subsidiary summit of about 17,000 feet. Both men followed the southern base of the range its entire length to Kashgar from Turfan. *References: 2, 82, 94*

1949–1955   Two unsuccessful Russian attempts on Mt. Tomur (Peak Pobeda), plus one repeat of Khan Tengri via the west ridge. *References: 62, 84*

1956   The great Russian climber Vitaly Abalakov led an ascent of Mt. Tomur (Peak Pobeda) with a large party that put many climbers on top. *References: 62, 84*

1956   Basil Davidson, a British adventurer, followed essentially the same grand circle of the Tian Shan as Skrede in 1941. *Reference: 19*

1977   A large Chinese expedition made the first Chinese ascent of Mt. Tomur (Peak Pobeda), while scientists studied the natural history and geology of the area. *Reference: 59*

EXPLORATION OF INNER TIBET

1624   Fathers Antonio de Andrade and Manuel Marques, Portuguese missionaries, entered western Tibet from India via the Mana Pass (18,400 feet) to investigate a rumor of a Christian community. *References: 53, 102*

1625   Andrade and Marques repeated their earlier route with another missionary, Gonzales de Souza, and founded a Christian church in Tsaparang. They left by way of Afghanistan, then ruled by the Huns. *References: 53, 102*

1626–1628   Stephen Cacella and John Cabral, Portuguese Jesuits, made separate journeys to Shigatse in central Tibet via the Chumbi Valley from Sikkim. *References: 53, 54, 102*

1661   Johann Grueber (Austrian) and Albert d'Orville (Belgian) were Jesuits stationed in Peking. When they were ordered back to Europe, they traveled overland through Tibet and Nepal, spending a month in Lhasa, the first recorded Europeans to reach the holy city. *References: 78, 102*

1708   Four Capuchin friars, names unknown, reached Lhasa via Gyantse from Nepal in 1708 to establish a mission, which was abandoned in 1711 due to lack of finances, then reestablished from 1715 to 1733 by another group of friars including Orazio della Penna, who returned again in 1741 with Cassiano Beligatti, who stayed until the mission was abandoned due to pressure by the lamas in 1745. *Reference: 78*

1714   Ippolito Desideri, a Portuguese Jesuit, reached Lhasa in 1716 after a journey through Ladakh and western Tibet in an attempt to compete with the Capuchins. He left in 1721. *References: 22, 53*

1728   Samuel Van der Putte, a Dutch layman, ventured into Mongolia and Tibet for trade and adventure. Details are unknown, but he passed through Lhasa in 1728 and 1730. *References: 53, 78*

1774   George Bogle, a Britisher on a trade mission for the East India Company, traveled through Bhutan into Tibet as far as Shigatse. *References: 54, 78*

1783   Samuel Turner, a British officer, was sent by the East India Company to Shigatse to acknowledge the new reincarnation of the Panchen Lama. *References: 54, 78*

1811-1812   Thomas Manning, a British civilian interested in China and its language, traveled through Tibet on his way from Canton to Calcutta. He was the first Britisher in Lhasa, and the first European since the Capuchins were expelled in 1745. *References: 53, 78*

1812   Thomas Moorcroft, a British veterinary surgeon, crossed the Himalaya in search of breeding animals. He was the first European to reach Lake Manasarovar since Desideri a century before. *References: 57, 78*

1844-1846   Evariste Regis Huc and Joseph Gabet, French Lazarist priests, traveled through Lhasa on a missionary journey from north China and Mongolia. *References: 78, 89*

1846   Henry Strachey, a British officer, surveyed Lake Manasarovar and the Kailas Range for the first accurate maps of the region. He returned with his brother, Richard, in 1848 and 1849 to continue the survey. *References: 78, 89*

1848   Joseph Hooker, a British botanist, and Dr. Campbell, a Darjeeling school superintendent, studied the Sikkim-Tibet border regions and brought back a voluminous amount of information on Tibetan culture, wildlife, and natural history. Hooker's studies formed much of the botanical basis of his friend Charles Darwin's theory of evolution, published over a decade later. *Reference: 78*

1865   Nain Singh, the first Indian pundit explorer, was sent by the British into Tibet disguised first as a pilgrim, then as a Ladakhi trader, to bring back geographical measurements. He surveyed from Kathmandu to Lhasa, charted the Tsangpo from its source to Lhasa, and surmised correctly that it was the same river as the Brahmaputra in India. In 1867 he visited Gartok and investigated the gold fields east of Rudok. *References: 53, 78*

1872   Kishen (A. K.) Singh, another pundit, reached Lhasa with four assistants and attempted to explore the Kokonor region of eastern Tibet. Golok raids near Tengri Nor forced them to retreat. *References: 53, 78*

1878   After a year in Lhasa, A. K. Singh left again with a well-prepared Mongolian caravan that repelled Golok attacks, although with a considerable loss of provisions. In the Tsaidam district one of his servants robbed him, and he had to work as a servant himself to earn his food and passage back to India. *References: 53, 78*

1879   Nicholas Przewalski, the premier Russian explorer of Central Asia, reached the village of Napchu within two hundred miles of Lhasa on his third unsuccessful attempt to penetrate Tibet. He made major botanical and zoological collections over the course of four journeys totaling twenty thousand miles. *References: 53, 66*

1879-1881   Sarat Chandra Das, Bengali headmaster of the Bhutia Boarding School in Darjeeling, trained prospective pundits and later became one himself. He negotiated for a legal travel permit to Shigatse, and stayed as a guest in the Tashilhunpo Monastery for four months, returning with invaluable political, cultural, and geographical information. A second illegal journey brought him briefly to Lhasa in 1881. From the fruits of his journeys he made a new map of central Tibet and what remains today as one of the two best Tibetan-English dictionaries. *References: 16, 53*

1880   Kintup Singh, a pundit explorer, disguised himself as the servant of a Mongolian lama to get into Tibet and sent marked logs down the Tsangpo River to see if they came out on the Brahmaputra. His mission took four years. After being betrayed, sold as a slave, escaping, and sending a message from Lhasa notifying the British of the exact date the logs were to be released, he carried out his task. Upon returning to India he found that his message had never arrived and the logs had apparently floated unnoticed into the Bay of Bengal. *References: 53, 78*

1883   Urgyen Gyatso, a Sikkimese pundit in the employ of the British, visited Lhasa, Shigatse, Shekar, and Gyantse, where he made extremely accurate and detailed notes on the geography and culture. Ethnically similar to Tibetans, Gyatso was an especially successful pundit explorer. *Reference: 78*

1889-1892   William W. Rockhill, an American diplomat in Peking, was a student of Tibetan language and culture who attempted to reach Lhasa twice by routes through Kham and Amdo. He traveled extensively through eastern Tibet, but failed to penetrate the heartland. *References: 53, 78*

1890-1899   Various European travelers—Carey, Dalgleish, Bonvalot, Bower, Littledale, Thorold, and Annie Taylor (the first European woman in Tibet)—explored the fringes of Tibet without reaching Lhasa. *Reference: 78*

1892-1900   Lieutenant Colonel L. Austine Waddell, a British officer, attempted unsuccessfully to reach Lhasa in disguise, then made several other penetrations of border regions of Tibet. He later was a member of the 1904 Younghusband expedition. *Reference: 100*

1894   Dutreuil de Rhins and Fernand Grenard, French adventurers, traveled from Khotan in Sinkiang to Tengri Nor north of Lhasa, but were not permitted to travel further. They headed northeast, and in the Kokonor region wandered into a Tibetan settlement where the inhabitants, probably Goloks, shot de Rhins, laced him into a yak skin, and threw him into the Yellow River. Grenard escaped. *Reference: 30*

1897   A. Henry Savage Landor, British adventurer, reached central Tibet by way of Lake Manasarovar. He was captured by the Tibetans, tortured, and finally released. *Reference: 50*

1898   Mr. and Mrs. Rijnhart, a Dutch and American missionary family, tried to penetrate to Lhasa. They were forced back at Nakchu, Tibetans stole their horses, their young son died, and Mr. Rijnhart drowned trying to swim the Tsachu River. Mrs. Rijnhart made it safely to eastern China. *References: 68, 78*

1900   Captain R. L. Kennian (British) and Kazi Ugyen (Bhutanese) both attempted to carry letters from the viceroy of India to the Dalai Lama in hopes of improving relations. Both missions failed, and the letters were not acknowledged. *Reference: 53*

1900   Aguan Dorjieff, a Mongolian lama who had traveled with Przewalski, carried a letter from the Dalai Lama in Lhasa to the Russian czar in St. Petersburg after presenting his view that Tibet should befriend Russia to protect itself from encroaching British and Chinese imperialism. *Reference: 53*

1900–1902   Ekai Kawaguchi, a Japanese intelligence agent (and Buddhist), spent two years in disguise in Lhasa. *Reference: 45*

1901   Zerempil, a Mongolian lama working for the Russians, brought two camel caravans of weapons and ammunition to Lhasa. *References: 25, 53*

1901   Sven Hedin, a Swedish explorer, tried to reach Lhasa disguised as a Mongolian pilgrim. His party was discovered just short of Lhasa, and it retreated across the Himalaya to Ladakh. *References: 33, 34, 36*

1903–1904   Francis Younghusband, a British colonel, entered Tibet from Sikkim to force the Tibetans into discussions about British/Tibetan/Russian relations. He waited five months at Khampa Dzong for word from Lhasa, then decided to bring a thousand soldiers under General J. R. L. Macdonald with him to Gyantse. En route near the town of Guru, hundreds of Tibetans were killed in an altercation. More died in a six-week siege of the fort in Gyantse. On August 2, 1904, Younghusband and 622 men entered Lhasa. The Dalai Lama had fled to Mongolia, so a treaty concerning relations and trade with Britain was signed by a high lama. Younghusband was severely criticized for pursuing a protocol of such international significance without clear authority from London. *References: 26, 109*

1905   Tom Longstaff, a legendary mountaineer, entered Tibet with two alpine guides, Alexis and Henri Brocherel, to attempt Gurla Mandhata (25,355 feet) in the Lake Manasarovar region. Near the summit the party was caught in an avalanche. Because they lost most of their equipment, they were forced to descend. Only one week was spent on the mountain in an amazingly high ascent for the times. *Reference: 51*

1906   Sven Hedin returned for a second attempt to reach Lhasa. Again he was refused a permit. He spent two years in Shigatse, eastern Tibet, and the Lake Manasarovar region before returning to India via the Sutlej River Valley. *References: 33, 34, 36*

1913   British Captains F. M. Bailey and H. T. Morshead, penetrated into Tibet from the northern tip of Assam. They traveled west along the Tsangpo and reached Tsetang, which was at the time the farthest anyone had penetrated the Tsangpo gorges. Morshead made an excellent map of the region, and Bailey discovered the famed Blue Poppy. *Reference: 4*

1917–1918   Edwin G. Schary, an American adventurer from San Francisco, traveled into southern Tibet from India by way of Lake Manasarovar to Shigatse and Gyantse before returning by way of the Chumbi Valley. *Reference: 79*

1920   Charles Bell, British political officer in charge of Bhutan, Sikkim, and Tibet, met the Thirteenth Dalai Lama in Darjeeling while he was in exile there. Bell was invited to Lhasa as both a personal friend and political officer, and he stayed for a year. After he retired, Bell revisited Tibet in 1934. *References: 7, 65*

c. 1920   Jacques Bacot, a French scholar, traveled through Tibet in search of information on language, religion, and art. He brought back one of the world's finest collections of Tibetan thangkas (painted scrolls), which now resides in the Musée Guimet in Paris. *Reference: 3*

c. 1920   Alexandra David-Neel, a French mystic, studied Sanskrit and Tibetan at the Sorbonne before spending fourteen years in Asia to further investigate Buddhism. The dates of her travels and her itineraries are as difficult to decipher as her obscure prose, but she definitely visited Shigatse and eastern Tibet on separate journeys from her travels around Kokonor and Lhasa. *References: 17, 18*

1921-1922   British Brigadier General George Pereira traveled through Lhasa and eastern Tibet on a grand loop from Peking through Tibet, India, Burma, and southern China. He died before reaching Peking. *Reference: 110*

1922-1923   William M. McGovern, a British anthropologist, accompanied a scientific expedition led by George Knight as far as Gyantse. After they were informed that they would not be allowed in Lhasa, McGovern returned to Darjeeling, disguised himself as a Tibetan coolie, and managed to reach Lhasa. He was discovered, declared a prisoner of state, and escorted back to India. *Reference: 55*

1927-1928   N. Roerich, a Russian scholar, was refused permission into Lhasa after traveling with a caravan through Central Asia, Mongolia, and Darjeeling. He was sent on a roundabout path west of Lhasa, then east to Gangtok. His keen insights into the culture, geography, and religion were eventually written into one of the best travel narratives on Tibet. *References: 74, 75*

1927-1948   Giuseppi Tucci, an Italian Tibetan scholar, visited all major areas of Tibet during this period on repeated ventures. This godfather of Tibetan studies walked thousands of miles on foot with such illustrious companions as Tenzing Norgay and Fosco Maraini doing archaeological and literary research for his many definitive books. *References: 52, 97, 98*

1931-1933   Robert Byron, an American traveling with two companions called only "G." and "M.," went to Gyantse via Darjeeling and the Chumbi Valley. *Reference: 12*

1933   A British mission visited Lhasa after the death of the Thirteenth Dalai Lama to determine if China would again pursue sovereignty over Tibet. *Reference: 104*

1935, 1937   Suydam Cutting, an American naturalist, went to Lhasa in 1935 alone, and again with his wife in 1937. He was the first American in Lhasa. Another American, Theos Bernard, visited Lhasa soon after. *References: 8, 15*

1936   B. J. Gould led another British political mission to Lhasa including Spencer Chapman and Hugh Richardson with the primary motive of bringing the Panchen Lama back to Tibet from Chinghai Province to counter growing Chinese power. The Panchen Lama refused. *References: 29, 104*

1936-1950   Reginald Fox, a British officer, stayed in Lhasa after the Gould mission, resigned his commission with British India, married a Tibetan woman, and became a radio operator for the Dalai Lama, who monitored foreign stations for news relating to Tibet. *Reference: 104*

1942   Lieutenant Colonel Ilya Tolstoy and Captain Brooke Dolan on a U.S. Army OSS mission had an audience with the Dalai Lama in Lhasa during a long journey to find supply routes through China and Tibet to aid the besieged Nationalist Chinese. *Reference: 92*

c. 1942-1945   Arch Steele, a correspondent for the *Chicago Daily News*, visited Lhasa and wrote a series of articles. *Reference: 92*

1944-1950   Peter Aufschnaiter and Heinrich Harrer, Austrian mountaineers, escaped from a POW camp in India, after returning from a Himalayan expedition at the beginning of the war, into the hands of the British. Disguised as pilgrims, they spent parts of two years walking over a thousand miles to Lhasa, where they were accepted into Tibetan society. Aufschnaiter worked on engineering projects, while Harrer became an advisor and tutor of the Dalai Lama. *Reference: 31*

1947-1949   Lama Anagarika Govinda, ethnically a German, and his Indian wife, Li Gotami Govinda, were sponsored by the Indian press to explore temples and art in the Tsaparang area of western Tibet. They circumambulated Mt. Kailas near Lake Manasarovar, and also visited Gyantse. *Reference: 28*

1949   Lowell Thomas, an American journalist, and his son, Lowell Thomas, Jr., were given permission to visit Lhasa by the Dalai Lama in exchange for their promoting the cause of Tibetan independence. *References: 92, 93*

1955   Alan Winnington, the first British journalist allowed to travel in Tibet after the Chinese invasion, traveled overland from Chengdu to Lhasa on a new road with a party of eight foreign journalists. They traversed eastern Tibet and left via the Chumbi Valley to India. *Reference: 104*

1961   Mt. Shisha Pangma, the only 26,000-foot peak wholly in Tibet or China (not a border peak), was explored at close hand for the first time by a Chinese team of surveyors and mountaineers. *Reference: 59*

1964   A 206-member Chinese expedition placed ten climbers on the summit of Shisha Pangma for the first time. Scientific work was done in the area as well. *Reference: 59*

EXPLORATION OF THE CHOMOLUNGMA REGION

1904   Captains Ryder and Rawling (British), members of the Younghusband military expedition, observed Mt. Everest from the Tingri plains (approximately sixty miles north of the mountain). This sighting was, most likely, the first from Tibet. *Reference: 60*

1913   Captain John B. L. Noel (British) attempted to reconnoiter Mt. Everest from Tibet, reaching a point about forty-five miles from the peak. *Reference: 60*

1921   Colonel C. K. Howard-Bury (British) led the first expedition to Mt. Everest. The team left Darjeeling via the traditional Chumbi Valley route west via Shekar, Tingri, and Rongbuk. They were unable to make a serious attempt on the mountain due to disorganization and bad weather, but they did pioneer several approach routes, discovering the feasibility of the North Col (the route of all prewar attempts). *References: 41, 70*

1922   General C. G. Bruce brought another British expedition from Darjeeling via the traditional approach route. They followed the East Rongbuk Glacier and placed an advanced base camp at the foot of the North Col (approximately 21,000 feet). The most experienced climbers, Mallory, Norton, Somervell, and Morshead, reached close to 27,000 feet without oxygen before they were forced to retreat. A second attempt by George Finch and Geoffrey Bruce (the general's nephew), reached 27,300 feet before wind and problems with oxygen equipment turned them back. A third attempt, including Mallory and Somervell, never got to the North Col after a giant snow slab avalanche devastated their roped party, killing seven Sherpas. *References: 9, 70*

1924   Bruce returned to Everest again, caught malaria on the approach march, and handed over the leadership to Colonel Norton. On the first attempt Norton made it to approximately 28,125 feet without oxygen. On the famed second attempt, George Mallory and Andrew Irvine were last seen close enough to the summit that their fate has remained a controversy to this day. *References: 23, 61, 70, 99*

1933   This British expedition, led by Hugh Ruttledge, made two summit attempts from Camp VI (27,400 feet). First Wyn Harris and L. R. Wager attempted the bands of the northwest face but gave up in deep snow just beyond the Main Couloir (approximately 28,125 feet). On the second attempt Eric Shipton and Frank Smythe left Camp VI together, but Smythe went on alone after Shipton had stomach problems. Smythe, too, made it as far as the Main Couloir, climbing alone with his hallucinations. *References: 23, 77, 86, 99*

1934   Maurice Wilson, an ex-captain of the British Army, flew a plane to India with the intention of landing on the Rongbuk Glacier. Grounded by authorities, he made his way to Rongbuk Monastery disguised as a deaf and dumb Tibetan. After reaching Camp III on the East Rongbuk Glacier, his three Sherpas refused to continue on to the North Col. He climbed on alone and died near Camp III, apparently from cold and exhaustion. His body was found by Shipton's expedition the following year. *References: 23, 69, 99*

1935   Eric Shipton brought a small British expedition to Rongbuk late in the climbing season, but still managed to reach the North Col in favorable weather. However, the monsoon forced them off the mountain before they could climb higher. Michael Spender's photogrammetric maps were one of the more valuable results of this expedition. *References: 23, 99*

1936   Hugh Ruttledge again led a British expedition through Tibet, but an early monsoon prevented it from going beyond the North Col. *References: 23, 99*

1938   H. W. Tilman led this British expedition to the North Col, where the team found it too cold and windy to climb. After waiting for nearly a month, the team made it to about 27,300 feet before the irascible monsoon drove them off the mountain. *References: 23, 95, 99*

1947   Earl Denman, a lone Canadian, tried to climb Everest via the North Col route with just two porters. He left from Gangtok disguised as a Tibetan, forgot to bring a sleeping bag, and never made it to the North Col. He survived to return to Darjeeling in less than five weeks. *References: 21, 23, 99*

1952   An unconfirmed but widely circulated news story told of a Russian expedition that met disaster high on the mountain. Reportedly, six summit climbers disappeared above 27,000 feet. The forty-two-member expedition has never been officially confirmed nor denied by either the Russians or the Chinese. *References: 23, 99*

1959   A Russian/Chinese reconnaissance of Everest was

successfully completed but did not result in a joint expedition due to political conflicts between the two nations in the intervening time. *Reference: 99*

1960   A 214-member Chinese expedition succeeded in making the first ascent of the North Col route tried by the early British expeditions. Three relatively inexperienced members made the summit from a high camp just above 28,000 feet. They reached the summit after nineteen grueling hours at 4:20 A.M. Chu Yin-hua led the infamous Second Step in his stocking feet, subsequently losing all ten toes. *References: 1, 99*

1962   Woodrow Wilson Sayre, grandson of President Wilson, applied for Gyachung Kang, a border peak between Nepal and Tibet. With three companions he crossed illegally into Tibet and attempted Everest via the North Col route, reaching about 24,500 feet. *References: 1, 99*

1975   A large Chinese expedition of climbers and scientific workers went to Everest both to climb the summit and do extensive geological and medical research on the East, West, and Central Rongbuk Glaciers. Nine members (eight of them Tibetan) reached the summit via the North Col route. *Reference: 59*

EXPLORATION OF MINYA KONKA

1877–1880   A Hungarian count, Bela Szechenyi, was the first person to make a scientific observation of Minya Konka. He measured its altitude to a remarkably accurate 24,936 feet (just 36 feet more than the current elevation). *Reference: 10*

1929   Joseph Rock, an American botanical explorer, went to the foot of Minya Konka, visited the monastery at its base, and brought back the first close photographs. Using only a compass and an aneroid, he estimated the altitude of the mountain to be 30,250 feet, a figure that *National Geographic* refused to publish. His estimate was modified to 25,600 feet. *Reference: 72*

1930   The Sun Yat Sen University Expedition, led by Dr. Arnold Heim (Swiss), carried out a formal geological survey of the Minya Konka region. A Swiss companion, Edward Imhof, published a remarkably accurate book about the region with superb cartography and original paintings of rare quality. *Reference: 44*

1931   Brooke Dolan, Gordon Bowles, and J. Huston Edgar (Americans) went on multipurpose expeditions to the Minya Konka region to bring back, respec-tively, zoological, ethnological, and geological/archaeological information. *Reference: 10*

1932   Richard Burdsall, Arthur Emmons, Terris Moore, and Jack Young arrived in Shanghai with the intention of going to Anye Machin with an American exploratory expedition. After they were denied permission because of the Japanese invasion, they stayed in China and put together the American Sikong Expedition to explore and possibly climb Minya Konka. After determining the summit to be 24,900 feet, Moore and Burdsall reached it on October 28. For the next one-quarter century, this remained the highest summit reached by Americans. *Reference: 10*

1957   A Chinese expedition led by Shih Chan Chun claimed that it put six climbers on the summit of Minya Konka and that accidents claimed four lives during the expedition. They repeated the American route, and for some time their ascent was in doubt in the Western world because of the sloppy wording of the government propaganda surrounding it. *Reference: 81*

EXPLORATION OF ANYE MACHIN

c. 1893   A French explorer, Dutreuil de Rhins, indicated Anye Machin as a peak of 6,500 meters (21,325 feet) in his 1894 book, *Mission Scientifique dans la Haute Asie*. *Reference: 24*

1895   Roborowski, a Russian explorer, reached the northeast side of Mangun Pass just short of the Anye Machin Range only to be turned back by Golok bandits. *Reference: 13*

1900   Captain P. K. Kozloff, a Russian explorer, traversed the series of alkaline lakes to the northwest of the Anye Machin Range, making numerous observations about the wildlife and flora. *References: 13, 48*

1923   British General George Pereira saw the peak of Anye Machin from about one hundred miles away on his way to Lhasa from Peking. He told Joseph Rock and others that the peak probably exceeded Mt. Everest in height, thus beginning the legend. Pereira died before returning from his journey. *Reference: 110*

1929   Joseph Rock, an American botanical explorer, approached Anye Machin to within fifty miles, and measured it as the second 30,000-footer of his life. *National Geographic* reduced his estimate to a mere 28,000 feet for publication in 1930. Rock brought back considerable information of the flora, fauna, and Tibetan culture of the Golok people. *References: 72, 90*

1943   Captain Brooke Dolan and Lieutenant Colonel Ilya Tolstoy passed the western edge of the Anye Machin Range while on an OSS mission during World War II. They brought back more information on the wildlife, but little about the mountain. *Reference: 13*

1944   Newspapers around the world reported that an American DC-3 crew blown off course while flying "The Hump" from Burma to China had sighted a mountain 30,000 feet high in the Anye Machin Range. *Reference: 13*

1948   Milton Reynolds, an American promoter of aircraft exploits, received premature publicity about his search for the 30,000-foot peak in the Anye Machin area. He made one illegal flight with his pilot, Bill Odom, which passed over the range in cloud cover below 30,000 feet. No peaks showed above the clouds. *Reference: 13*

1948   Jack Birns, a photographer on assignment for *Life* magazine, flew over Anye Machin in perfect weather with Chinese pilot Moon Chin. They estimated the high peaks to be not much more than 20,000 feet. The magazine decided not to publish a story which would only gratify Reynolds' desire for publicity, even though it might have set the dispute to rest. *Reference: 13*

1949   Leonard Clark, a former OSS officer in China, organized an expedition to Anye Machin, fought off Golok tribesmen with a cavalry armed with machine guns, and surveyed the peak from fifteen miles at 29,661 feet with crude instruments borrowed from a Chinese highway crew. His article in *Life* and his book, *The Marching Wind*, promoted once again the legend that Anye Machin surpassed Everest. *Reference: 13*

1960   A Chinese expedition from the Peking Geological Institute surveyed a peak in the Anye Machin Range at 23,491 feet. Eight members subsequently reached the summit. Chinese surveys as early as 1972 indicated that the peak climbed was not the highest in the range, but was just 20,524 feet. Another summit some miles to the north was the highest, measured at 20,610 feet. The maps, however, and the information on them were kept secret. Not until the summer of 1980 did the Chinese Mountaineering Association finally release the information that the real Anye Machin was unclimbed. *Reference: 59*

List of Color Photographs

185

186

Bibliography

1. Ahluwalia, Major H. P. S. *Faces of Everest*. New Delhi, 1978.
2. Anderson, J. R. L. *High Mountains and Cold Seas: A Biography of H. W. Tilman*. Seattle, 1980.
3. Bacot, J. *Le Tibet Révolté*. Paris, 1912.
4. Bailey, F. M. *No Passport to Tibet*. London, 1957.
5. Baume, Louis C. *Sivalaya: Explorations of the 8000-metre Peaks of the Himalaya*. Seattle, 1978.
6. Beal, Samuel. *Si-Yu-Ki: Buddhist Records of the Western World*. London, 1884. Reprinted 1969.
7. Bell, Sir Charles. *Portrait of the Dalai Lama*. London, 1946.
8. Bernard, Theos. *Penthouse of the Gods: A Pilgrimmage into the Heart of Tibet and the Sacred City of Lhasa*. New York, 1939.
9. Bruce, Charles G. *The Assault on Mount Everest, 1922*. London, 1923.
10. Burdsall, R.; Emmons, A.; Moore, T.; and Young, J. *Men Against the Clouds*. Seattle, 1935.
11. Burrard, S., and Hayden, H. *A sketch of the geography and geology of the Himalaya Mountains and Tibet*. Calcutta, 1907.
12. Byron, Robert. *First Russia Then Tibet*. London, 1933.
13. Clark, Leonard. *The Marching Wind*. New York, 1954.
14. Curzon, G. N. *The Pamir and the Source of the Oxus*. London, 1898.
15. Cutting, C. S. *The Fire Ox and Other Years*. New York, 1940.
16. Das, Sarat Chandra. *Journey to Lhasa and Central Tibet*. London, 1902. Reprinted. New York, 1970.
17. David-Neel, Alexandra. *My Journey to Lhasa*. New York, 1927.
18. ————. *Tibetan Journey*. London, 1936.
19. Davidson, Basil. *Turkestan Alive: New Travels in Chinese Central Asia*. London, 1957.
20. Debenham, Frank. *Discovery and Exploration*. London, 1960.
21. Denman, Earl L. *Alone to Everest*. London, 1954.
22. de Filippi, Filippo, ed. *An Account of Tibet: The Travels of Ippolito Desideri of Pistoia*. London, 1932.
23. Dhyrenfurth, G. O. *To the Third Pole: The History of the High Himalaya*. London, 1955.
24. Dutreuil de Rhins. *Mission Scientifique dans la Haute Asie, 1890-95*. Paris, 1897-8.
25. Filchner, Wilhelm. *Storm Over Asia: Experiences of Secret Diplomatic Agents*. Berlin, 1924.
26. Fleming, Peter. *Bayonets to Lhasa*. London, 1961.
27. ————. *News From Tartary*. London, 1936.
28. Govinda, Li Gotami. *Tibet in Pictures: A Journey into the Past*. Berkeley, 1979.
29. Gould, Sir B. J. *The Jewel in the Lotus*. London, 1956.
30. Grenard, F. *Tibet: The Country and Its Inhabitants*. Translated by A. T. de Mattos. London, 1904.
31. Harrer, H. *Seven Years in Tibet*. Translated by R. Graves. New York, 1953.
32. Hedin, Sven. *Central Asia and Tibet*. London, 1903.
33. ————. *My Life as an Explorer*. New York, 1925.
34. ————. *Southern Tibet*. Stockholm, 1922.
35. ————. *Through Asia*. Sweden, 1898.
36. ————. *Trans-Himalaya: Discoveries and Adventures in Tibet*. London, 1909.
37. Heim, Arnold. *Minya Gongkar*. Berlin, 1933.
38. ————. *The Throne of the Gods*. London, 1939.
39. Holdich, Sir Thomas. *Tibet the Mysterious (The Story of Exploration)*. London, 1921.
40. Hopkirk, Peter. *Foreign Devils on the Silk Road*. London, 1980.
41. Howard-Bury, C. K. *Mt. Everest: The Reconnaissance, 1921*. London, 1922.
42. Huc, R. E. *Souvenirs d'un voyage dans la Tartarie et le Thibet, 1844-48*. 2d ed. Paris, 1962.
43. Hui-Li, compiler. *The Life of Hsuan-Tsang*. Peking, 1959.
44. Imhof, Edward. *Die Grossen Kalten Berge von Szetschuan*. Zurich, 1974.
45. Kawaguchi, Ekai. *Three Years in Tibet*. Benares, 1909.
46. Keay, John. *The Gilgit Game*. London, 1979.
47. ————. *When Men and Mountains Meet*. London, 1977.
48. Kozloff, P. K. "The Russian Tibet Expedition, 1899-1901." R. G. S. N. S. vol. XIX, 1902.
49. Krader, Lawrence. *Peoples of Central Asia*. Bloomington, 1966.
50. Landor, A. Henry Savage. *In the Forbidden Land*. London and New York, 1899.
51. Longstaff, T. G. *This My Voyage*. London, 1950.
52. Maraini, Fosco. *Secret Tibet*. New York, 1952.
53. MacGregor, John. *Tibet: A Chronicle of Exploration*. London, 1970.
54. Mason, K. *Abode of Snow*. London, 1955.

55. McGovern, W. M. *To Lhasa in Disguise*. New York and London, 1924.
56. Mirsky, Jeannette. *Sir Aurel Stein: Archaeological Explorer*. Chicago, 1977.
57. Moorcroft, Thomas. *A Journey to Lake Manasarovara in Undes*. Calcutta, 1816.
58. Morgan, Gerald. *Ney Elias, Explorer and Envoy Extraordinary in High Asia*. London, 1971.
59. *Mountaineering in China*. Peking: Foreign Languages Press, 1965.
60. Noel, J. B. L. *Through Tibet to Everest*. London, 1927.
61. Norton, Edward F. *The Fight for Everest: 1924*. London, 1925.
62. Onishtchenko, W. "Khan Tengri, Lord of the Sky: 1964 Moscow Expedition." *The Mountain World*, vol. 66-67. London, 1968.
63. Pearse, Major H. *Memoirs of Alexander Gardiner*. London, 1898.
64. Polo, Marco. *The Travels of Marco Polo*. Translated by Ronald Latham. London, 1958.
65. Przewalski, N. M. *Mongolia, The Tangul Country, and the Solitudes of Northern Tibet*. Translated by E. D. Morgan. 2 vols. London, 1876.
66. ———. *Reisen in Tibet am oberen Lauf des Gelben Flusses in den Jahren 1879-1880*. Jena, 1884.
67. Richardson, H. E. *Tibet and Its History*. London, 1962. American edition: *A Short History of Tibet*. New York, 1962.
68. Rijnhart, S. C. *With the Tibetans in Tent and Temple*. New York and Chicago, 1901.
69. Robertson, David. *I'll Climb Everest Alone: The Story of Maurice Wilson*. London, 1957.
70. Robertson, Maz. *George Mallory*. London, 1969.
71. Roborovski, V. "Progress of the Russian Expedition to Central Asia Under Colonel Pievtsoff." R. G. S. N. S. vols. XII, XIII, 1890-91.
72. Rock, Joseph. *The Amnye Ma-Chhen Range and Adjacent Regions*. Rome, 1956.
73. Rockhill, W. W. *The Land of the Lamas*. New York, 1891.
74. Roerich, Nicholas. *Altai-Himalaya*. New York, 1929.
75. ———. *Heart of Asia*. New York, 1930.
76. Roosevelt, Theodore, and Roosevelt, Kermit. *East of the Sun—West of the Moon*. New York, 1926.
77. Ruttledge, Hugh. *Everest 1933*. London, 1934.
78. Sandberg, Graham. *The Exploration of Tibet: History and Particulars*. Delhi, 1973.
79. Schary, Edwin G. *In Search of the Mahatmas of Tibet*. London, 1946.
80. Schomberg, R. C. F. *Peaks and Plains of Central Asia*. London, 1933.
81. Shih Chan Chun. *Conquest of Minya Konka*. Peking, 1959.
82. Shipton, Eric. *Mountains of Tartary*. London, 1951.
83. ———. *That Untravelled World: An Autobiography*. London, 1969.
84. Simonov, Yevgeny. *Conquering the Celestial Mountains*. Moscow, 1958.
85. Skrede, Wilfred. *Across the Roof of the World*. New York, 1954.
86. Smythe, Frank. *Camp Six: an account of the 1933 Everest expedition*. London, 1937.
87. Stein, Sir Aurel. *On Ancient Central Asian Tracks*. London, 1933.
88. ———. "On Ancient Tracks Past the Pamirs." *Himalayan Journal*, vol. IV, 1932.
89. Strachey, Henry. *A Journey to Lake Manasarowar*. Calcutta, 1848.
90. Sutton, S. B. *In China's Border Provinces*. New York, 1974.
91. Suyin, Han. *Lhasa, the Open City*. New York, 1977.
92. Thomas, Lowell, Jr. *Out of This World: Across the Himalayas To Forbidden Tibet*. New York, 1950.
93. ———. *The Silent War in Tibet*. London, 1960.
94. Tilman, H. W. *China to Chitral*. Cambridge, 1951.
95. ———. *Mount Everest 1938*. Cambridge, 1948.
96. ———. *Two Mountains and a River*. London, 1949.
97. Tucci, Giuseppi. *Tibet: Land of Snows*. Translated by J. E. Stapleton Driver. London, 1967.
98. ———. *To Lhasa and Beyond*. Translated by Mario Carelli. Rome, 1956.
99. Unsworth, Walt. *Everest*. London, 1981.
100. Waddell, L. Austine. *Lhasa and Its Mysteries*. London, 1905.
101. Wallace, H. *The Big Game of Central and Western China*. London, 1913.
102. Wessels, Father C. J. *Early Jesuit Travellers in Central Asia: 1603-1721*. The Hague, 1924.
103. Whitaker, Donald P., et al. *Area Handbook for the People's Republic of China*. Washington, 1972.
104. Winnington, Alan. *Tibet: Record of a Journey*. London, 1957.
105. Wood, John. *Journey to the Source of the River Oxus*. London, 1841. 2d ed. 1872.
106. Woodcock, George. *Into Tibet: The Early British Explorers*. London, 1971.
107. Woodman, Dorothy. *Himalayan Frontiers*. New York, 1969.
108. Yang Ke-Hsien. *The Ascent of Mustagh Ata*. Peking, 1959.
109. Younghusband, Sir F. *India and Tibet*. London, 1910.
110. ———. *Peking to Lhasa* (The Narrative of Journeys Made by the Late Brigadier General George Pereira). London, 1925. New York, 1926.
111. ———. *The Heart of a Continent*. London, 1896.
112. Yutang, Lin. *My Country and My People*. New York, 1935.

Index

Photo: Harold Knutson

"GALEN ROWELL may be the foremost American practitioner of that hybrid art, photojournalism," said the *Washington Post* in reviewing one of Rowell's earlier books. ". . . Rowell has somehow overcome time; otherwise there's no accounting for his presence at so many sites of beauty on the verge of evanescence."

Galen Rowell was among the first foreign visitors allowed into China's mountainous West when its borders were reopened in 1980 after three decades, and his travels there, documented in this book, represent the most extensive exploration of Chinese mountain territory by any occidental since World War II. An experienced and active mountaineer, he has made notable ascents in China, as well as elsewhere in Asia and North America.

In addition to his extensive work for the *National Geographic*, Rowell's photographs have appeared in numerous other periodicals and calendars, and have been exhibited at New York's International Center of Photography and the California Academy of Sciences in San Francisco. He is the author of *The Vertical World of Yosemite; In the Throne Room of the Mountain Gods; High and Wild; Many People Come, Looking, Looking;* and, with John McPhee, *Alaska: Images of the Country*. He lives in Berkeley, California, with his wife, Barbara.